PEARSON ALWAYS LEARNING

Compiled by The Program in Writing and Rhetoric

Work in America

William Paterson University
English 1100: College Writing

Cover Art: *Courtesy of Digital Vision, Stockbyte/Getty Images*

Pearson Learning Solutions, 501 Boylston Street, Suite 900, Boston, MA 02116
A Pearson Education Company
www.pearsoned.com

Printed in the United States of America

2 3 4 5 6 7 8 9 10 V0CR 17 16 15 14 13 12

000200010271657547

KH/CB

PEARSON

ISBN 10: 1-256-81784-8
ISBN 13: 978-1-256-81784-0

COPYRIGHT ACKNOWLEDGMENTS

Grateful acknowledgment is made to the following sources for permission to reprint material copyrighted or controlled by them:

"Spheres of Power and Oppression," by Gregory Mantsios, reprinted from *Class in America: Myths and Realities* (2006), by permission of the author.

"What Work Is," by Philip Levine, reprinted from *What Work Is* (1992), Random House, Inc.

"The Inheritance of Tools," by Scott Russell Sanders, reprinted from *Paradise of Bombs* (1986), Beacon Press.

"Serve or Fail," by Dave Eggers, reprinted from the *New York Times*, June 13, 2004, by permission of The New York Times Company.

"On Dumpster Diving," by Lars Eighner, reprinted from *Travels with Lizbeth* (1993), Bedford St. Martin's Press.

"Why I Write," by George Orwell, reprinted from *Such, Such Were the Joys* (1953), by permission of Houghton Mifflin Harcourt Publishing Company.

"Is Everybody Happy?" by John Ciardi, reprinted from *The Saturday Review*, March 14, 1964, by permission of the Ciardi Family Publishing Trust.

"Dolores Dante, Waitress," by Studs Terkel, reprinted from *Working: People Talk About What They Do All Day and How They Feel About What They Do* (1997), by permission of The New Press.

"Excerpt from Jarhead," by Anthony Swofford, reprinted from *Jarhead : A Marine's Chronicle of the Gulf War and Other Battles* (2003), by permission of Simon & Schuster, Inc.

"Tip Jars and the New Economy," by Dalton Conley, reprinted from the *Chronicle of Higher Education* 49, no. 7, January 3, 2003, by permission of the author.

"Working at McDonald's," by Amitai Etzioni, reprinted from *The Miami Herald*, August 24, 1986, by permission of the author.

"Serving in Florida," by Barbara Ehrenreich, reprinted from *Nickel and Dimed: On (Not) Getting by in America* (2001), by permission of Henry Holt & Company.

"Raise Wages, Not Walls," by Michael S. Dukakis and Daniel J. B. Mitchell, reprinted from the *New York Times*, July 25, 2006, by permission of The New York Times Company.

"Living Wage Fight Goes On," by Molly Ivins, reprinted from the *San Francisco Chronicle*, September 9, 1998, by permission of Creators Syndicate, Inc.

"The Communist Manifesto," by Karl Marx and Frederick Engels, February 21, 1848, by permission of International Publishers.

"Social Responsibility of Business and Labor," by Milton Friedman, reprinted from *Capitalism & Freedom: With a New Preface* (1963), University of Chicago Press.

"Management Women and the New Facts of Life," by Felice N. Schwartz, reprinted from *The Harvard Business Review*, Jan—Feb 1989, by permission of Harvard Business School Publishing.

"Win-Win Flexibility," by Karen Kornbluh, reprinted from *New America Foundation*, June 29, 2005, New America Foundation.

"Beyond the Information Revolution," by Peter F. Drucker, reprinted from *The Atlantic Monthly*, October 1999, by permission of The Peter F. Drucker Literary Trust.

"Globalization: The Super-Story," by Thomas L. Friedman, reprinted from *Longitudes and Attitudes* (2002), by permission of Farrar, Straus and Giroux.

"What are 'Class' and 'Inequality'?" by Jeremy Seabrook, reprinted from *The No-Nonsense Guide to Class, Caste, & Hierarchies* (2002), by permission of New Internationalist.

"Class," by Sherman Alexie, reprinted from *The Toughest Indian in the World* (2000), Grove/Atlantic, Inc.

"Laid-Back Labor," by Stephen J. Dubner and Steven D. Levitt, reprinted from the *New York Times Magazine*, May 6, 2007, by permission of the authors.

"Social Class and the Hidden Curriculum of Work," by Jean Anyon, reprinted from *Journal of Education* 162, no.1 (fall 1980), by permission of the author.

"Class in America: Myths and Realities," by Gregory Mantsios, reprinted from *The American Dream: Class in America*, by permission of the author.

"Learning the Language," by Perri Klass, reprinted from *A Not Entirely Benign Procedure* (1987), by permission of Penguin Group USA, Inc.

"How to Lie with Statistics," by Darrell Huff, reprinted by permission from *Harper's Magazine*, August 1950.

"Streets of Gold: The Myth of the Model Minority," by Curtis Chang, reprinted from *Student Writers at Work*, Third Edition (1989), by permission of Bedford St. Martin's Press.

"The Human Cost of an Illiterate Society," by Jonathan Kozol, reprinted from *Illiterate America* (1985), Random House, Inc.

"The Limits to Growth," by Donella Meadows, Dennis L. Meadows, and Jorgen Randers, reprinted from *Limits to Growth* (1972), Universe Books.

"Pie in the Sky," by Bill McKibben, reprinted from *Orion*, March/April 2006, by permission of the author.

"No Logo," by Naomi Klein, reprinted from *No Logo: Taking Aim at the Brand Bullies* (2000), Bedford St. Martin's Press.

"Why I Want a Wife," by Judy Brady, reprinted from *Ms.*, December 31, 1971, by permission of the author.

"Woody Guthrie bio," by Judy Bell and Nora Guthrie, reprinted from *Woody Guthrie Classics Songbook* by permission of Woody Guthrie Publications.

"Plane Wreck at Los Gatos (Deportee)," by Woody Guthrie, (1948), Ludlow Music, Inc.

"Girl," by Jamaica Kincaid, reprinted from *At the Bottom of the River* (1983), by permission of Farrar, Straus and Giroux.

"A Nation of Welfare Families," by Stephanie Coontz, reprinted from *Harper's Magazine*, October 1992, by permission of the author.

CONTENTS

Personal Views of Work

Working for Wages

Theorizing about Work

Work: Issues, Problems, and Dilemmas

A Message to the Students in this Course from the William Paterson University Program in Writing and Rhetoric

What Is A Writing Workshop?

A writing workshop is a class where the main text is students' writing. That may seem like an odd beginning to a textbook that's a collection of other people's published work. Nonetheless, it's true. The main focus of this class is not the collection of essays that you hold in your hands. We hope that this collection will give you a lot to write about, but it's the writing that you generate and share with your classmates and your teacher that makes up the main focus of study in this class. What do *those* pieces say? How do they work? What effect do they have? What discussion do they provoke? These are the questions we want you ponder and discuss in the upcoming semester.

What kind of writing will you be doing? To a large extent, this is up to your teacher who has selected this textbook from among numerous different collections because the overall topic (work) presents interesting possibilities and because she thinks that the selections themselves are ones that will provoke discussion. But we hope that you'll experiment with different kinds of writing because there are a variety of ways to respond to these readings. We hope that you'll talk about your reactions to the selections, tell (or make up) your own stories, have discussions with each other in writing, analyze what the writers say, discuss how the readings work on you as a reader, and report on similarities and differences between how you responded and how other people responded—just to name a few possibilities. In other words, what we'd like you to come away with at the end of this course is a sense of how readings can provoke different kinds of responses in you as a reader and an appreciation of how writing can take different shapes and forms and lead you in different directions. As experts and teachers, that's what makes writing interesting to us and what we hope to transmit in a writing course.

So this will be a course where you read published work but spend just as much time (if not more) sharing and discussing your own pieces of writing. It's important, therefore, to emphasize a key difference between the writing you'll be doing and the writing in this textbook: the essays in this book are *finished*. The writers have worked on them, shared them with other writers and editors, revised them, and carefully prepared them for publication. What you don't get to see is how these pieces were written—where they started, how they developed, what wrong turns the writer took, or where he had a breakthrough. The author's writing process is hidden behind the final product.

Understanding the difference between the finished piece of writing and the writing process itself is also an important aspect of a workshop course. Many traditional English courses focus mainly on the finished product. If you're like most students, you've probably had a few English teachers who have talked about writing in terms of introductions, conclusions, thesis statements, topic sentences, evidence, and transitions. These are words that describe the way a piece of finished writing looks—how its parts fit together. Maybe you've even had teachers who asked that you make an outline of your writing before beginning, indicating that you have a plan for fitting the pieces together.

There's a problem with thinking about writing this way, and it's one that's worth mentioning here because using a book of essays in a writing course can make this problem even worse. There is a difference between *analyzing* a piece of writing and *creating* a piece of writing. We can look at a piece of writing and describe the parts of it and how those parts work. But you're only seeing the final step in the process. It's unlikely that the writer created her piece by figuring out all the parts she needed and then planning the way they would fit together best. Usually, writing just doesn't work that way.

So we want you to read these essays, react to them, talk about them, write about them, compare your responses, and write about them some more. Because this is how we think that writing works. It almost never progresses in a straight line, from idea to completion. A workshop class like this one is as concerned with the creative process as it is with the final piece of writing. These are the main activities of a workshop class—talking, writing, sharing, and revising. We think that most of the energy in the class—as well as most of the feedback from your teacher—should be directed towards these activities.

Sharing Drafts of Writing With Other Students: What Do They Know, Anyway?

Students (and sometimes even teachers) are skeptical about sharing writing with other students. You may be used to looking to your teacher for guidance with your writing, and you may worry that other students don't know enough to give good advice. Or you may not trust yourself to give good feedback to other people's writing. These are valid concerns. And yet, we believe that the act of sharing writing with other people is so important that it needs to be the central activity of any good writing course.

We think that sharing and responding to writing is a bit like writing itself: It's complex, it's messy, and there's no one right way to do it. That's frustrating if you're waiting for someone to tell you what to do. But we hope that it's also exciting. Writing and responding isn't like painting by numbers. It's a much richer experience than that.

Of course, your teacher will have a lot of good advice about the process of sharing your writing and responding to your classmates' drafts. He'll probably also have some suggestions about what questions to ask or what form your responses could take. But we have two pieces of advice about this process as you go through the semester:

1. Don't worry too much about giving or getting advice about how to make the writing better. Sometimes you can get good advice from readers about this, but not all of the time. If you think that this is the main benefit from sharing your writing, then you're likely to be disappointed more often than not. Remember that you'll always have your teacher to give you guidance and advice. Classroom readers aren't substitutes for your teacher. Your main job when you're in your writing groups or discussing a piece of writing with the class is to be engaged and interested readers—not to try to guess what your teacher would say.
2. Even if you don't get or give any feedback at all, you're still doing something crucial by sharing your writing with readers. Ask just about any writer, and they'll tell you this. There's something about bringing your words out in public—even if it's just a rough draft—that makes a difference. When you speak those words out loud, when you hear them read by other people, when you experience them through other people's eyes and ears—they take on a life that they didn't have before. Sharing is an act of commitment both for writers and for readers. What you need is readers who will take your writing seriously.

We know that everyone in this class begins in a different place, with different backgrounds, different levels of experience and success as writers. We don't think this matters much. What matters is that a writing workshop is a place where you will take writing seriously, where you will commit to this process of reading, talking, sharing, and revising. That's what we're asking of you in this course.

If you have any questions or comments about the Program in Writing and Rhetoric, we hope that you will stop by the English Department Office in the Atrium Building and talk with us about them. Good luck, and have a great semester!

–Chris Weaver (on behalf of the William Paterson University Program in Writing and Rhetoric)

What Work Is

Philip Levine [b. 1928]

We stand in the rain in a long line
waiting at Ford Highland Park. For work.
You know what work is—if you're
old enough to read this you know what
work is, although you may not do it.
Forget you. This is about waiting,
shifting from one foot to another.
Feeling the light rain falling like mist
into your hair, blurring your vision
until you think you see your own brother
ahead of you, maybe ten places.
You rub your glasses with your fingers,
and of course it's someone else's brother,
narrower across the shoulders than
yours but with the same sad slouch, the grin
that does not hide the stubbornness,
the sad refusal to give in to
rain, to the hours wasted waiting,
to the knowledge that somewhere ahead
a man is waiting who will say, "No,
we're not hiring today," for any
reason he wants. You love your brother,
now suddenly you can hardly stand
the love flooding you for your brother,
who's not beside you or behind or
ahead because he's home trying to
sleep off a miserable night shift
at Cadillac so he can get up
before noon to study his German.
Works eight hours a night so he can sing
Wagner, the opera you hate most,
the worst music ever invented.

How long has it been since you told him
you loved him, held his wide shoulders,
opened your eyes wide and said those words,
and maybe kissed his cheek? You've never
done something so simple, so obvious,
not because you're too young or too dumb,
not because you're jealous or even mean
or incapable of crying in
the presence of another man, no,
just because you don't know what work is.

[1991]

The Inheritance of Tools

Scott Russell Sanders [b. 1945]

Scott Russell Sanders (1945–) was born in Memphis, Tennessee, attended Brown University and took a Ph.D. at Cambridge University. He writes on a variety of subjects for "little" magazines such as The Georgia Review *and* The North American Review *and for more commercial publications such as* Omni *and* Isaac Asimov's Science Fiction Magazine. *His published books include* Wonders Hidden: Audubon's Early Years *(1984),* Hear the Wind Blow: American Folksongs Retold *(1985), and* The Paradise of Bombs *(1987). His writing is characteristically rich in detail and focused on the ironies and complexities of human experience. The essay that follows first appeared in* The North American Review *in 1986 and uses a story within a story to pay tribute to his father's teaching.*

At just about the hour when my father died, soon after dawn one February morning when ice coated the windows like cataracts, I banged my thumb with a hammer. Naturally I swore at the hammer, the reckless thing, and in the moment of swearing I thought of what my father would say: "If you'd try hitting the nail it would go in a whole lot faster. Don't you know your thumb's not as hard as that hammer?" We both were doing carpentry that day, but far apart. He was building cupboards at my brother's place in Oklahoma; I was at home in Indiana putting up a wall in the basement to make a bedroom for my daughter. By the time my mother called with news of his death—the long distance wires whittling her voice until it seemed too thin to bear the weight of what she had to say—my thumb was swollen. A week or so later a white scar in the shape of a crescent moon began to show above the cuticle, and month by month it rose across the pink sky of my thumbnail. It took the better part of a year for the scar to disappear, and every time I noticed it I thought of my father.

The hammer had belonged to him, and to his father before him. The three of us have used it to build houses and barns and chicken coops, to upholster chairs and crack walnuts, to make doll furniture and bookshelves and jewelry boxes. The head is scratched and pockmarked, like an old plowshare that has been working rocky fields, and it gives off the sort of dull sheen you see on fast creek water in the shade. It is a finishing hammer, about the weight of a bread loaf, too light really for framing walls, too heavy for cabinetwork, with a curved claw for pulling nails, a rounded head for pounding, a fluted neck for looks, and a hickory handle for strength.

The present handle is my third one, bought from a lumberyard in Tennessee down the road from where my brother and I were helping my father build his retirement house. I broke the previous one by trying to pull sixteen-penny nails out of floor joists—a foolish thing to do with a finishing hammer, as my father pointed out. "You ever hear of a crowbar?" he said. No telling how many handles he and my grandfather had gone through before me. My grandfather used to cut down hickory trees on his farm, saw them into slabs, cure the planks in his hayloft, and carve handles with a drawknife. The grain in hickory is crooked and knotty, and therefore tough, hard to split, like the grain in the two men who owned this hammer before me.

After proposing marriage to a neighbor girl, my grandfather used this hammer to build a house for his bride on a stretch of river bottom in northern Mississippi. The lumber for the place, like the hickory for the handle, was cut on his own land. By the day of the wedding he had not quite finished the house, and so right after the ceremony he took his wife home and put her to work. My grandmother had worn her Sunday dress for the wedding, with a fringe of lace tacked on around the hem in honor of the occasion. She removed this lace and folded it away before going out to help my grandfather nail siding on the house. "There she was in her good dress," he told me some fifty-odd years after that wedding day, "holding up them long pieces of clapboard while I hammered, and together we got the place covered up before dark." As the family grew to four, six, eight, and eventually thirteen, my grandfather used this hammer to enlarge his house room by room, like a chambered nautilus expanding its shell.

By and by the hammer was passed along to my father. One day he was up on the roof of our pony barn nailing shingles with it, when I stepped out the kitchen door to call him for supper. Before I could yell, something about the sight of him straddling the spine of that roof and swinging the hammer caught my eye and made me hold my tongue. I was five or six years old, and the world's commonplaces were still news to me. He would pull a nail from the pouch at his waist, bring the hammer down, and a moment later the *thunk* of the blow would reach my ears. And that is what had stopped me in my tracks and stilled my tongue, that momentary gap between seeing and hearing the blow. Instead of yelling from the kitchen door, I ran to the barn and climbed two rungs up the ladder—as far as I was allowed to go—and spoke quietly to my father. On our walk to the house he explained that sound takes time to make its way through air. Suddenly the world seemed larger, the air more dense, if sound could be held back like any ordinary traveler.

By the time I started using this hammer, at about the age when I discovered the speed of sound, it already contained houses and mysteries for me. The smooth handle was one my grandfather had made. In those days I needed both hands to swing it. My father would start a nail in a scrap of wood, and I would pound away until I bent it over.

"Looks like you got ahold of some of those rubber nails," he would tell me. "Here, let me see if I can find you some stiff ones." And he would rummage in a drawer until he came up with a fistful of more cooperative nails. "Look at the head," he would tell me. "Don't look at your hands, don't look at the hammer. Just look at the head of that nail and pretty soon you'll learn to hit it square."

Pretty soon I did learn. While he worked in the garage cutting dovetail joints for a drawer or skinning a deer or tuning an engine, I would hammer nails. I made innocent blocks of wood look like porcupines. He did not talk much in the midst of his tools, but he kept up a nearly ceaseless humming, slipping in and out of a dozen tunes in an afternoon, often running back over the same stretch of melody again and again, as if searching for a way out. When the humming did cease, I knew he was faced with a task requiring great delicacy or concentration, and I took care not to distract him.

He kept scraps of wood in a cardboard box—the ends of two-by-fours, slabs of shelving and plywood, odd pieces of molding—and everything in it was fair game. I nailed scraps together to fashion what I called boats or houses, but the results usually bore only faint resemblance to the visions I carried in my head. I would hold up these constructions to show my father, and he would turn them over in his hands admiringly, speculating about what they might be. My cobbled-together guitars might have been alien spaceships, my barns might have been models of Aztec temples, each wooden contraption might have been anything but what I had set out to make.

Now and again I would feel the need to have a chunk of wood shaped or shortened before I riddled it with nails, and I would clamp it in a vise and scrape at it with a handsaw. My father would let me lacerate the board until my arm gave out, and then he would wrap his hand around mine and help me finish the cut, showing me how to use my thumb to guide the blade, how to pull back on the saw to keep it from binding, how to let my shoulder do the work.

"Don't force it," he would say, "just drag it easy and give the teeth a chance to bite."

As the saw teeth bit down the wood released its smell, each kind with its own fragrance, oak or walnut or cherry or pine—usually pine, because it was the softest and the easiest for a child to work. No matter how weathered and gray the board, no matter how warped and cracked, inside there was this smell waiting, as of something freshly baked. I gathered every smidgen of sawdust and stored it away in coffee cans, which I kept in a drawer of the workbench. When I did not feel like hammering nails I would dump my sawdust on the concrete floor of the garage and landscape it into highways and farms and towns, running miniature cars and trucks along miniature roads. Looming as huge as a colossus, my father worked over and around me, now and again bending down to inspect my work, careful not to trample my creations. It was a landscape that smelled dizzyingly of wood. Even after a bath my skin would carry the smell, and so would my father's hair, when he lifted me for a bedtime hug.

I tell these things not only from memory but also from recent observation, because my own son now turns blocks of wood into nailed porcupines, dumps cans full of sawdust at my feet, and sculpts highways on the floor. He learns how to swing a hammer from the elbow instead of the wrist, how to lay his thumb beside the blade to guide a saw, how to tap a chisel with a wooden mallet, how to mark a hole with an awl before starting a drill bit. My daughter did the same before him, and even now, on the brink of teenage aloofness, she will occasionally drag out my box of wood scraps and carpenter something. So I have seen my apprenticeship to wood and tools reenacted in each of my children, as my father saw his own apprenticeship renewed in me.

The saw I use belonged to him, as did my level and both of my squares, and all four tools had belonged to his father. The blade of the saw is the bluish color of gun barrels, and the maple handle, dark from the sweat of hands, is inscribed with curving leaf designs. The level is a shaft of walnut two feet long, edged with brass and pierced by three round windows in which air bubbles float in oil-filled tubes of glass. The middle window serves for testing if a surface is horizontal, the others for testing whether it is plumb or vertical. My grandfather used to carry this level on the gun rack behind the seat in his pickup, and when I rode with him I would turn around to watch the bubbles dance. The larger of the two squares is called a framing square, a flat steel elbow so beat up and tarnished you can barely make out the rows of numbers that show how to figure the cuts on rafters. The smaller one is called a try square, for marking right angles, with a blued steel blade for the shank and a brass-faced block of cherry for the head.

I was taught early on that a saw is not to be used apart from a square: "If you're going to cut a piece of wood," my father insisted, "you owe it to the tree to cut it straight."

Long before studying geometry, I learned there is a mystical virtue in right angles. There is an unspoken morality in seeking the level and the plumb. A house will stand, a table will bear weight, the sides of a box will hold together only if the joints are square and the members upright. When the bubble is lined up between two marks etched in the glass tube of a level, you have aligned yourself with the forces that hold the universe together. When you miter the corners of a picture frame, each angle must be exactly forty-five degrees, as they are in the perfect triangles of Pythagoras, not a degree more or less. Otherwise the frame will hang crookedly, as if ashamed of itself and of its maker. No matter if the joints you are cutting do not show. Even if you are butting two pieces of wood together inside a cabinet, where no one except a wrecking crew will ever see them, you must take pains to ensure that the ends are square and the studs are plumb.

I took pains over the wall I was building on the day my father died. Not long after that wall was finished—paneled with tongue-and-groove boards of yellow pine, the nail holes filled with putty and the wood all stained and sealed—I came close to wrecking it one afternoon when my daughter ran howling up the stairs to announce that her gerbils had escaped from their cage and were hiding in my brand-new wall. She could hear them scratching and squeaking behind her bed. Impossible! I said. How on earth could they get inside my drum-tight wall? Through the heating vent, she answered. I went downstairs, pressed my ear to the honey-colored wood, and heard the scritch scritch of tiny feet.

"What can we do?" my daughter wailed. "They'll starve to death, they'll die of thirst, they'll suffocate."

"Hold on," I soothed. "I'll think of something."

While I thought and she fretted, the radio on her bedside table delivered us the headlines: Several thousand people had died in a city in India from a poisonous cloud that had leaked overnight from a chemical plant. A nuclear-powered submarine had been launched. Rioting continued in South Africa. An airplane had been hijacked in the Mediterranean. Authorities calculated that several thousand homeless people slept on the streets within sight of the Washington Monument. I felt my usual helplessness in the face of all these calamities. But here was my daughter weeping because her gerbils were holed up in a wall. This calamity I could handle.

"Don't worry," I told her. "We'll set food and water by the heating vent and lure them out. And if that doesn't do the trick, I'll tear the wall apart until we find them."

She stopped crying and gazed at me. "You'd really tear it apart? Just for my gerbils? The *wall?*" Astonishment slowed her down only for a second, however, before she ran to the workbench and began tugging at drawers, saying, "Let's see, what'll we need? Crowbar. Hammer. Chisels. I hope we don't have to use them—but just in case."

We didn't need the wrecking tools. I never had to assault my handsome wall, because the gerbils eventually came out to nibble at a dish of popcorn. But for several hours I studied the tongue-and-groove skin I had nailed up on the day of my father's death, considering where to begin prying. There were no gaps in that wall, no crooked joints.

I had botched a great many pieces of wood before I mastered the right angle with a saw, botched even more before I learned to miter a joint. The knowledge of these things resides in my hands and eyes and the webwork of muscles, not in the tools. There are machines for sale—powered miter boxes and radial arm saws, for instance—that will enable any casual soul to cut proper angles in boards. The skill is invested in the gadget instead of the person who uses it, and this is what distinguishes a machine from a tool. If I had to earn my keep by making furniture or building houses, I suppose I would buy powered saws and pneumatic nailers; the need for speed would drive me to it. But since I carpenter only for my own pleasure or to help neighbors or to remake the house around the ears of my family, I stick with hand tools. Most of the ones I own were given to me by my father, who also taught me how to wield them. The tools in my workbench are a double inheritance, for each hammer and level and saw is wrapped in a cloud of knowing.

All of these tools are a pleasure to look at and to hold. Merchants would never paste NEW NEW NEW$ signs on them in stores. Their designs are old because they work, because they serve their purpose well. Like folk songs and aphorisms and the grainy bits of language, these tools have been pared down to essentials. I look at my claw hammer, the distillation of a hundred generations of carpenters, and consider that it holds up well beside those other classics—Greek vases, Gregorian chants, *Don Quixote,* barbed fish-hooks, candles, spoons. Knowledge of hammering stretches back to the earliest humans who squatted beside fires chipping flints. Anthropologists have a lovely name for those unworked rocks that served as the earliest hammers. "Dawn stones" they are called. Their only qualification for the work, aside from hardness, is that they fit the hand. Our ancestors used them for grinding corn, tapping awls, smashing bones. From dawn stones to the claw hammer is a great leap in time, but no great distance in design or imagination.

On that iced-over February morning when I smashed my thumb with the hammer, I was down in the basement framing the wall that my daughter's gerbils would later hide in. I was thinking of my father, as I always did whenever I built anything, thinking how he would have gone about the work, hearing in memory what he would have said about the wisdom of hitting the nail instead of my thumb. I had the studs and plates nailed together all square and trim, and was lifting the wall into place when the phone rang upstairs. My wife answered, and in a moment she came to the basement door and called down softly to me. The stillness in her voice made me drop the framed wall and hurry upstairs. She told me my father was dead. Then I heard the details over the phone from my mother. Building a set of cupboards for my brother in Oklahoma, he had knocked off work early the previous afternoon because of cramps in his stomach. Early this morning, on his way into the kitchen of my brother's trailer, maybe going for a glass of water, so early that no one else was awake, he slumped down on the linoleum and his heart quit.

For several hours I paced around inside my house, upstairs and down, in and out of every room, looking for the right door to open and knowing there was no such door. My wife and children followed me and wrapped me in arms and backed away again, circling and staring as if I were on fire. Where was the door, the door, the door? I kept wondering. My smashed thumb turned purple and throbbed, making me furious. I wanted to cut it off and rush outside and scrape away the snow and hack a hole in the frozen earth and bury the shameful thing.

I went down into the basement, opened a drawer in my workbench, and stared at the ranks of chisels and knives. Oiled and sharp, as my father would have kept them, they gleamed at me like teeth. I took up a clasp knife, pried out the longest blade, and tested the edge on the hair of my forearm. A tuft came away cleanly, and I saw my father testing the sharpness of tools on his own skin, the blades of axes and knives and gouges and hoes, saw the red hair shaved off in patches from his arms and the backs of hands. "That will cut bear," he would say. He never cut a bear with his blades, now my blades, but he cut deer, dirt, wood. I closed the knife and put it away. Then I took up the hammer and went back to work on my daughter's wall, snugging the bottom plate against a chalk line on the floor, shimming the top plate against the joists overhead, plumbing the studs with my level, making sure before I drove the first nail that every line was square and true.

[1986]

Serve or Fail

Dave Eggers [b. 1971]

About now, most recent college graduates, a mere week or two beyond their last final, are giving themselves a nice respite. Maybe they're on a beach, maybe they're on a road trip, maybe they're in their rooms, painting their toenails black with a Q-tip and shoe polish. Does it matter? What's important is that they have some time off.

Do they deserve the time off? Well, yes and no. Yes, because finals week is stressful and sleep-deprived and possibly involves trucker-style stimulants. No, because a good deal of the four years of college is spent playing foosball.

I went to a large state school—the University of Illinois—and during my time there, I became one of the best two or three foosball players in the Land of Lincoln. I learned to pass deftly between my rigid players, to play the corners, to strike the ball like a cobra would strike something a cobra would want to strike. I also mastered the dart game called Cricket, and the billiards contest called Nine-ball. I became expert at whiffle ball, at backyard archery, and at a sport we invented that involved one person tossing roasted chickens from a balcony to a group of us waiting below. We got to eat the parts that didn't land on the patio.

The point is that college is too long—it should be three years—and that even with a full course load and part-time jobs (I had my share) there are many hours in the days and weeks that need killing. And because most of us, as students, saw our hours as in need of killing—as opposed to thinking about giving a few of these hours to our communities in one way or another—colleges should consider instituting a service requirement for graduation.

I volunteered a few times in Urbana-Champaign—at a Y.M.C.A. and at a home for senior citizens—and in both cases it was much too easy to quit. I thought the senior home smelled odd, so I left, and though the Y.M.C.A. was a perfect fit, I could have used nudging to continue—nudging the university might have provided. Just as parents and schools need to foster in young people a "reading habit"—a love of reading that becomes a need, almost an addiction—colleges are best-poised to create in their students a lifelong commitment to volunteering even a few hours a month.

Some colleges, and many high schools, have such a thing in place, and last year Michael R. Veon, a Democratic member of Pennsylvania's House of Representatives, introduced a bill that would require the more than 90,000 students at 14 state-run universities to perform 25 hours of community service annually. That comes out to more than two million volunteer hours a year.

College students are, for the most part, uniquely suited to have time for and to benefit from getting involved and addressing the needs of those around them. Unlike high school students, they're less programmed, less boxed-in by family and after-school obligations. They're also more mature, and better able to handle a wide range of tasks. Finally, they're at a stage where exposure to service—and to the people whose lives non-profit service organizations touch—would have a profound effect on them. Meeting a World War II veteran who needs meals brought to him would be educational for the deliverer of that meal, I would think. A college history major might learn something by tutoring a local middle school class that's studying the Underground Railroad. A connection would be forged; a potential career might be discovered.

A service requirement won't work everywhere. It probably wouldn't be feasible, for example, for community college students, who tend to be transient and who generally have considerable family and work demands. But exempt community colleges and you would still have almost 10 million college students enrolled in four-year colleges in the United States. If you exempted a third of them for various reasons, that would leave more than 6 million able-bodied young people at the ready. Even with a modest 10-hour-a-year requirement (the equivalent of two mornings a year) America would gain 60 million volunteer hours to invigorate the nation's nonprofit organizations, churches, job corps, conservation groups and college outreach programs.

And with some flexibility, it wouldn't have to be too onerous. Colleges could give credit for service. That is, at the beginning of each year, a student could opt for service, and in return he or she might get credits equal to one class period. Perhaps every 25 hours of service could be traded for one class credit, with a maximum of three credits a year. What a student would learn from working in a shelter for the victims of domestic abuse would surely equal or surpass his or her time spent in racquetball class—at my college worth one full unit.

Alternatively, colleges could limit the service requirement to a student's junior year—a time when the students are settled and have more hours and stability in their schedules. Turning the junior year into a year when volunteering figures prominently could also help colleges bridge the chasm that usually stands between the academic world and the one that lies beyond it.

When Gov. Gray Davis of California proposed a service requirement in 1999, an editorial in *The Daily Californian,* the student newspaper at the University of California at Berkeley, opposed the plan: "Forced philanthropy will be as much an oxymoron in action as it is in terms. Who would want to receive community service from someone who is forced to serve? Is forced community service in California not generally reserved for criminals and delinquents?"

First of all, that's putting forth a pretty dim view of the soul of the average student. What, is the unwilling college volunteer going to *throw food* at visitors to the soup kitchen? Volunteering is by nature transformative—reluctant participants become quick converts every day, once they meet those who need their help.

Second, college is largely about fulfilling requirements, isn't it? Students have to complete this much work in the sciences, that much work in the arts. Incoming freshmen accept a tacit contract, submitting to the wisdom of the college's founders and shapers, who decide which experiences are necessary to create a well-rounded scholar, one ready to make a contribution to the world. But while colleges give their students the intellectual tools for life beyond campus, they largely ignore the part about how they might contribute to the world. That is, until the commencement speech, at which time all the "go forth's" and "be helpful's" happen.

But what if such a sentiment happened on the student's first day? What if graduating seniors already knew full well how to balance jobs, studies, family, and volunteer work in the surrounding community? What if campuses were full of underserved high school students meeting with their college tutors? What if the tired and clogged veins of thousands of towns and cities had the energy of millions of college students coursing through them? What if the student who might have become a foosball power—and I say this knowing how much those skills have enhanced my life and those who had the good fortune to have watched me—became instead a lifelong volunteer? That might be pretty good for everybody.

[2004]

On Dumpster Diving

Lars Eighner [b. 1948]

Long before I began Dumpster diving I was impressed with Dumpsters, enough so that I wrote the Merriam-Webster research service to discover what I could about the word "Dumpster." I learned from them that "Dumpster" is a proprietary word belonging to the Dempster Dumpster company.

Since then I have dutifully capitalized the word although it was lower-cased in almost all of the citations Merriam-Webster photocopied for me. Dempster's word is too apt. I have never heard these things called anything but Dumpsters. I do not know anyone who knows the generic name for these objects. From time to time, however, I hear a wino or hobo give some corrupted credit to the original and call them Dipsy Dumpsters.

I began Dumpster diving about a year before I became homeless.

I prefer the term "scavenging" and use the word "scrounging" when I mean to be obscure. I have heard people, evidently meaning to be polite, using the word "foraging," but I prefer to reserve that word for gathering nuts and berries and such which I do also according to the season and the opportunity. "Dumpster diving" seems to me to be a little too cute and, in my case, inaccurate because I lack the athletic ability to lower myself into the Dumpsters as the true divers do, much to their increased profit.

I like the frankness of the word "scavenging," which I can hardly think of without picturing a big black snail on an aquarium wall. I live from the refuse of others. I am a scavenger. I think it a sound and honorable niche, although if I could I would naturally prefer to live the comfortable consumer life, perhaps—and only perhaps—as a slightly less wasteful consumer owing to what I have learned as a scavenger.

While my dog Lizbeth and I were still living in the house on Avenue B in Austin, as my savings ran out, I put almost all my sporadic income into rent. The necessities of daily life I began to extract from Dumpsters. Yes, we ate from Dumpsters. Except for jeans, all my clothes came from Dumpsters. Boom boxes, candles, bedding, toilet paper, medicine, books, a typewriter, a virgin male love doll, change sometimes amounting to many dollars: I acquired many things from the Dumpsters.

I have learned much as a scavenger. I mean to put some of what I have learned down here, beginning with the practical art of Dumpster diving and proceeding to the abstract.

What is safe to eat?

After all, the finding of objects is becoming something of an urban art. Even respectable employed people will sometimes find something tempting sticking out of a Dumpster or standing beside one. Quite a number of people, not all of them of the bohemian type, are willing to brag that they found this or that piece in the trash. But eating from Dumpsters is the thing that separates the dilettanti from the professionals.

Eating safely from the Dumpsters involves three principles: 10
using the senses and common sense to evaluate the condition of the found materials, knowing the Dumpsters of a given area and checking them regularly, and seeking always to answer the question "Why was this discarded?"

Perhaps everyone who has a kitchen and a regular supply of groceries has, at one time or another, made a sandwich and eaten half of it before discovering mold on the bread or got a mouthful of milk before realizing the milk had turned. Nothing of the sort is likely to happen to a Dumpster diver because he is constantly reminded that most food is discarded for a reason. Yet a lot of perfectly good food can be found in Dumpsters.

Canned goods, for example, turn up fairly often in the Dumpsters I frequent. All except the most phobic people would be willing to eat from a can even if it came from a Dumpster. Canned goods are among the safest of foods to be found in Dumpsters, but are not utterly foolproof.

Although very rare with modern canning methods, botulism is a possibility. Most other forms of food poisoning seldom do lasting harm to a healthy person. But botulism is almost certainly fatal and often the first symptom is death. Except for carbonated beverages, all canned goods should contain a slight vacuum and suck air when first punctured. Bulging, rusty, dented cans and cans that spew when punctured should be avoided, especially when the contents are not very acidic or syrupy.

Heat can break down the botulin, but this requires much more cooking than most people do to canned goods. To the extent that botulism occurs at all, of course, it can occur in cans on pantry shelves as well as in cans from Dumpsters. Need I say that home-canned goods found in Dumpsters are simply too risky to be recommended.

From time to time one of my companions, aware of the source of my provisions, will ask, "Do you think these crackers are really safe to eat?" For some reason it is most often the crackers they ask about.

This question always makes me angry. Of course I would not offer my companion anything I had doubts about. But more than that I wonder why he cannot evaluate the condition of the crackers for himself. I have no special knowledge and I have been wrong before. Since he knows where the food comes from, it seems to me he ought to assume some of the responsibility for deciding what he will put in his mouth.

For myself I have few qualms about dry foods such as crackers, cookies, cereal, chips, and pasta if they are free of visible contaminates and still dry and crisp. Most often such things are found in the original packaging, which is not so much a positive sign as it is the absence of a negative one.

Raw fruits and vegetables with intact skins seem perfectly safe to me, excluding of course the obviously rotten. Many are discarded for minor imperfections which can be pared away. Leafy vegetables, grapes, cauliflower, broccoli, and similar things may be contaminated by liquids and may be impractical to wash.

Candy, especially hard candy, is usually safe if it has not drawn ants. Chocolate is often discarded only because it has become discolored as the cocoa butter de-emulsified. Candying after all is one method of food preservation because pathogens do not like very sugary substances.

All of these foods might be found in any Dumpster and can be 20
evaluated with some confidence largely on the basis of appearance. Beyond these are foods which cannot be correctly evaluated without additional information.

I began scavenging by pulling pizzas out of the Dumpster behind a pizza delivery shop. In general prepared food requires caution, but in this case I knew when the shop closed and went to the Dumpster as soon as the last of the help left.

Such shops often get prank orders, called "bogus." Because help seldom stays long at these places pizzas are often made with the wrong topping, refused on delivery for being cold, or baked incorrectly. The products to be discarded are boxed up because inventory is kept by counting boxes: A boxed pizza can be written off; an unboxed pizza does not exist.

I never placed a bogus order to increase the supply of pizzas and I believe no one else was scavenging in this Dumpster. But the people in the shop became suspicious and began to retain their garbage in the shop overnight.

While it lasted I had a steady supply of fresh, sometimes warm pizza. Because I knew the Dumpster I knew the source of the pizza, and because I visited the Dumpster regularly I knew what was fresh and what was yesterday's.

The area I frequent is inhabited by many affluent college stu- 25
dents. I am not here by chance; the Dumpsters in this area are very rich. Students throw out many good things, including food. In particular they tend to throw everything out when they move at the end of a semester, before and after breaks, and around midterm when many of them despair of college. So I find it advantageous to keep an eye on the academic calendar.

The students throw food away around the breaks because they do not know whether it has spoiled or will spoil before they return. A typical discard is a half jar of peanut butter. In fact nonorganic peanut butter does not require refrigeration and is unlikely to spoil in any reasonable time. The student does not know that, and since it is Daddy's money, the student decides not to take a chance.

Opened containers require caution and some attention to the question "Why was this discarded?" But in the case of discards from student apartments, the answer may be that the item was discarded through carelessness, ignorance, or wastefulness. This can sometimes be deduced when the item is found with many others, including some that are obviously perfectly good.

Some students, and others, approach defrosting a freezer by chucking out the whole lot. Not only do the circumstances of such a find tell the story, but also the mass of frozen goods stays cold for a long time and items may be found still frozen or freshly thawed.

Yogurt, cheese, and sour cream are items that are often thrown out while they are still good. Occasionally I find a cheese with a spot of mold, which of course I just pare off, and because it is obvious why such a cheese was discarded, I treat it with less suspicion than an apparently perfect cheese found in similar circumstances. Yogurt is often discarded, still sealed, only because the expiration date on the carton had passed. This is one of my favorite finds because yogurt will keep for several days, even in warm weather.

Students throw out canned goods and staples at the end of semesters and when they give up college at midterm. Drugs, pornography, spirits, and the like are often discarded when parents are expected—Dad's day, for example. And spirits also turn up after big party weekends, presumably discarded by the newly reformed. Wine and spirits, of course, keep perfectly well even once opened.

My test for carbonated soft drinks is whether they still fizz vigorously. Many juices or other beverages are too acid or too syrupy to cause much concern provided they are not visibly contaminated. Liquids, however, require some care.

One hot day I found a large jug of Pat O'Brien's Hurricane mix. The jug had been opened, but it was still ice cold. I drank three large glasses before it became apparent to me that someone had added the rum to the mix, and not a little rum. I never tasted the rum and by the time I began to feel the effects I had already ingested a very large quantity of the beverage. Some divers would have considered this a boon, but being suddenly and thoroughly intoxicated in a public place in the early afternoon is not my idea of a good time.

I have heard of people maliciously contaminating discarded food and even handouts, but mostly I have heard of this from people with vivid imaginations who have had no experience with the Dumpsters themselves. Just before the pizza shop stopped discarding its garbage at night, jalapeños began showing up on most of the discarded pizzas. If indeed this was meant to discourage me it was a wasted effort because I am native Texan.

For myself, I avoid game, poultry, pork, and egg-based foods whether I find them raw or cooked. I seldom have the means to cook what I find, but when I do I avail myself of plentiful supplies of beef which is often in very good condition. I suppose fish becomes disagreeable before it becomes dangerous. The dog is happy to have any such thing that is past its prime and, in fact, does not recognize fish as food until it is quite strong.

Home leftovers, as opposed to surpluses from restaurants, are 35
very often bad. Evidently, especially among students, there is a common type of personality that carefully wraps up even the smallest leftover and shoves it into the back of the refrigerator for six months or so before discarding it. Characteristic of this type are the reused jars and margarine tubs which house the remains.

I avoid ethnic foods I am unfamiliar with. If I do not know what it is supposed to look like when it is good, I cannot be certain I will be able to tell if it is bad.

No matter how careful I am I still get dysentery at least once a month, oftener in warm weather. I do not want to paint too romantic a picture. Dumpster diving has serious drawbacks as a way of life.

* * *

I learned to scavenge gradually, on my own. Since then I have initiated several companions into the trade. I have learned that there is a predictable series of stages a person goes through in learning to scavenge.

At first the new scavenger is filled with disgust and self-loathing. He is ashamed of being seen and may lurk around, trying to duck behind things, or he may try to dive at night.

(In fact, most people instinctively look away from a scavenger. 40
By skulking around, the novice calls attention to himself and arouses suspicion. Diving at night is ineffective and needlessly messy.)

Every grain of rice seems to be a maggot. Everything seems to stink. He can wipe the egg yolk off the found can, but he cannot erase the stigma of eating garbage out of his mind.

That stage passes with experience. The scavenger finds a pair of running shoes that fit and look and smell brand new. He finds a pocket calculator in perfect working order. He finds pristine ice cream, still frozen, more than he can eat or keep. He begins to understand: People do throw away perfectly good stuff, a lot of perfectly good stuff.

At this stage, Dumpster shyness begins to dissipate. The diver, after all, has the last laugh. He is finding all manner of good things which are his for the taking. Those who disparage his profession are the fools, not he.

He may begin to hang onto some perfectly good things for which he has neither a use nor a market. Then he begins to take note of the things which are not perfectly good but are nearly so. He mates a Walkman with broken earphones and one that is missing a battery cover. He picks up things which he can repair.

At this stage he may become lost and never recover. Dump- 45
sters are full of things of some potential value to someone and also of things which never have much intrinsic value but are interesting. All the Dumpster divers I have known come to the point of trying to acquire everything they touch. Why not take it, they reason, since it is all free.

This is, of course, hopeless. Most divers come to realize that they must restrict themselves to items of relatively immediate utility. But in some cases the diver simply cannot control himself. I have met several of these pack-rat types. Their ideas of the values of various pieces of junk verge on the psychotic. Every bit of glass may be a diamond, they think, and all that glistens, gold.

I tend to gain weight when I am scavenging. Partly this is because I always find far more pizza and doughnuts than water-packed tuna, nonfat yogurt, and fresh vegetables. Also I have not developed much faith in the reliability of Dumpsters as a food source, although it has been proven to me many times. I tend to eat as if I have no idea where my next meal is coming from. But mostly I just hate to see food go to waste and so I eat much more than I should. Something like this drives the obsession to collect junk.

As for collecting objects, I usually restrict myself to collecting one kind of small object at a time, such as pocket calculators, sunglasses, or campaign buttons. To live on the street I must anticipate my needs to a certain extent: I must pick up and save warm bedding I find in August because it will not be found in Dumpsters in November. But even if I had a home with extensive storage space I could not save everything that might be valuable in some contingency.

I have proprietary feelings about my Dumpsters. As I have suggested, it is no accident that I scavenge from Dumpsters where good finds are common. But my limited experience with Dumpsters in other areas suggests to me that it is the population of competitors rather than the affluence of the dumpers that most affects the feasibility of survival by scavenging. The large number of competitors is what puts me off the idea of trying to scavenge in places like Los Angeles.

50 Curiously, I do not mind my direct competition, other scavengers, so much as I hate the can scroungers.

People scrounge cans because they have to have a little cash. I have tried scrounging cans with an able-bodied companion. Afoot a can scrounger simply cannot make more than a few dollars a day. One can extract the necessities of life from the Dumpsters directly with far less effort than would be required to accumulate the equivalent value in cans.

Can scroungers, then, are people who *must* have small amounts of cash. These are drug addicts and winos, mostly the latter because the amounts of cash are so small.

Spirits and drugs do, like all other commodities, turn up in Dumpsters and the scavenger will from time to time have a half bottle of a rather good wine with his dinner. But the wino cannot survive on these occasional finds; he must have his daily dose to stave off the DTs. All the cans he can carry will buy about three bottles of Wild Irish Rose.

I do not begrudge them the cans, but can scroungers tend to tear up the Dumpsters, mixing the contents and littering the area. They become so specialized that they can see only cans. They earn my contempt by passing up change, canned goods, and readily hockable items.

There are precious few courtesies among scavengers. But it is a common practice to set aside surplus items: pairs of shoes, clothing, canned goods, and such. A true scavenger hates to see good stuff go to waste and what he cannot use he leaves in good condition in plain sight.

Can scroungers lay waste to everything in their path and will stir one of a pair of good shoes to the bottom of a Dumpster, to be lost or ruined in the muck. Can scroungers will even go through individual garbage cans, something I have never seen a scavenger do.

Individual garbage cans are set out on the public easement only on garbage days. On other days going through them requires trespassing close to a dwelling. Going through individual garbage cans without scattering litter is almost impossible. Litter is likely to reduce the public's tolerance of scavenging. Individual garbage cans are simply not as productive as Dumpsters; people in houses and duplexes do not move as often and for some reason do not tend to discard as much useful material. Moreover, the time required to go through one garbage can that serves one household is not much less than the time required to go through a Dumpster that contains the refuse of twenty apartments.

But my strongest reservation about going through individual garbage cans is that this seems to me a very personal kind of invasion to which I would object if I were a householder. Although many things in Dumpsters are obviously meant never to come to light, a Dumpster is somehow less personal.

I avoid trying to draw conclusions about the people who dump in the Dumpsters I frequent. I think it would be unethical to do so, although I know many people will find the idea of scavenger ethics too funny for words.

Dumpsters contain bank statements, bills, correspondence, 60
and other documents, just as anyone might expect. But there are also less obvious sources of information. Pill bottles, for example. The labels on pill bottles contain the name of the patient, the name of the doctor, and the name of the drug. AIDS drugs and antipsychotic medicines, to name but two groups, are specific and are seldom prescribed for any other disorders. The plastic compacts for birth control pills usually have complete label information.

Despite all of this sensitive information, I have had only one apartment resident object to my going through the Dumpster. In that case it turned out the resident was a university athlete who was taking bets and who was afraid I would turn up his wager slips.

Occasionally a find tells a story. I once found a small paper bag containing some unused condoms, several partial tubes of flavored sexual lubricant, a partially used compact of birth control pills, and the torn pieces of a picture of a young man. Clearly she was through with him and planning to give up sex altogether.

Dumpster things are often sad—abandoned teddy bears, shredded wedding books, despaired-of sales kits. I find many pets lying in state in Dumpsters. Although I hope to get off the streets so that Lizbeth can have a long and comfortable old age, I know this hope is not very realistic. So I suppose when her time comes she too will go into a Dumpster. I will have no better place for her. And after all, for most of her life her livelihood has come from the Dumpster. When she finds something I think is safe that has been spilled from the Dumpster I let her have it. She already knows the route around the best Dumpsters. I like to think that if she survives me she will have a chance of evading the dog catcher and of finding her sustenance on the route.

Silly vanities also come to rest in the Dumpsters. I am a rather accomplished needleworker. I get a lot of materials from the Dumpsters. Evidently sorority girls, hoping to impress someone, perhaps themselves, with their mastery of a womanly art, buy a lot of embroider-by-number kits, work a few stitches horribly, and eventually discard the whole mess. I pull out their stitches, turn the canvas over, and work an original design. Do not think I refrain from chuckling as I make original gifts from these kits.

I find diaries and journals. I have often thought of compiling a book of literary found objects. And perhaps I will one day. But what I find is hopelessly commonplace and bad without being, even unconsciously, camp. College students also discard their papers. I am horrified to discover the kind of paper which now merits an A in an undergraduate course. I am grateful, however, for the number of good books and magazines the students throw out.

In the area I know best I have never discovered vermin in the Dumpsters, but there are two kinds of kitty surprise. One is alley cats which I meet as they leap, claws first, out of Dumpsters. This is especially thrilling when I have Lizbeth in tow. The other kind of kitty surprise is a plastic garbage bag filled with some ponderous, amorphous mass. This always proves to be used cat litter.

City bees harvest doughnut glaze and this makes the Dumpster at the doughnut shop more interesting. My faith in the instinctive wisdom of animals is always shaken whenever I see Lizbeth attempt to catch a bee in her mouth, which she does whenever bees are present. Evidently some birds find Dumpsters profitable, for birdie surprise is almost as common as kitty surprise of the first kind. In hunting season all kinds of small game turn up in Dumpsters, some of it, sadly, not entirely dead. Curiously, summer and winter, maggots are uncommon.

The worst of the living and near-living hazards of the Dumpsters are the fire ants. The food that they claim is not much of a loss, but they are vicious and aggressive. It is very easy to brush against some surface of the Dumpster and pick up half a dozen or more fire ants, usually in some sensitive area such as the underarm. One advantage of bringing Lizbeth along as I make Dumpster rounds is that, for obvious reasons, she is very alert to ground-based fire ants. When Lizbeth recognizes the signs of fire ant infestation around our feet she does the Dance of the Zillion Fire Ants. I have learned not to ignore this warning from Lizbeth, whether I perceive the tiny ants or not, but to remove ourselves at Lizbeth's first pas de bourrée.° All the more so because the ants are the worst in the months I wear flip-flops, if I have them.

(Perhaps someone will misunderstand the above. Lizbeth does the Dance of the Zillion Fire Ants when she recognizes more fire ants than she cares to eat, not when she is being bitten. Since I have learned to react promptly, she does not get bitten at all. It is the isolated patrol of fire ants that falls in Lizbeth's range that deserves pity. Lizbeth finds them quite tasty.)

70 By far the best way to go through a Dumpster is to lower yourself into it. Most of the good stuff tends to settle at the bottom because it is usually weightier than the rubbish. My more athletic companions have often demonstrated to me that they can extract much good material from a Dumpster I have already been over.

To those psychologically or physically unprepared to enter a Dumpster, I recommend a stout stick, preferably with some barb or hook at one end. The hook can be used to grab plastic garbage bags. When I find canned goods or other objects loose at the bottom of a Dumpster I usually can roll them into a small bag that I can then hoist up. Much Dumpster diving is a matter of experience for which nothing will do except practice.

Dumpster diving is outdoor work, often surprisingly pleasant. It is not entirely predictable; things of interest turn up every day and some days there are finds of great value. I am always very pleased when I can turn up exactly the thing I most wanted to find. Yet in spite of the element of chance, scavenging more than most other pursuits tends to yield returns in some proportion to the effort and intelligence brought to bear. It is very sweet to turn up a few dollars in change from a Dumpster that has just been gone over by a wino.

The land is now covered with cities. The cities are full of Dumpsters. I think of scavenging as a modern form of self-reliance. In any event, after ten years of government service, where everything is geared to the lowest common denominator, I find work

pas de bourrée: A ballet step (French).

that rewards initiative and effort refreshing. Certainly I would be happy to have a sinecure again, but I am not heartbroken not to have one anymore.

I find from the experience of scavenging two rather deep lessons. The first is to take what I can use and let the rest go by. I have come to think that there is no value in the abstract. A thing I cannot use or make useful, perhaps by trading, has no value however fine or rare it may be. I mean useful in a broad sense—so, for example, some art I would think useful and valuable, but other art might be otherwise for me.

I was shocked to realize that some things are not worth ac- 75
quiring, but now I think it is so. Some material things are white elephants that eat up the possessor's substance.

The second lesson is of the transience of material being. This has not quite converted me to a dualist, but it has made some headway in that direction. I do not suppose that ideas are immortal, but certainly mental things are longer-lived than other material things.

Once I was the sort of person who invests material objects with sentimental value. Now I no longer have those things, but I have the sentiments yet.

Many times in my travels I have lost everything but the clothes I was wearing and Lizbeth. The things I find in Dumpsters, the love letters and ragdolls of so many lives, remind me of this lesson. Now I hardly pick up a thing without envisioning the time I will cast it away. This I think is a healthy state of mind. Almost everything I have now has already been cast out at least once, proving that what I own is valueless to someone.

Anyway, I find my desire to grab for the gaudy bauble has been largely sated. I think this is an attitude I share with the very wealthy—we both know there is plenty more where what we have came from. Between us are the rat-race millions who have confounded their selves with the objects they grasp and who nightly scavenge the cable channels looking for they know not what.

I am sorry for them. 80

[1993]

Why I Write

George Orwell [1903–1950]

George Orwell is the pen name used by the British author Eric Blair (1903-1950). Orwell was born in the Indian village of Motihari, near Nepal where his father was stationed in the Civil Service. India was then part of the British Empire. From 1907 to 1922, Orwell lived in England returning to India and Burma and a position in the Imperial Police, which he held until 1927. Thereafter, he lived in England, Paris, Spain, and elsewhere, writing on a wide range of topics. He fought in the Spanish Civil War and was actively engaged in several political movements, always against totalitarianism of any kind. He is best known today for two novels of political satire: Animal Farm *(1945) and 1984 (1949). He was also a prolific journalist and essayist, with his essays collected in five volumes. Orwell wrote "Why I Write" near the end of his life, looking back and writing autobiographically about his own experiences and writing even as he generalizes about all writers. Though Orwell asserts that he, like all writers, is "vain, selfish and lazy," we take this with a grain of salt even as he gives us many insights into the writer's motivations.*

From a very early age, perhaps the age of five or six, I knew that when I grew up I should be a writer. Between the ages of about seventeen and twenty-four I tried to abandon this idea, but I did so with the consciousness that I was outraging my true nature and that sooner or later I should have to settle down and write books.

I was the middle child of three, but there was a gap of five years on either side, and I barely saw my father before I was eight. For this and other reasons I was somewhat lonely, and I soon developed disagreeable mannerisms which made me unpopular throughout my schooldays. I had the lonely child's habit of making up stories and holding conversations with imaginary persons, and I think from the very start my literary ambitions were mixed up with the feeling of being isolated and undervalued. I knew that I had a facility with words and a power of facing unpleasant facts, and I felt that this created a sort of private world in which I could get my own back for my failure in everyday life. Nevertheless the volume of serious—i.e., seriously intended—writing which I produced all through my childhood and boyhood would not amount to half a dozen pages. I wrote my first poem at the age of four or five, my mother taking it down to dictation. I cannot remember anything about it except that it was about a tiger and the tiger had "chair-like teeth"—a good enough phrase, but I fancy the poem was a plagiarism of Blake's "Tiger, Tiger." At eleven when the war of 1914-18 broke out, I wrote a patriotic poem which was printed in the local newspaper, as was another, two years later, on the death of Kitchener. From time to time, when I was a bit older, I wrote bad and usually unfinished "nature poems" in the Georgian style. I also, about twice, attempted a short story which was a ghastly failure. That was the total of the would-be serious work that I actually set down on paper during all those years.

However, throughout this time I did in a sense engage in literary activities. To begin with there was the made-to-order stuff which I produced quickly, easily and without much pleasure to myself. Apart from school work, I wrote *vers d'occasion,* semicomic poems which I could turn out at what now seems to me astonishing speed—at fourteen I wrote a whole rhyming play, in imitation of Aristophanes, in about a week—and helped to edit school magazines, both printed and in manuscript. These magazines were the most pitiful burlesque stuff that you could imagine, and I took far less trouble with them than I now would with the cheapest journalism. But side by side with all this, for fifteen years or more, I was carrying out a literary exercise of a quite different kind: this was the making up of a continuous "story" about myself, a sort of diary existing only in the mind. I believe this is a common habit of children and adolescents. As a very small child I used to imagine that I was, say, Robin Hood, and picture myself as the hero of thrilling adventures, but quite soon my "story" ceased to be narcissistic in a crude way and became more and more a mere description of what I was doing and the things I saw. For minutes at a time this kind of thing would be running through my head: "He pushed the door open and entered the room. A yellow beam of sunlight, filtering through the muslin curtains, slanted on to the table, where a matchbox, half open, lay beside the inkpot. With his right hand in his pocket he moved across to the window. Down in the street a tortoiseshell cat was chasing a dead leaf," etc. etc. This habit continued till I was about twenty-five, right through my non-literary years. Although I had to search, and did search, for the right words, I seemed to be making this descriptive effort almost against my will, under a kind of compulsion from outside. The "story" must, I suppose, have reflected the styles of the various writers I admired at different ages, but so far as I remember it always had the same meticulous descriptive quality.

When I was about sixteen I suddenly discovered the joy of mere words, i.e., the sounds and associations of words. The lines from *Paradise Lost,*

So hee with difficulty and labour hard
Moved on: with difficulty and labour hee,

which do not now seem to me so very wonderful, sent shivers down my backbone; and the spelling "hee" for "he" was an added pleasure. As for the need to describe things, I knew all about it already. So it is clear what kind of books I wanted to write, in so far as I could be said to want to write books at that time. I wanted to write enormous naturalistic novels with unhappy endings, full of detailed descriptions and arresting similes, and also full of purple passages in which words were used partly for the sake of their sound. And in fact my first completed novel, *Burmese Days,* which I wrote when I was thirty but projected much earlier, is rather that kind of book.

I give all this background information because I do not think one can assess a writer's motives without knowing something of his early development. His subject matter will be determined by the age he lives in—at least this is true in tumultuous, revolutionary ages like our own—but before he ever begins to write he will have acquired an emotional attitude from which he will never completely escape. It is his job, no doubt, to discipline his temperament and avoid getting stuck at some immature stage, or in some perverse mood: but if he escapes from his early influences altogether, he will have killed his impulse to write. Putting aside the need to earn a living, I think there are four great motives for writing, at any rate for writing prose. They exist in different degrees in every writer, and in any one writer the proportions will vary from time to time, according to the atmosphere in which he is living. They are:

1. Sheer egoism. Desire to seem clever, to be talked about, to be remembered after death, to get your own back on grown-ups who snubbed you in childhood, etc. etc. It is humbug to pretend that this is not a motive, and a strong one. Writers share this characteristic with scientists, artists, politicians, lawyers, soldiers, successful businessmen—in short, with the whole top crust of humanity. The great mass of human beings are not acutely selfish. After the age of about thirty they abandon individual ambition—in many cases, indeed, they almost abandon the sense of being individuals at all—and live chiefly for others, or are simply smothered under drudgery. But there is also the minority of gifted, wilful people who are determined to live their own lives to the end, and writers belong in this class. Serious writers, I should say, are on the whole more vain and self-centered than journalists, though less interested in money.
2. Aesthetic enthusiasm. Perception of beauty in the external world, or, on the other hand, in words and their right arrangement. Pleasure in the impact of one sound on another, in the firmness of good prose or the rhythm of a good story. Desire to share an experience which one feels is valuable and ought not to be missed. The aesthetic motive is very feeble in a lot of writers, but even a pamphleteer or a writer of textbooks will have pet words and

phrases which appeal to him for non-utilitarian reasons; or he may feel strongly about typography, width of margins, etc. Above the level of a railway guide, no book is quite free from aesthetic considerations.

3. Historical impulse. Desire to see things as they are, to find out true facts and store them up for the use of posterity.
4. Political purpose—using the word "political" in the widest possible sense. Desire to push the world in a certain direction, to alter other people's idea of the kind of society that they should strive after. Once again, no book is genuinely free from political bias. The opinion that art should have nothing to do with politics is itself a political attitude.

It can be seen how these various impulses must war against one 10
another, and how they must fluctuate from person to person and from time to time. By nature—taking your "nature" to be the state you have attained when you are first adult—I am a person in whom the first three motives would outweigh the fourth. In a peaceful age I might have written ornate or merely descriptive books, and might have remained almost unaware of my political loyalties. As it is I have been forced into becoming a sort of pamphleteer. First I spent five years in an unsuitable profession (the Indian Imperial Police, in Burma), and then I underwent poverty and the sense of failure. This increased my natural hatred of authority and made me for the first time fully aware of the existence of the working classes, and the job in Burma had given me some understanding of the nature of imperialism: but these experiences were not enough to give me an accurate political orientation. Then came Hitler, the Spanish civil war, etc. By the end of 1935 I had still failed to reach a firm decision. I remember a little poem that I wrote at that date, expressing my dilemma:

A happy vicar I might have been
Two hundred years ago,
To preach upon eternal doom
And watch my walnuts grow;

But born, alas, in an evil time,
I missed that pleasant haven,
For the hair has grown on my upper lip
And the clergy are all clean-shaven.

And later still the times were good,
We were so easy to please,
We rocked our troubled thoughts to sleep
On the bosoms of the trees.

All ignorant we dared to own
The joys we now dissemble;
The greenfinch on the apple bough
Could make my enemies tremble.

But girls' bellies and apricots,
Roach in a shaded stream,
Horses, ducks in flight at dawn,
All these are a dream.

It is forbidden to dream again;
We maim our joys or hide them;
Horses are made of chromium steel
And little fat men shall ride them.

I am the worm who never turned,
The eunuch without a harem;
Between the priest and the commissar
I walk like Eugene Aram;

And the commissar is telling my fortune
While the radio plays,
But the priest has promised an Austin Seven,
For Duggie always pays.

I dreamed I dwelt in marble halls,
And woke to find it true;
I wasn't born for an age like this;
Was Smith? Was Jones? Were you?

The Spanish War and other events in 1936-37 turned the scale and thereafter I knew where I stood. Every line of serious work that I have written since 1936 has been written, directly or indirectly, *against* totalitarianism and *for* democratic Socialism, as I understand it. It seems to me nonsense, in a period like our own, to think that one can avoid writing of such subjects. Everyone writes of them in one guise or another. It is simply a question of which side one takes and what approach one follows. And the more one is conscious of one's political bias, the more chance one has of acting politically without sacrificing one's aesthetic and intellectual integrity.

What I have most wanted to do throughout the past ten years is to make political writing into an art. My starting point is always a feeling of partisanship, a sense of injustice. When I sit down to write a book, I do not say to myself, "I am going to produce a work of art." I write it because there is some lie that I want to expose, some fact to which I want to draw attention, and my initial concern is to get a hearing. But I could not do the work of writing a book, or even a long magazine article, if it were not also an aesthetic experience. Anyone who cares to examine my work will see that even when it is downright propaganda it contains much that a full-time politician would consider irrelevant. I am not able, and I do not want, completely to abandon the world-view that I acquired in childhood. So long as I remain alive and well I shall continue to feel strongly about prose style, to love the surface of the earth and to take pleasure in solid objects and scraps of useless information. It is no use trying to suppress that side of myself. The job is to reconcile my ingrained likes and dislikes with the essentially public, non-individual activities that this age forces on all of us.

It is not easy. It raises problems of construction and of language, and it raises in a new way the problem of truthfulness. Let me give just one example of the cruder kind of difficulty that arises. My book about the Spanish civil war, *Homage to Catalonia,* is, of course, a frankly political book, but in the main it is written with a certain detachment and regard for form. I did try very hard in it to tell the whole truth without violating my literary instincts. But among other things it contains a long chapter, full of newspaper quotations and the like, defending the Trotskyists who were accused of plotting with France. Clearly such a chapter, which after a year or two would lose its interest for any ordinary reader, must ruin the book. A critic whom I respect read me a lecture about it. "Why did you put in all that stuff?" he said. "You've turned what might have been a good book into journalism." What he said was true, but I could not have done otherwise. I happened to know, what very few people in England have been allowed to know, that innocent men were being falsely accused. If I had not been angry about that I should never have written the book.

In one form or another this problem comes up again. The problem of language is subtler and would take too long to discuss. I will only say that of late years I have tried to write less picturesquely and more exactly. In any case I find that by the time you have perfected any style of writing, you have always outgrown it. *Animal Farm* was the first book in which I tried, with full consciousness of what I was doing, to fuse political purpose and artistic purpose into one whole. I have not written a novel for seven years, but I hope to write another fairly soon. It is bound to be a failure, every book is a failure, but I know with some clarity what kind of book I want to write.

Looking back through the last page or two, I see that I have made it appear as though my motives in writing were wholly public-spirited. I don't want to leave that as the final impression. All writers are vain, selfish, and lazy, and at the very bottom of their motives there lies a mystery. Writing a book is a horrible, exhausting struggle, like a long bout of some painful illness. One would never undertake such a thing if one were not driven on by some demon whom one can neither resist nor understand. For all one knows that demon is simply the same instinct that makes a baby squall for attention. And yet it is also true that one can write nothing readable unless one constantly struggles to efface one's own personality. Good prose is like a window pane. I cannot say with certainty which of my motives are the strongest, but I know which of them deserve to be followed. And looking back through my work, I see that it is invariably where I lacked a *political* purpose that I wrote lifeless books and was betrayed into purple passages, sentences without meaning, decorative adjectives and humbug generally.

Is Everybody Happy?

John Ciardi [1916–1986]

The right to pursue happiness is issued to Americans with their birth certificates, but no one seems quite sure which way it ran. It may be we are issued a hunting license but offered no game. Jonathan Swift seemed to think so when he attacked the idea of happiness as "the possession of being well-deceived," the felicity of being "a fool among knaves." For Swift saw society as Vanity Fair, the land of false goals.

It is, of course, un-American to think in terms of fools and knaves. We do, however, seem to be dedicated to the idea of buying our way to happiness. We shall all have made it to Heaven when we possess enough.

And at the same time the forces of American commercialism are hugely dedicated to making us deliberately unhappy. Advertising is one of our major industries, and advertising exists not to satisfy desires but to create them—and to create them faster than any man's budget can satisfy them. For that matter, our whole economy is based on a dedicated insatiability. We are taught that to possess is to be happy, and then we are made to want. We are even told it is our duty to want. It was only a few years ago, to cite a single example, that car dealers across the country were flying banners that read "You Auto Buy Now." They were calling upon Americans, as an act approaching patriotism, to buy at once, with money they did not have, automobiles they did not really need, and which they would be required to grow tired of by the time the next year's models were released.

Or look at any of the women's magazines. There, as Bernard DeVoto once pointed out, advertising begins as poetry in the front pages and ends as pharmacopoeia and therapy in the back pages. The poetry of the front matter is the dream of perfect beauty. This is the baby skin that must be hers. These, the flawless teeth. This, the perfumed breath she must exhale. This, the sixteen-year-old figure she must display at forty, at fifty, at sixty, and forever.

Once past the vaguely uplifting fiction and feature articles, the reader finds the other face of the dream in the back matter. This is the harness into which Mother must strap herself in order to display that perfect figure. These, the chin straps she must sleep in. This is the salve that restores all, this is her laxative, these are the tablets that melt away fat, these are the hormones of perpetual youth, these are the stockings that hide varicose veins.

Obviously no half-sane person can be completely persuaded either by such poetry or by such pharmacopoeia and orthopedics. Yet someone is obviously trying to buy the dream as offered and spending billions every year in the attempt. Clearly the happiness market is not running out of customers, but what are we trying to buy?

The idea "happiness," to be sure, will not sit still for easy definition: the best one can do is to try to set some extremes to the idea and then work in toward the middle. To think of happiness as acquisitive and competitive will do to set the materialistic extreme. To think of it as the idea one senses in, say, a holy man of India will do to set the spiritual extreme. That holy man's ideal of happiness is in needing nothing from outside himself. In wanting nothing, he lacks nothing. He sits immobile, rapt in contemplation, free even of his own body. Or nearly free of it. If devout admirers bring him food he eats it; if not, he starves indifferently. Why be concerned? What is physical is an illusion to him. Contemplation is his joy and he achieves it through a fantastically demanding discipline, the accomplishment of which is itself a joy within him.

Is he a happy man? Perhaps his happiness is only another sort of illusion. But who can take it from him? And who will dare say it is more illusory than happiness on the installment plan?

But, perhaps because I am Western, I doubt such catatonic happiness, as I doubt the dreams of the happiness market. What is certain is that his way of happiness would be torture to almost any

Western man. Yet these extremes will still serve to frame the area within which all of us must find some sort of balance. Thoreau—a creature of both Eastern and Western thought—had his own firm sense of that balance. His aim was to save on the low levels in order to spend on the high.

Possession for its own sake or in competition with the rest of 1
the neighborhood would have been Thoreau's idea of the low levels. The active discipline of heightening one's perception of what is enduring in nature would have been his idea of the high. What he saved from the low was time and effort he could spend on the high. Thoreau certainly disapproved of starvation, but he would put into feeding himself only as much effort as would keep him functioning for more important efforts.

Effort is the gist of it. There is no happiness except as we take on life-engaging difficulties. Short of the impossible, as Yeats put it, the satisfactions we get from a lifetime depend on how high we choose our difficulties. Robert Frost was thinking in something like the same terms when he spoke of "the pleasure of taking pains." The mortal flaw in the advertised version of happiness is in the fact that it purports to be effortless.

We demand difficulty even in our games. We demand it because without difficulty there can be no game. A game is a way of making something hard for the fun of it. The rules of the game are an arbitrary imposition of difficulty. When the spoilsport ruins the fun, he always does so by refusing to play by the rules. It is easier to win at chess if you are free, at your pleasure, to change the wholly arbitrary rules, but the fun is in winning within the rules. No difficulty, no fun.

The buyers and sellers at the happiness market seem too often to have lost their sense of the pleasure of difficulty. Heaven knows what they are playing, but it seems a dull game. The Indian holy man seems dull to us, I suppose, because he seems to be refusing to play anything at all. The Western weakness may be in the illusion that happiness can be bought. Perhaps the Eastern weakness is in the idea that there is such a thing as perfect (and therefore static) happiness.

Happiness is never more than partial. There are no pure states of mankind. Whatever else happiness may be, it is neither in having nor in being, but in becoming. What the Founding Fathers declared for us as an inherent right, we should do well to remember, was not happiness but the *pursuit* of happiness. What they might have underlined, could they have foreseen the happiness market, is the cardinal fact that happiness is in the pursuit itself, in the meaningful pursuit of what is life-engaging and life-revealing, which is to say, in the idea of *becoming*. A nation is not measured by what it possesses or wants to possess, but by what it wants to become.

By all means let the happiness market sell us minor satisfac- 15
tions and even minor follies so long as we keep them in scale and buy them out of spiritual change. I am no customer for either puritanism or asceticism. But drop any real spiritual capital at those bazaars, and what you come home to will be your own poorhouse.

FROM *WORKING*, DOLORES DANTE, WAITRESS

Studs Terkel (1912–2008)

Louis "Studs" Terkel was born to Russian–Jewish parents in New York City. When he was eleven years old, his family moved to Chicago, where Terkel lived most of his life. Although he graduated from the University of Chicago Law School, he never pursued a career in law. Instead, he acted, hosted a radio show, and wrote. He had his own television show called Studs' Place, *in which he played himself as a restaurant owner. The contract for the show was cancelled when Terkel refused to testify against other left-wing activists to Senator Joseph McCarthy and the House Un-American Activities Committee. His popular radio show remained on air in Chicago from 1952 to 1997.*

Terkel gained a national audience, however, through his books, especially his oral histories. In Hard Times: An Oral History of the Great Depression *(1970), he documents the struggle through the memories of those who endured the Depression. In 1985, he won a Pulitzer Prize for* "The Good War": An Oral History of World War II. *The selections in this text come from* Working: People Talk about What They Do All Day and How They Feel about What They Do *(1974), which was transformed into a Broadway musical and a Public Broadcasting Service special. These and Terkel's other books helped to establish oral history as a serious genre.*

Dolores Dante

She has been a waitress in the same restaurant for twenty-three years. Many of its patrons are credit card carriers on an expense account— conventioneers, politicians, labor leaders, agency people. Her hours are from 5:00 p.m. to 2:00 a.m. six days a week. She arrives earlier "to get things ready, the silverware, the butter. When people come in and ask for you, you would like to be in a position to handle them all, because that means more money for you."

"I became a waitress because I needed money fast and you don't get it in an office. My husband and I broke up and he left me with debts and three children. My baby was six months. The fast buck, your tips. The first ten-dollar bill that I got as a tip, a Viking guy gave to me. He was a very robust, terrific atheist. Made very good conversation for us, 'cause I am too."

"Everyone says all waitresses have broken homes. What they don't realize is when people have broken homes they need to make money fast, and do this work. They don't have broken homes because they're waitresses."

I have to be a waitress. How else can I learn about people? How else does the world come to me? I can't go to everyone. So they have to come to me. Everyone wants to eat, everyone has hunger. And I serve them. If they've had a bad day, I nurse them, cajole them. Maybe with coffee I give them a little philosophy. They have cocktails, I give them political science.

I'll say things that bug me. If they manufacture soap, I say what I think about pollution. If it's automobiles, I say what I think about them. If I pour water I'll say, "Would you like your quota of mercury today?" If I serve cream, I say, "Here is your substitute. I think you're drinking plastic." I just can't keep quiet. I have an opinion on every single subject there is. In the beginning it was theology, and my bosses didn't like it. Now I am a political and my bosses don't like it. I speak *sotto voce*. But if I get heated, then I don't give a damn. I speak like an Italian speaks. I can't be servile. I give service. There is a difference.

I'm called by my first name. I like my name. I hate to be called Miss. Even when I serve a lady, a strange woman, I will not say madam. I hate ma'am. I always say milady. In the American language there is no word to address a woman, to indicate whether she's married or unmarried. So I say milady. And sometimes I playfully say to the man milord.

It would be very tiring if I had to say, "Would you like a cocktail?" and say that over and over. So I come out different for my own enjoyment. I would say, "What's exciting at the bar that I can offer?" I can't say, "Do you want coffee?" Maybe I'll say, "Are you in the mood for coffee?" Or, "The coffee sounds exciting." Just rephrase it enough to make it interesting for me. That would make them take an interest. It becomes theatrical and I feel like Mata Hari and it intoxicates me.

People imagine a waitress couldn't possibly think or have any kind of aspiration other than to serve food. When somebody says to me, "You're great, how come you're *just* a waitress?" *Just* a waitress. I'd say, "Why, don't you think you deserve to be served by me?" It's implying that he's not worthy, not that I'm not worthy. It makes me irate. I don't feel lowly at all. I myself feel sure. I don't want to change the job. I love it.

Tips? I feel like Carmen. It's like a gypsy holding out a tambourine and they throw the coin. (Laughs.) If you like people, you're not thinking of the tips. I never count my money at night. I always wait till morning. If I thought about my tips I'd be uptight. I never look at a tip. You pick it up fast. I would do my bookkeeping in the morning. It would be very dull for me to know I was making so much and no more. I do like challenge. And it isn't demeaning, not for me.

There might be occasions when the customers might intend to make it demeaning—the man about town, the conventioneer. When the time comes to pay the check, he would do little things, "How much should I give you?" He might make an issue about it. I did say to one, "Don't play God with me. Do what you want." Then it really didn't matter whether I got a tip or not. I would spit it out, my resentment—that he dares make me feel I'm operating only for a tip.

He'd ask for his check. Maybe he's going to sign it. He'd take a very long time and he'd make me stand there, "Let's see now, what do you think I ought to give you?" He would not let go of that moment. And you knew it. You know he meant to demean you. He's holding the change in his hand, or if he'd sign, he'd flourish the pen and wait. These are the times I really get angry. I'm not reticent. Something would come out. Then I really didn't care. "Goddamn, keep your money!"

There are conventioneers, who leave their lovely wives or their bad wives. They approach you and say, "Are there any hot spots?"

"Where can I find girls?" It is, of course, first directed at you. I don't mean that as a compliment, 'cause all they're looking for is females. They're not looking for companionship or conversation. I am quite adept at understanding this. I think I'm interesting enough that someone may just want to talk to me. But I would philosophize that way. After all, what is left after you talk? The hours have gone by and I could be home resting or reading or studying guitar, which I do on occasion. I would say, "What are you going to offer me? Drinks?" And I'd point to the bar, "I have it all here." He'd look blank and then I'd say, "A man? If I need a man, wouldn't you think I'd have one of my own? Must I wait for you?"

Life doesn't frighten me any more. There are only two things that relegate us—the bathroom and the grave. Either I'm gonna have to go to the bathroom now or I'm gonna die now. I go to the bathroom.

And I don't have a high opinion of bosses. The more popular you are, the more the boss holds it over your head. You're bringing them business, but he knows you're getting good tips and you won't leave. You have to worry not to overplay it, because the boss becomes resentful and he uses this as a club over your head.

If you become too good a waitress, there's jealousy. They don't come in and say, "Where's the boss?" They'll ask for Dolores. It doesn't make a hit. That makes it rough. Sometimes you say. Aw hell, why am I trying so hard? I did get an ulcer. Maybe the things I kept to myself were twisting me.

It's not the customers, never the customers. It's injustice. My dad came from Italy and I think of his broken English—*injoost*. He hated injustice. If you hate injustice for the world, you hate more than anything injustice toward you. Loyalty is never appreciated, particularly if you're the type who doesn't like small talk and are not the type who makes reports on your fellow worker. The boss wants to find out what is going on surreptitiously. In our society today you have informers everywhere. They've informed on cooks, on coworkers. "Oh, someone wasted this." They would say I'm talking to all the customers. "I saw her carry such-and-such out. See if she wrote that on her check." "The salad looked like it was a double salad." I don't give anything away. I just give myself. Informers will manufacture things in order to make their job worthwhile. They're not sure of themselves as workers. There's always someone who wants your station, who would be pretender to the crown. In life there is always someone who wants somebody's job.

I'd get intoxicated with giving service. People would ask for me and I didn't have enough tables. Some of the girls are standing and don't have customers. There is resentment. I feel self-conscious. I feel a sense of guilt. It cramps my style. I would like to say to the customer, "Go to so-and-so." But you can't do that, because you feel a sense of loyalty. So you would rush, get to your customers quickly. Some don't care to drink and still they wait for you. That's a compliment.

There is plenty of tension. If the cook isn't good, you fight to see that the customers get what you know they like. You have to use diplomacy with cooks, who are always dangerous. (Laughs.) They're madmen. (Laughs.) You have to be their friend. They better like you. And your bartender better like you too, because he may do something to the drink. If your bartender doesn't like you, your cook doesn't like you, your boss doesn't like you, the other girls don't like you, you're in trouble.

And there will be customers who are hypochondriacs, who feel they can't eat, and I coax them. Then I hope I can get it just the right way from the cook. I may mix the salad myself, just the way they want it.

Maybe there's a party of ten. Big shots, and they'd say, "Dolores, I have special clients, do your best tonight." You just hope you have the right cook behind the broiler. You really want to pleasure your guests. He's selling something, he wants things right, too. You're giving your all. How does the steak look? If you cut his steak, you look at it surreptitiously. How's it going?

Carrying dishes is a problem. We do have accidents. I spilled a tray once with steaks for seven on it. It was a big, gigantic T-bone, all sliced.

But when that tray fell. I went with it, and never made a sound, dish and all (softly) never made a sound. It took about an hour and a half to cook that steak. How would I explain this thing? That steak was salvaged. (Laughs.)

Some don't care. When the plate is down you can hear the sound. I try not to have that sound. I want my hands to be right when I serve. I pick up a glass, I want it to be just right. I get to be almost Oriental in the serving. I like it to look nice all the way. To be a waitress, it's an art. I feel like a ballerina, too. I have to go between those tables, between those chairs . . . Maybe that's the reason I always stayed slim. It is a certain way I can go through a chair no one else can do. I do it with an air. If I drop a fork, there is a certain way I pick it up. I know they can see how delicately I do it. I'm on stage.

I tell everyone I'm a waitress and I'm proud. If a nurse gives service, I say, "You're a professional." Whatever you do, be professional. I always compliment people.

I like to have my station looking nice. I like to see there's enough ash trays when they're having their coffee and cigarettes. I don't like ash trays so loaded that people are not enjoying the moment. It offends me. I don't do it because I think that's gonna make a better tip. It offends me as a person.

People say, "No one does good work any more." I don't believe it. You know who's saying that? The man at the top, who says the people beneath him are not doing a good job. He's the one who always said, "You're nothing." The housewife who has all the money, she believed housework was demeaning, 'cause she hired someone else to do it. If it weren't so demeaning, why didn't *she* do it? So anyone who did her housework was a person to be demeaned. The maid who did all the housework said, "Well hell, if this is the way you feel about it, I won't do your housework. You tell me I'm no good. I'm nobody. Well, maybe I'll go out and be somebody." They're only mad because they can't find someone to do it now. The fault is not in the people who did the—quote— lowly work.

Just a waitress. At the end of the night I feel drained. I think a lot of waitresses become alcoholics because of that. In most cases, a waiter or a waitress doesn't eat. They handle food, they don't have time. You'll pick at something in the kitchen, maybe a piece of bread. You'll have a cracker, a little bit of soup. You go back and take a teaspoonful of something. Then maybe sit down afterwards and have a drink, maybe three, four, five. And bartenders, too. most of them are alcoholics. They'd go out in a group. There are after-hour places. You've got to go release your tension. So they go out before they go to bed. Some of them stay out all night.

It's tiring, it's nerve-racking. We don't ever sit down. We're on stage and the bosses are watching. If you get the wrong shoes and you get the wrong stitch in that shoe, that does bother you. Your feet hurt, your body aches. If you come out in anger at things that were done to you, it would only make you feel cheapened. Really I've been keeping it to myself. But of late. I'm beginning to spew it out. It's almost as though I sensed my body and soul had had quite enough.

It builds and builds and builds in your guts. Near crying. I can think about it . . . (She cries softly.) Cause you're tired. When the night is done, you're tired. You've had so much, there's so much going . . . You had to get it done. The dread that something wouldn't be right, because you want to please. You hope everyone is satisfied. The night's done, you've done your act. The curtains close.

The next morning is pleasant again. I take out my budget book, write down how much I made, what my bills are. I'm managing. I won't give up this job as long as I'm able to do it. I feel out of contact if I just sit at home. At work they all consider me a kook. (Laughs.) That's okay. No matter where I'd be, I would make a rough road for me. It's just me, and I can't keep still. It hurts, and what hurts has to come out.

POSTSCRIPT: *After sixteen years—that was seven years ago—I took a trip to Hawaii and the Caribbean for two weeks. Went with a lover. The kids saw it—they're all married now. (Laughs.) One of my daughters said, "Act your age." I said, "Honey, if I were acting my age, I wouldn't be walking. My bones would ache. You don't want to hear about my arthritis. Aren't you glad I'm happy?"*

Girl

Jamaica Kincaid

Born Elaine Potter Richardson in St. John's, Antigua, in the West Indies, Jamaica Kincaid (1949-) left Antigua for New York when she was seventeen, took classes at a community college, studied photography at the New School for Social Research, and attended Franconia College. She has been a staff writer for The New Yorker *and has published her work in* Rolling Stone, The Village Voice, *and* The Paris Review. *Her first book,* At the Bottom of the River *(1983) won an award from the American Academy and Institute of Arts and Letters. Her more recent works include* The Autobiography of My Mother *(1996) and* My Brother *(1997). The following selection originally appeared in* The New Yorker *and was included in* At the Bottom of the River. *It vividly narrates a relationship between a powerful mother and her young daughter and confronts us with the advice the daughter must listen to.*

Wash the white clothes on Monday and put them on the stone heap; wash the color clothes on Tuesday and put them on the clothesline to dry; don't walk barehead in the hot sun; cook pumpkin fritters[1] in very hot sweet oil; soak your little cloths right after you take them off; when buying cotton to make yourself a nice blouse, be sure that it doesn't have gum[2] on it, because that way it won't hold up well after a wash; soak salt fish overnight before you cook it; is it true that you sing benna[3] in Sunday school?; always eat your food in such a way that it won't turn someone else's stomach; on Sundays try to walk like a lady and not like the slut you are so bent on becoming; don't sing benna in Sunday school; you mustn't speak to wharf-rat boys, not even to give directions; don't eat fruits on the street—flies will follow you; *but I don't sing benna on Sundays at all and never in Sunday school*; this is how to sew on a button; this is how to make a button hole for the button you have just sewed on; this is how to hem a dress when you see the hem coming down and so to prevent yourself from looking like the slut

[1] *fritters:* small fried cakes of batter, often containing vegetables, fruit, or other fillings.
[2] *gum:* plant residue on cotton.
[3] *sing benna:* sing popular music (not appropriate for Sunday school).

I know you are so bent on becoming; this is how you iron your father's khaki shirt so that it doesn't have a crease; this is how you iron your father's khaki pants so that they don't have a crease; this is how you grow okra—far from the house, because okra[4] tree harbors red ants; when you are growing dasheen[5], make sure it gets plenty of water or else it makes your throat itch when you are eating it; this is how you sweep a corner; this is how you sweep a whole house; this is how you sweep a yard; this is how you smile to someone you don't like too much; this is how you smile to someone you don't like at all; this is how you smile to someone you like completely; this is how you set a table for tea; this is how you set a table for dinner; this is how you set a table for dinner with an important guest; this is how you set a table for lunch; this is how you set a table for breakfast; this is how to behave in the presence of men who don't know you very well, and this way they won't recognize immediately the slut I have warned you against becoming; be sure to wash every day, even if it is with your own spit; don't squat down to play marbles—you are not a boy, you know; don't pick people's flowers—you might catch something; don't throw stones at blackbirds, because it might not be a blackbird at all; this is how to make a bread pudding; this is how to make doukona[6]; this is how to make pepper pot[7]; this is how to make a good medicine for a cold; this is how to make a good medicine to throw away a child before it even becomes a child; this is how to catch a fish; this is how to throw back a fish you don't like, and that way something bad won't fall on you; this is how to bully a man; this is how a man bullies you; this is how to love a man; and if this doesn't work there are other ways, and if they don't work don't feel too bad about giving up; this is how to spit up in the air if you feel like it, and this is how to move quick so that it doesn't fall on you; this is how to make ends meet; always squeeze bread to make sure it's fresh; *but what if the baker won't let me feel the bread?*; you mean to say that after all you are really going to be the kind of woman who the baker won't let near the bread?

---

[4] *okra:* a shrub whose pods are used in soups, stews, and gumbo.

[5] *dasheen:* the taro plant, cultivated, like the potato, for its edible tuber.

[6] *doukona:* plantain pudding; the plantain fruit is similar to the banana.

[7] *pepper pot:* a spicy West Indian stew.

]XCERPT FROM JARHEAD: \ MARINE'S CHRONICLE OF THE]ULF WAR AND OTHER BATTLES

Anthony Swofford

ʒo to the basement and open my ruck. The basement is in Iowa, ter a long, harsh winter, and deep in the ruck where I reach for my mmies, I still feel the cold of February. We were supposed to turn our desert cammies, but I kept mine. They're ratty and bleached sand and sun and blemished with the petroleum rain that fell from e oil-well fires in Kuwait. The cammies don't fit. While in the arines, I exercised thirty hours a week. Since I've been out, I've ercised about thirty hours a year. The waist stops at my thighs. ne blouse buttons, but barely. I pull out maps of Kuwait and Saudi abia. Patrol books. Pictures. Letters. My journal with its sparse tries. Coalition propaganda pamphlets. Brass bore punch for the 40A1 sniper rifle. A handful of 50-caliber projectiles. I think of hat I must look like to the late-night walker peering through the sement windows: the movie cliché, the mad old warrior going rough his memorabilia, juicing up before he runs off and kills a few ith precision fire. But, no, I am not mad. I am not well, but I am ɔt mad. I'm after something. Memory, yes. A reel. More than just ne. Years pass. But more than just time. I've been working toward is—I've opened the ruck and now I must open myself.

It would've been easy to sell my gear to a surplus store. After e war, when I spent most of my monthly pay on the bars in Palm rings and Newport Beach, Las Vegas and Santa Monica, I'd steal ase or two of MREs meals ready to call from supply each week, d on my way out of town for the weekend I'd sell the meals for 0 per case in an army/navy store in San Bernardino. And occa- ɔnally I'd steal more than meals. Or I wouldn't necessarily steal. metimes I'd happen along a Sergeant Smith's ruck, and he'd be where near, and I'd remember the saying *Gear left adrift, must be a gift,* and I knew that the ex-marine who ran the army/navy store would give me $300 for the sergeant's misfortune.

So my ruck didn't have to be here, in my basement, six or seven moves and eight and a half years after my discharge. I could've sold it for one outrageous bar tab or given it to Goodwill or thrown it away—or set it afire as some jarheads did.

I open a map of southern Kuwait. Sand falls from between the folds.

As a lance corporal in a U.S. Marine Corps scout/sniper platoon, I saw more of the Gulf War than the average grunt. Still, my vision was blurred—by wind and sand and distance, by false signals, poor communication, and bad coordinates, by stupidity and fear and ignorance, by valor and false pride. By the mirage.

Thus what follows is neither true nor false but *what I know.* I have forgotten most of the statistics and must look them up. I remember the weapons, though not their capabilities, so I must look those up as well. For the place names I refer to maps. For unit deployments and order of battle, I must consult published charts. I search through congressional reports and presidential statements at the Federal depository Library. I remember most of the names and faces of my platoon mates. I remember the names and faces of some of their girlfriends and wives. I think I know who cheated and who stayed faithful. I remember who wrote letters and who drove their men mad with silence. I remember some of the lies and most of the questions. I remember the dreams and the naive wishes, the pathetic pleas and the trouser pissing horror.

I remember some of the sand, but there was so much of it, I should be forgiven.

I remember about myself a loneliness and poverty of spirit; mental collapse; brief jovial moments after weeks of exhaustion; discomfiting bodily pain; constant ringing in my ears; sleeplessness and drunkenness and desperation; fits of rage and despondency; mutiny of the self; lovers to whom I lied; lovers who lied to me. I remember going in one end and coming out the other. I remember being told I must remember and then for many years forgetting.

On August 2, 1990, Iraqi troops drive east to Kuwait City and start killing soldiers and civilians and capturing gold heavy palaces and expensive German sedans—though it is likely that the Iraqi atrocities are being exaggerated by Kuwaitis and Saudis and certain elements of the U. S. government, so as to gather more coalition support from the UN, the American people, and the international community generally.

Also on August 2 my platoon—STA (pronounced *stay*), the Surveillance and Target Acquisition Platoon, scout/snipers, of the Second Battalion, Seventh Marines—is put on standby. We're currently stationed at Twentynine Palms Marine Corps Base, in California's Mojave Desert.

After hearing the news of imminent war in the Middle East, we march in a platoon formation to the base barber and get fresh high-and-tight haircuts. And no wonder we call ourselves jarheads—our heads look just like jars.

Then we send a few guys downtown to rent all of the war movies they can get their hands on. They also buy a hell of a lot of beer. For three days we sit in our rec room and drink all of the beer and watch all of those damn movies, and we yell *Semper fi* and we head-butt and beat the crap out of each other and we get off on the various visions of carnage and violence and decent, the raping and killing and pillaging. We concentrate on the Vietnam films because it's the most recent war, and the successes and failures of that war helped write our training manuals. We rewind and review famous scenes, such as Robert Duvall and his helicopter gunships during *Apocalypse Now,* and in the same film Martin Sheen floating up the fake Vietnamese Congo; we watch Willem Dafoe get shot by a friendly and left on the battlefield in *Platoon;* and we listen closely as Matthew Modine talks trash to a streetwalker in *Full Metal Jacket*. We watch again the ragged, tired, burnt-out fighters walking through the villes and the pretty native women smiling because if they don't smile, the fighters might kill their pigs or burn their cache of rice. We rewind the rape scenes when American soldiers return from the bush after killing many VC to sip cool beers in a thatch bar while whores sit on their laps for a song to two (a song from the fifties when America was still sweet) before they retire to rooms and fuck the whores sweetly. The American boys, brutal, young farm boys or tough city boys, sweetly fuck the whores. Yes, somehow the films convince us that these boys are sweet, even though we know we are much like these boys and that we are no longer sweet.

There is talk that many Vietnam films are antiwar, that the message is war is inhumane and look what happens when you train young American men to fight and kill, they turn their fighting and killing everywhere, they ignore their targets and desecrate the entire country, shooting fully automatic, forgetting they were trained to aim. But actually, Vietnam war films are all pro-war, no matter what the supposed message, what Kubrick or Coppola or Stone intended. Mr. and Mrs. Johnson in Omaha or San Francisco or Manhattan will watch the films and weep and decide once and for all that war is inhumane and terrible, and they will tell their friends at church and their family this, but Corporal Johnson at Camp Pendleton and Sergeant Johnson at Travis Air Force Base and Seaman Johnson at Coronado Naval Station and Spec 4 Johnson at Fort Bragg and Lance Corporal Swofford at Twentynine Palms Marine Corps Base watch the same films and are excited by them, because the magic brutality of the films celebrates the terrible and despicable beauty of their fighting skills. Fight, rape, war, pillage, burn. Filmic images of death and carnage are pornography for the military man: with film you are stroking his cock, tickling his balls with the pink feather of history, getting him ready for his real First Fuck. It doesn't matter how many Mr. and Mrs. Johnsons are antiwar—the actual killers who know how to use the weapons are not.

We watch our films and drink our beer and occasionally someone begins weeping and exits the room to stand on the catwalk and stare at the Bullion Mountains, the treacherous, craggy range that borders our barracks. Once, this person is me. It's nearly midnight, the temperature still in the upper nineties, and the sky is wracked with stars. Moonlight spreads across the desert like a white fire. The door behind me remains open, and on the TV screen an ambush erupts on one of the famous murderous hills of Vietnam.

I reenter the room and look at the faces of my fellows. We are all afraid, but show this in various ways—violent indifference, fake ease, standard-issue bravura. We are afraid, but that doesn't ıean we don't want to fight. It occurs to me that we will never be oung again. I take my seat and return to the raging battle. The supposedly antiwar films have failed. Now is my time to step into the ewest combat zone. And as a young man raised on the films of the ietnam War. I want ammunition and alcohol and dope, I want to rew some whores and kill some Iraqi motherfuckers.

Tip Jars and the New Economy

Dalton Conley [b. 1969]

In all the hubbub about the rise and fall of the "new economy," one important trend has gone undocumented: the steady increase in the number of tip jars at restaurants, cafes, and other stores.

As far as I can tell, no official statistics are kept on the number of tip jars in consumer establishments, but over the last few years, I have noticed a staggering increase. Today you cannot order a coffee, buy a bagel, or pay for a photocopy without being asked to leave your change behind for "better service" or, alternatively, "good karma."

Their expansion to every service establishment seems to march onward independent of the state of the economy. In good times the supply of tips may be greater and thus drives their spread. But during a recession, demand may increase as low-wage workers rely on tips more than ever, and thus the proliferation of jars continues unabated. One way to view the spread of tipping culture is that it represents the triumph of the free market: The promise of 15 percent (or more) may spur better service through direct economic incentives. That view rests on a number of assumptions, however, most notably the promise of repeat business. After all, why tip a taxi driver when you are about as likely to get him again (and have him recognize you, the "big tipper") as to find a pot of gold on Sixth Avenue?

In fact, the origins of the multibillion-dollar culture of tipping are as vague as the reasons for its continuance. Scholars are not even sure of the origins of the word. Some historians attribute the habit and the word to 18th-century English coffeehouses, where collection boxes (not unlike the tip jars of today) were often emblazoned with the words "To Insure Promptitude" (TIP).

Other researchers date its ancestry to the Middle Ages (before capitalism), when feudal lords tossed coins to beggars on the road to insure safe passage. And others see the origins in the Dutch word *tippen*—that is, to tap on a table for service—or the Latin word *stips,* which translates as "gift." Although the word may be fairly recent in history, the practice most likely long predates any of these records.

So while the benefits and origins of tipping are questionable, the social costs may be large, even as they remain hidden. About 100 years ago the German social philosopher Georg Simmel wrote a series of lectures and essays that would come to be the largest philosophical treatise on money. One of his keenest observations was the way that forms of payment affect social relations. In Simmel's view, modern society has gone through an evolution of sorts in payment schemes. First there was "in kind" payment. For example, a serf received some food and shelter for tilling the soil. She wasn't much different than oxen who were fed and stored for the night. Basic human needs were taken care of, but the dependence of the worker on the largess of the master was, in Simmel's view, dehumanizing.

Then came the "good old" days of craftsmen and cottage industry, when workers were paid on a per-unit basis. That is, you agree on the price for, say, a chair. The furniture maker procures the raw materials, fashions the chair, and delivers it "on spec." If the wood is rotten, or he makes a mistake and has to start over again, there goes his profit margin. He bears all the risk. His wages are dependent on the quality of the capital goods.

One step up the ladder from per-unit payment is hourly wages. While many social theorists (most notably Karl Marx) saw the advent of wage labor as something to be mourned, Simmel saw it as a further step toward worker liberation. Now the worker was privileged over the raw materials. If the wood were rotten, and the chair turned out to be no good, the worker would be paid all the same.

Even better is a salary. Now the worker is not even dependent on how much work there is to do. His salary is based on what the employer thinks is a reasonable standard of living for someone occupying that kind of position. Still better are honoraria and grants, since they are promised before the work is even performed and are totally independent of the outcome.

Tips, in this schema, are a big step backward. It is already bad 10
enough that service workers are programmed to wish us a "nice day" and to plaster a perma-grin on their faces from the moment they show up to work.

The imposing tip jar further muddles business and sociability. If the promise of a dollar in the jar is what compels someone to be friendly, does that not cheapen smiles in general? Conversely, how can service workers and customers be on equal footing if the cashier's livelihood depends on the largess of the person ordering the mochachino? Also, studies show that aspects of the servers do affect tipping, although in a meritocratic world they should not. For instance, attractive females receive higher tips, according to at least one psychology study.

The presence of in-your-face money not only hurts the relationship between the customer and the service worker, it also damages the relationship between the worker and the firm. Tipping creates what economists call a principal-agent problem. In other words, it creates different incentives for the worker and the owner of an establishment. A waiter whose income largely derives from tips is more likely to give an extra scoop of ice cream to a customer. Research shows that these kinds of acts do increase tips on average, but they, of course, cut into the profit margin of the ice-cream parlor.

More importantly, tipping also is not good for the workers themselves. While often appearing to be tax-free revenue, tips create a high degree of income insecurity. Public-opinion research has shown that most customers would prefer that service workers were paid better wages and thereby the need for and practice of tipping could be eliminated—which leads us to the age-old debate over the minimum wage.

The empirical arguments against raising the minimum wage focus on the perceived loss of jobs. If workers cost more, goes the neoclassical economics argument, then employers will hire fewer of them. While the debate is far from settled, a study by economists David Card and Alan Krueger has seriously challenged that view. By comparing the changes in employment rates in neighboring areas across state lines after one state raised its minimum wage and the other did not, they found no detrimental effect on labor-market opportunities resulting from wage increases. The demand for unskilled labor, it seems, may not be as elastic (that is, responsive) to price as once thought. Of course, those relationships may vary by other factors such as the state of the national and local economy, labor laws, and the local cost of living.

So—in light of research and public opinion that casts the expansion of tipping and tip jars in a negative light—why the proliferation? Again, while the lack of official statistics makes any analysis nothing more than educated conjecture, my guess is that the proliferation is at least partially the result of rising income and wealth inequality in the United States. In a recent article, the economist Paul Krugman cites a Congressional Budget Office study that found "that between 1979 and 1997, the after-tax incomes of the top 1 percent of families rose 157 percent, compared with only a 10-percent gain for families near the middle of the income distribution." The result, he writes, is that we are now at a point where the richest one-hundredth of a percent of households—a mere 13,000 households in all—enjoy "almost as much income as the 20 million poorest households."

While the rich get richer, those who serve the rich are increasingly left to appeal to the better instincts of the well off. The rich also need to have a way to release their guilt. If they tip big, then how bad can they feel for driving $40,000 SUVs and drinking their $4 coffees? (Of course, often it is the less well off who tip the most, out of insecurity.)

The cruelest irony, is that, of course, the worst-paid jobs do not even afford their workers the option to garner tips. The men and women who take the orders and bus the tables at the McDonald's and KFC restaurants of the world earn minimal (if not minimum) wages, receive no health benefits, and cannot even ask for tips. Also in this category of the untipped are maintenance and domestic workers, dishwashers, security personnel, and many other hidden service workers who work hard to ensure that we "have a nice day."

In fact, at one time, McDonald's allowed the practice, but the managers pocketed the money. When the public discovered this practice, outrage boiled over, and it was ended. So now it is only the employees in the middlebrow and high-end service establishments—ranging from Starbucks (whose employees at least get health insurance) to the funky coffee shops it competes with—who are able to paint the side of a sugar canister in bright letters asking for donations. And those of us who can afford to tip are placed in one more daily bind—do we encourage the spread of tip jars by giving? Or do we find time in our busy days to rally for better wages for the hardest working, worst paid among us?

Another double latte, please.

Working at McDonald's

Amitai Etzioni [b. 1929]

McDonald's is bad for your kids. I do not mean the flat patties and the white-flour buns; I refer to the jobs teen-agers undertake, mass-producing these choice items.

As many as two-thirds of America's high school juniors and seniors now hold down part-time paying jobs, according to studies. Many of these are in fast-food chains, of which McDonald's is the pioneer, trendsetter, and symbol.

At first, such jobs may seem right out of the Founding Fathers' educational manual for how to bring up self-reliant, work-ethic-driven, productive youngsters. But in fact, these jobs undermine school attendance and involvement, impart few skills that will be useful in later life, and simultaneously skew the values of teen-agers—especially their ideas about the worth of a dollar.

It has been a longstanding American tradition that youngsters ought to get paying jobs. In folklore, few pursuits are more deeply revered than the newspaper route and the sidewalk lemonade stand. Here the youngsters are to learn how sweet are the fruits of labor and self-discipline (papers are delivered early in the morning, rain or shine), and the ways of trade (if you price your lemonade too high or too low . . .).

Roy Rogers, Baskin Robbins, Kentucky Fried Chicken, *et al.*, may at first seem nothing but a vast extension of the lemonade stand. They provide very large numbers of teen jobs, provide regular employment, pay quite well compared to many other teen jobs, and, in the modern equivalent of toiling over a hot stove, test one's stamina.

Closer examination, however, finds the McDonald's kind of job highly uneducational in several ways. Far from providing opportunities for entrepreneurship (the lemonade stand) or self-discipline, self-supervision, and self-scheduling (the paper route), most teen jobs these days are highly structured—what social scientists call "highly routinized."

True, you still have to have the gumption to get yourself over to the hamburger stand, but once you don the prescribed uniform, your task is spelled out in minute detail. The franchise prescribes the shape of the coffee cups; the weight, size, shape, and color of the patties; and the texture of the napkins (if any). Fresh coffee is to be made every eight minutes. And so on. There is no room for initiative, creativity, or even elementary rearrangements. These are breeding grounds for robots working for yesterday's assembly lines, not tomorrow's high-tech posts.

There are very few studies of the matter. One of the few is a 1984 study by Ivan Charper and Bryan Shore Fraser. The study relies mainly on what teen-agers write in response to questionnaires rather than actual observations of fast-food jobs. The authors argue that the employees develop many skills such as how to operate a food-preparation machine and a cash register. However, little attention is paid to how long it takes to acquire such a skill, or what its significance is.

What does it matter if you spend 20 minutes to learn to use a cash register, and then—"operate" it? What skill have you acquired? It is a long way from learning to work with a lathe or carpenter tools in the olden days or to program computers in the modern age.

A 1980 study by A. V. Harrell and P. W. Wirtz found that, 10
among those students who worked at least 25 hours per week while in school, their unemployment rate four years later was half of that of seniors who did not work. This is an impressive statistic. It must be seen, though, together with the finding that many who begin as part-time employees in fast-food chains drop out of high school and are gobbled up in the world of low-skill jobs.

Some say that while these jobs are rather unsuited for college-bound, white, middle-class youngsters, they are "ideal" for lower-class, "non-academic," minority youngsters. Indeed, minorities are "over-represented" in these jobs (21 percent of fast-food employees). While it is true that these places provide income, work, and even some training to such youngsters, they also tend to perpetuate their disadvantaged status. They provide no career ladders, few marketable skills, and undermine school attendance and involvement.

The hours are often long. Among those 14 to 17, a third of fast-food employees (including some school dropouts) labor more than 30 hours per week, according to the Charper-Fraser study. Only 20 percent work 15 hours or less. The rest: between 15 to 30 hours.

Often the stores close late, and after closing one must clean up and tally up. In affluent Montgomery County, Md., where child labor would not seem to be a widespread economic necessity, 24 percent of the seniors at one high school in 1985 worked as much as five to seven days a week; 27 percent, three to five. There is just no way such amounts of work will not interfere with school work, especially homework. In an informal survey published in the most recent yearbook of the high school, 58 percent of the seniors acknowledged that their jobs interfere with their school work.

The Charper-Fraser study sees merit in learning teamwork and working under supervision. The authors have a point here. However, it must be noted that such learning is not automatically educational or wholesome. For example, much of the supervision in fast-food places leans toward teaching one the wrong kinds of compliance: blind obedience, or shared alienation with the "boss."

Supervision is often both tight and woefully inappropriate. To- 1
day, fast-food chains and other such places of work (record shops, bowling alleys) keep costs down by having teens supervise teens with often no adult on the premises.

There is no father or mother figure with which to identify, to emulate, to provide a role model and guidance. The work-culture varies from one place to another: Sometimes it is a tightly ran shop (must keep the cash registers ringing); sometimes a rather loose pot party interrupted by customers. However, only rarely is there a master to learn from, or much worth learning. Indeed, far from being places where solid adult work values are being transmitted, these are places where all too often delinquent teen values dominate. Typically, when my son Oren was dishing out ice cream for

Baskin Robbins in upper Manhattan, his fellow teen-workers considered him a sucker for not helping himself to the till. Most youngsters felt they were entitled to $50 severance "pay" on their last day on the job.

The pay, oddly, is the part of the teen work-world that is most difficult to evaluate. The lemonade stand or paper route money was for your allowance. In the old days, apprentices learning a trade from a master contributed most, if not all of their income to their parents' household. Today, the teen pay may be low by adult standards, but it is often, especially in the middle class, spent largely or wholly by the teens. That is, the youngsters live free at home ("after all, they are high school kids") and are left with very substantial sums of money.

Where this money goes is not quite clear. Some use it to support themselves, especially among the poor. More middle-class kids set some money aside to help pay for college, or save it for a major purchase—often a car. But large amounts seem to flow to pay for an early introduction into the most trite aspects of American consumerism: Flimsy punk clothes, trinkets, and whatever else is the last fast-moving teen craze.

One may say that this is only fair and square; they are being good American consumers and spend their money on what turns them on. At least, a cynic might add, these funds do not go into illicit drugs and booze. On the other hand, an educator might bemoan that these young, yet unformed individuals, so early in life are driven to buy objects of no intrinsic educational, cultural, or social merit, learn so quickly the dubious merit of keeping up with the Joneses in ever-changing fads, promoted by mass merchandising.

Many teens find the instant reward of money, and the youth 20
status symbols it buys, much more alluring than credits in calculus courses, European history, or foreign languages. No wonder quite a few would rather skip school—and certainly homework—and instead work longer at a Burger King. Thus, most teen work these days is not providing early lessons in work ethic; it fosters escape from school and responsibilities, quick gratification, and a short cut to the consumeristic aspects of adult life.

Thus, parents should look at teen employment not as automatically educational. It is an activity—like sports—that can be turned into an educational opportunity. But it can also easily be abused. Youngsters must learn to balance the quest for income with the needs to keep growing and pursue other endeavors that do not pay off instantly—above all education.

Go back to school.

Serving in Florida

Barbara Ehrenreich [b. 1941]

Barbara Ehrenreich (1941–) was born in Montana and earned a Ph.D. from Rockefeller University. She is known as—and speaks of herself as—an independent and outspoken feminist, liberal, and democratic socialist. Most of her nonfiction can be classified as social criticism, including a number of books: The Hearts of Men *(1983);* Fear of Falling *(1989);* The Worst Years of Our Lives *(1990); and* Bait and Switch: The (Futile) Pursuit of the American Dream *(2005). Her* New York Times *best seller* Nickel and Dimed: On (Not) Getting By in America *(2001) exposed the reality of the working poor. Her novel* Kipper's Game *was published in 1993. She is a regular essayist for* Time *and other magazines. In this excerpt from* Nickel and Dimed: On (Not) Getting By in America, *Ehrenreich embarks on an experiment starting in a low-wage life. In doing so she learns much about the people she encounters and about herself.*

I could drift along like this, in some dreamy proletarian idyll, except for two things. One is management. If I have kept this subject to the margins so far it is because I still flinch to think that I spent all those weeks under the surveillance of men (and later women) whose job it was to monitor my behavior for signs of sloth, theft, drug abuse, or worse. Not that managers and especially "assistant managers" in low-wage settings like this are exactly the class enemy. Mostly, in the restaurant business, they are former cooks still capable of pinch-hitting in the kitchen, just as in hotels they are likely to be former clerks, and paid a salary of only about $400 a week. But everyone knows they have crossed over to the other side, which is, crudely put, corporate as opposed to human. Cooks want to prepare tasty meals, servers want to serve them graciously, but managers are there for only one reason—to make sure that money is made for some theoretical entity, the corporation, which exists far away in Chicago or New York, if a corporation can be said to have a physical existence at all. Reflecting on her career,

Gail tells me ruefully that she swore, years ago, never to work for a corporation again. "They don't cut you no slack. You give and you give and they take."

Managers can sit—for hours at a time if they want—but it's their job to see that no one else ever does, even when there's nothing to do, and this is why, for servers, slow times can be as exhausting as rushes. You start dragging out each little chore because if the manager on duty catches you in an idle moment he will give you something far nastier to do. So I wipe, I clean, I consolidate catsup bottles and recheck the cheesecake supply, even tour the tables to make sure the customer evaluation forms are all standing perkily in their places—wondering all the time how many calories I burn in these strictly theatrical exercises. In desperation, I even take the desserts out of their glass display case and freshen them up with whipped cream and bright new maraschino cherries; anything to look busy. When, on a particularly dead afternoon, Stu finds me glancing at a *USA Today* a customer has left behind, he assigns me to vacuum the entire floor with the broken vacuum cleaner, which has a handle only two feet long, and the only way to do that without incurring orthopedic damage is to proceed from spot to spot on your knees.

On my first Friday at Hearthside there is a "mandatory meeting for all restaurant employees," which I attend, eager for insight into our overall marketing strategy and the niche (your basic Ohio cuisine with a tropical twist?) we aim to inhabit. But there is no "we" at this meeting. Phillip, our top manager except for an occasional "consultant" sent out by corporate headquarters, opens it with a sneer: "The break room—it's disgusting. Butts in the ashtrays, newspapers lying around, crumbs." This windowless little room, which also houses the time clock for the entire hotel, is where we stash our bags and civilian clothes and take our half-hour meal breaks. But a break room is not a right, he tells us, it can be taken away. We should also know that the lockers in the break room and whatever is in them can be searched at any time. Then comes gossip; there has been gossip; gossip (which seems to mean employees talking among themselves) must stop. Off-duty employees are henceforth barred from eating at the restaurant, because "other servers gather around them and gossip." When Phillip has exhausted his agenda of rebukes, Joan complains about the conditions of the ladies' room and I throw in my two bits about the vacuum cleaner. But I don't see any backup coming from my fellow servers, each of whom has slipped into her own personal funk; Gail, my role model, stares sorrowfully at a point six inches from her nose. The meeting ends when Andy, one of the cooks, gets up, muttering about breaking up his day off for this almighty bullshit.

Just four days later we are suddenly summoned into the kitchen at 3:30 s ip i, even though there are live tables on the floor. We all—about ten of us—stand around Phillip, who announces grimly that there has been a report of some "drug activity" on the night shift and that, as a result, we are now to be a "drug-free" workplace, meaning that all new hires will be tested and possibly also current employees on a random basis. I am glad that this part of the kitchen is so dark because I find myself blushing as hard as if I had been caught toking up in the ladies' room myself: I haven't been treated this way—lined up in the corridor, threatened with locker searches, peppered with carelessly aimed accusations—since at least junior high school. Back on the floor, Joan cracks, "Next they'll be telling us we can't have *sex* on the job." When I ask Stu what happened to inspire the crackdown, he just mutters about "management decisions" and takes the opportunity to upbraid Gail and me for being too generous with the rolls. From now on there's to be only one per customer and it goes out with the dinner, not with the salad. He's also been riding the cooks, prompting Andy to come out of the kitchen and observe—with the serenity of a man whose customary implement is a butcher knife—that "Stu has a death wish today."

Later in the evening, the gossip crystallizes around the theo- 5
ry that Stu is himself the drug culprit, that he uses the restaurant
phone to order up marijuana and sends one of the late servers out
to fetch it for him. The server was caught and she may have ratted

out Stu, at least enough to cast some suspicion on him, thus accounting for his pissy behavior. Who knows? Personally, I'm ready to believe anything bad about Stu, who serves no evident function and presumes too much on our common ethnicity, sidling up to me one night to engage in a little nativism directed at the Haitian immigrants: "I feel like I'm the foreigner here. They're taking over the country." Still later that evening, the drug in question escalates to crack. Lionel, the busboy, entertains us for the rest of the shift by standing just behind Stu's back and sucking deliriously on an imaginary joint or maybe a pipe.

The other problem, in addition to the less-than-nurturing management style, is that this job shows no sign of being financially viable. You might imagine, from a comfortable distance, that people who live, year in and year out, on $6 to $10 an hour have discovered some survival stratagems unknown to the middle class. But no. It's not hard to get my coworkers talking about their living situations, because housing, in almost every case, is the principal source of disruption in their lives, the first thing they fill you in on when they arrive for their shifts. After a week, I have compiled the following survey:

> Gail is sharing a room in a well-known downtown flophouse for $250 a week. Her roommate, a male friend, has begun hitting on her, driving her nuts, but the rent would be impossible alone.
>
> Claude, the Haitian cook, is desperate to get out of the two-room apartment he shares with his girlfriend and two other, unrelated people. As far as I can determine, the other Haitian men live in similarly crowded situations.
>
> Annette, a twenty-year-old server who is six months pregnant and abandoned by her boyfriend, lives with her mother, a postal clerk.
>
> Marianne, who is a breakfast server, and her boyfriend are paying $170 a week for a one-person trailer.
>
> Billy, who at $10 an hour is the wealthiest of us, lives in the trailer he owns, paying only the $400-a-month lot fee.
>
> The other white cook, Andy, lives on his dry-docked boat, which, as far as I can tell from his loving descriptions, can't be more than twenty feet long. He offers to take me out on it once it's repaired,

but the offer comes with inquiries as to my marital status, so I do not follow up on it.

Tina, another server, and her husband are paying $60 a night for a room in the Days Inn. This is because they have no car and the Days Inn is in walking distance of the Hearthside. When Marianne is tossed out of her trailer for subletting (which is against trailer park rules), she leaves her boyfriend and moves in with Tina and her husband.

Joan, who had fooled me with her numerous and tasteful outfits (hostesses wear their own clothes), lives in a van parked behind a shopping center at night and showers in Tina's motel room. The clothes are from thrift shops.[1]

It strikes me, in my middle-class solipsism, that there is gross improvidence in some of these arrangements. When Gail and I are wrapping silverware in napkins—the only task for which we are permitted to sit—she tells me she is thinking of escaping from her roommate by moving into the Days Inn herself. I am astounded: how she can even think of paying $40 to $60 a day? But if I was afraid of sounding like a social worker, I have come out just sounding like a fool. She squints at me in disbelief: "And where am I supposed to get a month's rent and a month's deposit for an apartment?" I'd been feeling pretty smug about my $500 efficiency, but of course it was made possible only by the $1,300 I had allotted myself for start-up costs when I began my low-wage life: $1,000 for the first month's rent and deposit, $100 for initial groceries and cash in my pocket, $200 stuffed away for emergencies. In poverty, as in certain propositions in physics, starting conditions are everything.

There are no secret economies that nourish the poor; on the contrary, there are a host of special costs. If you can't put up the two months' rent you need to secure an apartment, you end up paying through the nose for a room by the week. If you have only a room, with a hot plate at best, you can't save by cooking up huge lentil stews that can be frozen for the week ahead. You eat fast

[1] I could find no statistics on the number of employed people living in cars or vans, but according to a 1997 report of the National Coalition for the Homeless, "Myths and Facts about Homelessness." nearly one-fifth of all homeless people (in twenty-nine cities across the nation) are employed in full-or part-time jobs.

food or the hot dogs and Styrofoam cups of soup that can be microwaved in a convenience store. If you have no money for health insurance—and the Hearthside's niggardly plan kicks in only after three months—you go without routine care or prescription drugs and end up paying the price. Gail, for example, was doing fine, healthwise anyway, until she ran out of money for estrogen pills. She is supposed to be on the company health plan by now, but they claim to have lost her application form and to be beginning the paperwork all over again. So she spends $9 a pop for pills to control the migraines she wouldn't have, she insists, if her estrogen supplements were covered. Similarly, Marianne's boyfriend lost his job as a roofer because he missed so much time after getting a cut on his foot for which he couldn't afford the prescribed antibiotic.

My own situation, when I sit down to assess it after two weeks of work, would not be much better if this were my actual life. The seductive thing about waitressing is that you don't have to wait for payday to feel a few bills in your pocket, and my tips usually cover meals and gas, plus something left over to stuff into the kitchen drawer I use as a bank. But as the tourist business slows in the summer heat, I sometimes leave work with only $20 in tips (the gross is higher, but servers share about 15 percent of their tips with the busboys and bartenders). With wages included, this amounts to about the minimum wage of $5.15 an hour. The sum in the drawer is piling up but at the present rate of accumulation will be more than $100 short of my rent when the end of the month comes around. Nor can I see any expenses to cut. True, I haven't gone the lentil stew route yet, but that's because I don't have a large cooking pot, potholders, or a ladle to stir with (which would cost a total of about $30 at Kmart, somewhat less at a thrift store), not to mention onions, carrots, and the indispensable bay leaf. I do make my lunch almost every day—usually some slow-burning, high-protein combo like frozen chicken patties with melted cheese on top and canned pinto beans on the side. Dinner is at the Hearthside, which offers its employees a choice of BLT, fish sandwich, or hamburger for only $2. The burger lasts longest, especially if it's heaped with gut-puckering jalapeños, but by midnight my stomach is growling again.

So unless I want to start using my car as a residence, I have to find a 10
second or an alternative job. I call all the hotels I'd filled out housekeeping applications at weeks ago—the Hyatt, Holiday Inn, Econo Lodge, HoJo's, Best Western, plus a half dozen locally run guest houses. Nothing. Then I start making the rounds again, wasting whole mornings waiting for some assistant manager to show up, even dipping into places so creepy that the front-desk clerk greets you from behind bullet-proof glass and sells pints of liquor over the counter. But either someone has exposed my real-life housekeeping habits—which are, shall we say, mellow—or I am at the wrong end of some infallible ethnic equation: most, but by no means all, of the working housekeepers I see on my job searches are African Americans, Spanish speaking, or refugees from the Central European post-Communist world, while servers are almost invariably white and monolingually English speaking. When I finally get a positive response, I have been identified once again as server material. Jerry's—again, not the real name—which is part of a well-known national chain and physically attached here to another budget hotel, is ready to use me at once. The prospect is both exciting and terrifying because, with about the same number of tables and counter seats, Jerry's attracts three or four times the volume of customers as the gloomy old Hearthside.

Picture a fat person's hell, and I don't mean a place with no food. Instead there is everything you might eat if eating had no bodily consequences—the cheese fries, the chicken-fried steaks, the fudge-laden desserts—only here every bite must be paid for, one way or another, in human discomfort. The kitchen is a cavern, a stomach leading to the lower intestine that is the garbage and dishwashing area, from which issue bizarre smells combining the edible and the offal: creamy carrion, pizza barf, and that unique and enigmatic Jerry's scent, citrus fart. The floor is slick with spills, forcing us to walk through the kitchen with tiny steps, like Susan McDougal in leg irons. Sinks everywhere are clogged with scraps of lettuce, decomposing lemon wedges, water-logged toast crusts.

Put your hand down on any counter and you risk being stuck to it by the film of ancient syrup spills, and this is unfortunate because hands are utensils here, used for scooping up lettuce onto the salad plates, lifting out pie slices, and even moving hash browns from one plate to another. The regulation poster in the single unisex rest room admonishes us to wash our hands thoroughly, and even offers instructions for doing so, but there is always some vital substance missing—soap, paper towels, toilet paper—and I never found all three at once. You learn to stuff your pockets with napkins before going in there, and too bad about the customers, who must eat, although they don't realize it, almost literally out of our hands.

The break room summarizes the whole situation: there is none, because there are no breaks at Jerry's. For six to eight hours in a row, you never sit except to pee. Actually, there are three folding chairs at a table immediately adjacent to the bathroom, but hardly anyone ever sits in this, the very rectum of the gastroarchitectural system. Rather, the function of the peritoilet area is to house the ashtrays in which servers and dishwashers leave their cigarettes burning at all times, like votive candles, so they don't have to waste time lighting up again when they dash back here for a puff. Almost everyone smokes as if their pulmonary well-being depended on it—the multinational mélange of cooks; the dishwashers, who are all Czechs here; the servers, who are American natives—creating an atmosphere in which oxygen is only an occasional pollutant. My first morning at Jerry's, when the hypoglycemic shakes set in, I complain to one of my fellow servers that I don't understand how she can go so long without food. "Well, I don't understand how *you* can go so long without a cigarette," she responds in a tone of reproach. Because work is what you do for others; smoking is what you do for yourself. I don't know why the anti-smoking crusaders have never grasped the element of defiant self-nurturance that makes the habit so endearing to its victims—as if, in the American workplace, the only thing people have to call their own is the tumors they are nourishing and the spare moments they devote to feeding them.

Now, the Industrial Revolution is not an easy transition, especially, in my experience, when you have to zip through it in just a couple of days. I have gone from craft work straight into the factory, from the air-conditioned morgue of the Hearthside directly into the flames. Customers arrive in human waves, sometimes disgorged fifty at a time from their tour buses, peckish and whiny. Instead of two "girls" on the floor at once, there can be as many as six of us running around in our brilliant pink-and-orange Hawaiian shirts. Conversations, either with customers or with fellow employees, seldom last more than twenty seconds at a time. On my first day, in fact, I am hurt by my sister servers' coldness. My mentor for the day is a supremely competent, emotionally uninflected twenty-three-year-old, and the others, who gossip a little among themselves about the real reason someone is out sick today and the size of the bail bond someone else has had to pay, ignore me completely. On my second day, I find out why. "Well, it's good to see *you* again," one of them says in greeting. "Hardly anyone comes back after the first day." I feel powerfully vindicated—a survivor—but it would take a long time, probably months, before I could hope to be accepted into this sorority.

I start out with the beautiful, heroic idea of handling the two jobs at once, and for two days I almost do it: working the breakfast/lunch shift at Jerry's from 8:00 till 2:00, arriving at the Hearthside a few minutes late, at 2:10, and attempting to hold out until 10:00. In the few minutes I have between jobs, I pick up a spicy chicken sandwich at the Wendy's drive-through window, gobble it down in the car, and change from khaki slacks to black, from Hawaiian to rust-colored polo. There is a problem, though. When, during the 3:00–4:00 o'clock dead time, I finally sit down to wrap silver, my flesh seems to bond to the seat. I try to refuel with a purloined cup of clam chowder, as I've seen Gail and Joan do dozens of time, but Stu catches me and hisses "No *eating!*" although there's not a customer around to be offended by the sight of food making contact with a server's lips. So I tell Gail I'm going to quit, and she hugs me and says she might just follow me to Jerry's herself.

But the chances of this are minuscule. She has left the flophouse 15
and her annoying roommate and is back to living in her truck. But,

guess what, she reports to me excitedly later that evening, Phillip has given her permission to park overnight in the hotel parking lot, as long as she keeps out of sight, and the parking lot should be totally safe since it's patrolled by a hotel security guard! With the Hearthside offering benefits like that, how could anyone think of leaving? This must be Phillip's theory, anyway. He accepts my resignation with a shrug, his main concern being that I return my two polo shirts and aprons.

Gail would have triumphed at Jerry's, I'm sure, but for me it's a crash course in exhaustion management. Years ago, the kindly fry cook who trained me to waitress at a Los Angeles truck stop used to say: never make an unnecessary trip; if you don't have to walk fast, walk slow; if you don't have to walk, stand. But at Jerry's the effort of distinguishing necessary from unnecessary and urgent from whenever would itself be too much of an energy drain. The only thing to do is to treat each shift as a one-time-only emergency: you've got fifty starving people out there, lying scattered on the battlefield, so get out there and feed them! Forget that you will have to do this again tomorrow, forget that you will have to be alert enough to dodge the drunks on the drive home tonight—just burn, burn, burn! Ideally, at some point you enter what servers call a "rhythm" and psychologists term a "flow state," where signals pass from the sense organs directly to the muscles, bypassing the cerebral cortex, and a Zen-like emptiness sets in. I'm on a 2:00–10:00 p.m. shift now, and a male server from the morning shift tells me about the time he "pulled a triple"—three shifts in a row, all the way around the clock—and then got off and had a drink and met this girl, and maybe he shouldn't tell me this, but they had sex right then and there and it was like *beautiful*. . . .

Raise Wages, Not Walls

Michael S. Dukakis
Daniel J. B. Mitchell

There are two approaches to illegal immigration currently being debated in Congress. One, supported by the House, emphasizes border control and law enforcement, including a wall along the Mexican border and increased border patrols. The other, which is supported by the Bush administration and has been passed by the Senate, relies on employers to police the workplace. Both proposals have serious flaws.

As opponents of the House plan have rightly pointed out, walls rarely work; illegal immigrants will get around them one way or another. Unless we erect something akin to the Berlin Wall, which would cost billions to build and police, a barrier on the border would be monitored by largely symbolic patrols and easily evaded.

The Senate approach is more realistic but it, too, has problems. It creates a temporary worker program but requires employers first to attempt to recruit American workers to fill job openings. It allows for more border fencing, but makes no effort to disguise the basic futility of the enterprise. Instead, it calls on employers to enforce immigration laws in the workplace, a plan that can only succeed through the creation and distribution of a costly national identification card.

A national ID card raises serious questions about civil liberties, but they are not the sole concern. The cost estimates for producing and distributing a counterfeit-proof card for the roughly 150 million people currently in the labor force—and the millions more who will seek work in the near future—extend into the billions of dollars. Employers would have to verify the identity of every American worker, otherwise the program would be as unreliable as the one in place now. Anyone erroneously denied a card in this bureaucratic labyrinth would be unemployable.

There is a simpler alternative. If we are really serious about turning back the tide of illegal immigration, we should start by raising the minimum wage from $5.15 per hour to something closer to $8. The Massachusetts legislature recently voted to raise the state minimum to $8 and California may soon set its minimum even higher. Once the minimum wage has been significantly increased, we can begin vigorously enforcing the wage law and other basic labor standards.

Millions of illegal immigrants work for minimum and even subminimum wages in workplaces that don't come close to meeting health and safety standards. It is nonsense to say, as President Bush did recently, that these jobs are filled by illegal immigrants because Americans won't do them. Before we had mass illegal immigration in this country, hotel beds were made, office floors were cleaned, restaurant dishes were washed and crops were picked—by Americans.

Americans will work at jobs that are risky, dirty or unpleasant so long as they provide decent wages and working conditions, especially if employers also provide health insurance. Plenty of Americans now work in such jobs, from mining coal to picking up garbage. The difference is they are paid a decent wage and provided benefits for their labor.

However, Americans won't work for peanuts, and these days the national minimum wage is less than peanuts. For full-time work, it doesn't even come close to the poverty line for an individual, let alone provide a family with a living wage. It hasn't been raised since 1997 and isn't enforced even at its currently ridiculous level.

Yet enforcing the minimum wage doesn't require walling off a porous border or trying to distinguish yesterday's illegal immigrant from tomorrow's "guest worker." All it takes is a willingness by the federal government to inspect workplaces to determine which employers obey the law.

Curiously, most members of Congress who take a hard line on 10
immigration also strongly oppose increasing the minimum wage, claiming it will hurt businesses and reduce jobs. For some reason, they don't seem eager to acknowledge that many of the jobs they claim to hold dear are held by the same illegal immigrants they are trying to deport.

But if we want to reduce illegal immigration, it makes sense to reduce the abundance of extremely low-paying jobs that fuels it. If we raise the minimum wage, it's possible some low-end jobs may be lost; but more Americans would also be willing to work in such jobs, thereby denying them to people who aren't supposed to be here in the first place. And tough enforcement of wage rules would curtail the growth of an underground economy in which both illegal immigration and employer abuses thrive.

Raising the minimum wage and increasing enforcement would prove far more effective and less costly than either proposal currently under consideration in Congress. If Congress would only remove its blinders about the minimum wage, it may see a plan to deal effectively with illegal immigration, too.

[2006]

Living Wage Fight Goes On

Molly Ivins [b. 1944]

Amid the mountains of evidence of increasing economic inequality in this country, it might be useful to focus on the solutions rather than the problem.

Here's the bottom line: Low-wage workers in this country—working forty hours a week, fifty-two weeks a year—make $10,700 a year, which is $2,900 below the poverty level for a family of three. On September 15, Senator Edward Kennedy offered a minimum-wage increase as an amendment to the bankruptcy bill, announcing in a news release: "These Americans are just one paycheck away from bankruptcy. If faced with divorce, an unexpected health crisis, or another family emergency, these families often have no option but to declare bankruptcy.

"My Republican friends have their own answer—legislation to make it easier for banks and credit card companies to squeeze these already-struggling families even harder."

Kennedy offers a minimum-wage increase that would get workers up to $6.15 an hour by the end of the century. He is in the happy position of being able to say, "I told you so."

Kennedy wrote and passed the last increase, which took effect in 1996 and 1997, amid the usual cries from the usual suspects—the Business Round Table, Senator Phil Gramm, the National Restaurant Association, and others—that doom and chaos would result. All the hoary arguments were trotted out: small businesses would be driven to the brink, massive layoffs would result, inflation would spiral out of control, etc., etc.

One can forgive Kennedy his polite, senatorial har-de-har-har about this because, as he points out, "Since the last increase, inflation has gone down. Unemployment has dropped. Jobs have been added, not lost, in low-wage industries. Retail employment has been growing almost one-third faster in the eleven months since the last increase than it did the year before. Five hundred seventeen thousand new retail jobs have been added since the wage increased to $5.15 last September."

But the Kennedy amendment hasn't the proverbial snowball's chance for political reasons—the pleasing economic good sense of it making no difference at a time when Our Nation's Capital is focused on something else—so let us consider some other solutions that apply here.

While Washington dithers, the people are already at work on a solution. The living-wage campaign is one of the most underreported movements in the United States. (Sorry, the media are busy with something else.) Unions, community groups, and religious organizations have won living-wage campaigns in Baltimore, Los Angeles, Milwaukee, and New York (and busted out in Houston, swamped by a ton of business money).

The premise is simple—you start by targeting city government with a requirement that any firm holding a service contract with the city pay enough (with gradual increases over about three years) to get their workers out of poverty. It's a concept, no? It's a sort of roundabout way of increasing the minimum wage because as city contractors bump up, other local employers are forced to follow. (Same concept as the Davis-Bacon Act, so loathed by the right wing, which obliges government contractors to meet the prevailing wage.)

An alert reader called the other day to propose still another 10
partial solution for inequality: a maximum wage, to apply to those obscene takeover deals in which the top execs collect tens of millions in exchange for firing thousands of workers. I like it.

SEÑOR PAYROLL

William E. Barrett

Larry and I were Junior Engineers in the gas plant which means that we were clerks. Anything that could be classified as paper work came to the flat double desk across which we faced each other. The Main Office downtown sent us a bewildering array of orders and rules that were to be put into effect.

Junior Engineers were beneath the notice of everyone except the Mexican laborers at the plant. To them we were the visible form of a distant, unknowable paymaster. We were Señor Payroll.

Those Mexicans were great workmen; the aristocrats among them were the stokers big men who worked Herculean eight-hour shifts in the fierce heat of the retorts. They scooped coal with huge shovels and hurled it with uncanny aim at tiny doors. The coal streamed out from the shovels like black water from a high-pressure nozzle, and never missed the narrow opening. The stokers worked stripped to the waist, and there was pride and dignity in them. Few men could do such work, and they were the few.

The Company paid its men only twice a month, on the fifth and on the twentieth. To a Mexican, this was absurd. What man with money will make it last fifteen days? If he hoarded money beyond the spending of three days, he was a miser—and when, Señor did the blood of Spain flow in the veins of misers? Hence, it was the custom for our stokers to appear every third or fourth day to draw the money due to them.

There was a certain elasticity in the Company rules, and Larry and I sent the necessary forms to the Main Office and received an "advance" against a man's pay check. Then, one day, Downtown favored us with a memorandum:

"There have been too many abuses of the advance-against-wages privilege. Hereafter, no advance against wages will be made to any employee except in a case of genuine emergency."

We had no sooner posted the notice when in came stoker Juan Garcia. He asked for an advance. I pointed to the notice. He spelled it through slowly, then said, "What does this mean, this 'genuine emergency'?"

I explained to him patiently that the Company was kind and sympathetic, but that it was a great nuisance to have to pay wages every few days. If someone was ill or if money was urgently needed for some other good reason, then the Company would make an exception to the rule.

Juan Garcia turned his hat over and over slowly in his big hands. "I do not get my money?"

"Next payday, Juan. On the twentieth."

He went out silently and I felt a little ashamed of myself. I looked across the desk at Larry. He avoided my eyes.

In the next hour two other stokers came in, looked at the notice, had it explained and walked solemnly out; then no more came. What we did not know was that Juan Garcia, Pete Mendoza, and Francisco Gonzalez had spread the word, and that every Mexican in the plant was explaining the order to every other Mexican. "To get money now, the wife must be sick. There must be medicine for the baby."

The next morning Juan Garcia's wife was practically dying, Pete Mendoza's mother would hardly last the day, there was a veritable epidemic among children and, just for variety, there was one sick father. We always suspected that the old man was really sick; no Mexican would otherwise have thought of him. At any rate, nobody paid Larry and me to examine private lives; we made out our forms with an added line describing the "genuine emergency." Our people got paid.

That went on for a week. Then came a new order, curt and to the point: "Hereafter, employees will be paid ONLY on the fifth and the twentieth of the month. No exceptions will be made except in the cases of employees leaving the service of the Company."

The notice went up on the board, and we explained its significance gravely. "No, Juan Garcia, we cannot advance your wages.

It is too bad about your wife and your cousins and your aunts, but there is a new rule."

Juan Garcia went out and thought it over. He thought out loud with Mendoza and Gonzalez and Ayala, then, in the morning, he was back. "I am quitting this company for different job. You pay me now?"

We argued that it was a good company and that it loved its employees like children, but in the end we paid off, because Juan Garcia quit. And so did Gonzalez Mendoza, Obregon, Ayala and Ortez, the best stokers, men who could not be replaced.

Larry and I looked at each other; we knew what was coming in about three days. One of our duties was to sit on the hiring line early each morning, engaging transient workers for the handy gangs. Any man was accepted who could walk up and ask for a job without falling down. Never before had we been called upon to hire such skilled virtuosos as stokers for handy-gang work, but we were called upon to hire them now.

The day foreman was wringing his hands and asking the Almighty if he was personally supposed to shovel this condemned coal, while there in a stolid, patient line were skilled men—Garcia, Mendoza, and others—waiting to be hired. We hired them, of course. There was nothing else we could do.

Every day we had a line of resigning stokers, and another line of stokers seeking work. Our paper work became very complicated. At the Main Office they were jumping up and down. The procession of forms showing Juan Garcia's resigning and being hired over and over again was too much for them. Sometimes Downtown had Garcia on the payroll twice at the same time when someone down there was slow in entering a resignation. Our phone rang early and often.

Tolerantly and patiently we explained: "There's nothing we can do if a man wants to quit, and if there are stokers available when the plant needs stokers, we hire them."

Out of chaos, Downtown issued another order. I read it and whistled. Larry looked at it and said, "It is going to be very quiet around here."

The order read: "Hereafter, no employee who resigns may be rehired within a period of 30 days."

Juan Garcia was due for another resignation, and when he came in we showed him the order and explained that standing in line the next day would do him no good if he resigned today. "Thirty days is a long time, Juan."

It was a grave matter and he took time to reflect on it. So did Gonzalez, Mendoza, Ayala and Ortez. Ultimately, however, they were all back—and all resigned.

We did our best to dissuade them and we were sad about the parting. This time it was for keeps and they shook hands with us solemnly. It was very nice knowing us. Larry and I looked at each other when they were gone and we both knew that neither of us had been pulling for Downtown to win this duel. It was a blue day.

In the morning, however, they were all back in line. With the utmost gravity, Juan Garcia informed me that he was a stoker looking for a job.

"No dice, Juan," I said. "Come back in thirty days. I warned you."

His eyes looked straight into mine, without a flicker. "There is some mistake, Señor," he said. "I am Manuel Hernandez. I work as the stoker in Pueblo, in Santa Fe, in many places."

I stared back at him, remembering the sick wife and the babies without medicine, the mother-in-law in the hospital, the many resignations and the rehirings. I knew that there was a gas plant in Pueblo, and that there wasn't any in Santa Fe; but who was I to argue with a man about his own name? A stoker is a stoker.

So I hired him. I hired Gonzalez, too, who swore that his name was Carrera and Ayala, who had shamelessly become Smith.

Three days later the resigning started.

Within a week our payroll read like a history of Latin America. Everyone was on it: Lopez and Obregon, Villa, Diaz, Batista, Gomez, and even San Martín and Bolívar. Finally Larry and I, growing weary of staring at familiar faces and writing unfamiliar names, went to the Superintendent and told him the whole story. He tried not to grin, and said, "Damned nonsense!"

The next day the orders were taken down. We called our most prominent stokers into the office and pointed to the board. No rules any more.

"The next time we hire you hombres," Larry said grimly, "come in under the names you like best, because that's the way you are going to stay on the books."

They looked at us and they looked at the board; then for the first time in the long duel, their teeth flashed white. "Si, Señores," they said.

And so it was.

The Communist Manifesto

Karl Marx [1818–1883]
Frederick Engels [1920–1895]

A spectre is haunting Europe—the spectre of Communism. All the Powers of old Europe have entered into a holy alliance to exorcise this spectre: Pope and Czar, Metternich and Guizot, French Radicals and German police-spies.

Where is the party in opposition that has not been decried as Communistic by its opponents in power? Where the Opposition that has not hurled back the branding reproach of Communism, against the more advanced opposition parties, as well as against its reactionary adversaries?

Two things result from this fact:

I. Communism is already acknowledged by all European Powers to be itself a Power.

II. It is high time that Communists should openly, in the face of the whole world, publish their views, their aims, their tendencies, and meet this nursery tale of the Spectre of Communism with a Manifesto of the party itself.

To this end, Communists of various nationalities have assembled in London, and sketched the following Manifesto, to be published in the English, French, German, Italian, Flemish and Danish languages.

I. Bourgeois and Proletarians

The history of all hitherto existing society is the history of class struggles.

Freeman and slave, patrician and plebeian, lord and serf, guild-master and journeyman, in a word, oppressor and oppressed, stood in constant opposition to one another, carried on an uninterrupted, now hidden, now open fight, a fight that each time ended, either in a revolutionary re-constitution of society at large, or in the common ruin of the contending classes.

In the earlier epochs of history, we find almost everywhere a complicated arrangement of society into various orders, a manifold gradation of social rank. In ancient Rome we have patricians, knights, plebeians, slaves; in the Middle Ages, feudal lords, vassals, guild-masters, journeymen, apprentices, serfs; in almost all of these classes, again, subordinate gradations.

The modern bourgeois society that has sprouted from the ru- 1
ins of feudal society has not done away with class antagonisms. It
has but established new classes, new conditions of oppression, new
forms of struggle in place of the old ones.

Our epoch, the epoch of the bourgeoisie, possesses, however, this distinctive feature: it has simplified the class antagonisms. Society as a whole is more and more splitting up into two great hostile camps, into two great classes directly facing each other: Bourgeoisie and Proletariat.

From the serfs of the Middle Ages sprang the chartered burghers of the earliest towns. From these burgesses the first elements of the bourgeoisie were developed.

The discovery of America, the rounding of the Cape, opened up fresh ground for the rising bourgeoisie. The East-Indian and Chinese markets, the colonisation of America, trade with the colonies, the increase in the means of exchange and in commodities generally, gave to commerce, to navigation, to industry, an impulse never before known, and thereby, to the revolutionary element in the tottering feudal society, a rapid development.

The feudal system of industry, under which industrial production was monopolised by closed guilds, now no longer sufficed for the growing wants of the new markets. The manufacturing system took its place. The guild-masters were pushed on one side by the manufacturing middle class; division of labour between the different corporate guilds vanished in the face of division of labour in each single workshop.

Meantime the markets kept ever growing, the demand ever 15
rising. Even manufacture no longer sufficed. Thereupon, steam and machinery revolutionised industrial production. The place of manufacture was taken by the giant, Modern Industry, the place of the industrial middle class, by industrial millionaires, the leaders of whole industrial armies, the modern bourgeois.

Modern industry has established the world market, for which the discovery of America paved the way. This market has given an immense development to commerce, to navigation, to communication by land. This development has, in its turn, reacted on the extension of industry; and in proportion as industry, commerce, navigation, railways extended, in the same proportion the bourgeoisie developed, increased its capital, and pushed into the background every class handed down from the Middle Ages.

We see, therefore, how the modern bourgeoisie is itself the product of a long course of development, of a series of revolutions in the modes of production and of exchange.

Each step in the development of the bourgeoisie was accompanied by a corresponding political advance of that class. An oppressed class under the sway of the feudal nobility, an armed and self-governing association in the medieval commune; here independent urban republic (as in Italy and Germany), there taxable "third estate" of the monarchy (as in France), afterwards, in the period of manufacture proper, serving either the semi-feudal or the absolute monarchy as a counterpoise against the nobility, and, in fact, cornerstone of the great monarchies in general, the bourgeoisie has at last, since the establishment of Modern Industry and of the world market, conquered for itself, in the modern representative State, exclusive political sway. The executive of the modern State is but a committee for managing the common affairs of the whole bourgeoisie.

The bourgeoisie, historically, has played a most revolutionary part.

The bourgeoisie, wherever it has got the upper hand, has put 20
an end to all feudal, patriarchal, idyllic relations. It has pitilessly torn asunder the motley feudal ties that bound man to his "natural

superiors," and has left remaining no other nexus between man and man than naked self-interest, than callous "cash payment." It has drowned the most heavenly ecstasies of religious fervour, of chivalrous enthusiasm, of philistine sentimentalism, in the icy water of egotistical calculation. It has resolved personal worth into exchange value, and in place of the numberless indefeasible chartered freedoms, has set up that single, unconscionable freedom—Free Trade. In one word, for exploitation, veiled by religious and political illusions, it has substituted naked, shameless, direct, brutal exploitation.

The bourgeoisie has stripped of its halo every occupation hitherto honoured and looked up to with reverent awe. It has converted the physician, the lawyer, the priest, the poet, the man of science, into its paid wage-labourers.

The bourgeoisie has torn away from the family its sentimental veil, and has reduced the family relation to a mere money relation.

The bourgeoisie has disclosed how it came to pass that the brutal display of vigour in the Middle Ages, which Reactionists so much admire, found its fitting complement in the most slothful indolence. It has been the first to show what man's activity can bring about. It has accomplished wonders far surpassing Egyptian pyramids, Roman aqueducts, and Gothic cathedrals; it has conducted expeditions that put in the shade all former Exoduses of nations and crusades.

The bourgeoisie cannot exist without constantly revolutionising the instruments of production, and thereby the relations of production, and with them the whole relations of society. Conservation of the old modes of production in unaltered form, was, on the contrary, the first condition of existence for all earlier industrial classes. Constant revolutionising of production, uninterrupted disturbance of all social conditions, everlasting uncertainty and agitation distinguish the bourgeois epoch from all earlier ones. All fixed, fast-frozen relations, with their train of ancient and venerable prejudices and opinions, are swept away, all new-formed ones become antiquated before they can ossify. All that is solid melts into air, all that is holy is profaned, and man is at last compelled to face with sober senses, his real conditions of life, and his relations with his kind.

The need of a constantly expanding market for its products chases the bourgeoisie over the whole surface of the globe. It must nestle everywhere, settle everywhere, establish connexions everywhere. 25

The bourgeoisie has through its exploitation of the world market given a cosmopolitan character to production and consumption in every country. To the great chagrin of Reactionists, it has drawn from under the feet of industry the national ground on which it stood. All old-established national industries have been destroyed or are daily being destroyed. They are dislodged by new industries, whose introduction becomes a life and death question for all civilised nations, by industries that no longer work up indigenous raw material, but raw material drawn from the remotest zones; industries whose products are consumed, not only at home, but in every quarter of the globe. In place of the old wants, satisfied by the productions of the country, we find new wants, requiring for their satisfaction the products of distant lands and climes. In place of the old local and national seclusion and self-sufficiency, we have intercourse in every direction, universal inter-dependence of nations. And as in material, so also in intellectual production. The intellectual creations of individual nations become common property. National one-sidedness and narrow-mindedness become more and more impossible, and from the numerous national and local literatures, there arises a world literature.

The bourgeoisie, by the rapid improvement of all instruments of production, by the immensely facilitated means of communication, draws all, even the most barbarian, nations into civilisation. The cheap prices of its commodities are the heavy artillery with which it batters down all Chinese walls, with which it forces the barbarians' intensely obstinate hatred of foreigners to capitulate. It compels all nations, on pain of extinction, to adopt the bourgeois mode of production; it compels them to introduce what it calls civilisation into their midst, i.e., to become bourgeois themselves. In one word, it creates a world after its own image.

The bourgeoisie has subjected the country to the rule of the towns. It has created enormous cities, has greatly increased the urban population as compared with the rural, and has thus rescued a considerable part of the population from the idiocy of rural life. Just as it has made the country dependent on the towns, so it has made barbarian and semi-barbarian countries dependent on the civilised ones, nations of peasants on nations of bourgeois, the East on the West.

The bourgeoisie keeps more and more doing away with the scattered state of the population, of the means of production, and of property. It has agglomerated population, centralised means of production, and has concentrated property in a few hands. The necessary consequence of this was political centralisation. Independent, or but loosely connected provinces with separate interests, laws, governments and systems of taxation, became lumped together into one nation, with one government, one code of laws, one national class-interest, one frontier and one customs-tariff.

The bourgeoisie, during its rule of scarce one hundred years, has created more massive and more colossal productive forces than have all preceding generations together. Subjection of Nature's forces to man, machinery, application of chemistry to industry and agriculture, steam-navigation, railways, electric telegraphs, clearing of whole continents for cultivation, canalisation of rivers, whole populations conjured out of the ground—what earlier century had even a presentiment that such productive forces slumbered in the lap of social labour?

We see then: the means of production and of exchange, on whose foundation the bourgeoisie built itself up, were generated in feudal society. At a certain stage in the development of these means of production and of exchange, the conditions under which feudal society produced and exchanged, the feudal organisation of agriculture and manufacturing industry, in one word, the feudal relations of property became no longer compatible with the already developed productive forces; they became so many fetters. They had to be burst asunder; they were burst asunder.

Into their place stepped free competition, accompanied by a social and political constitution adapted to it, and by the economical and political sway of the bourgeois class.

A similar movement is going on before our own eyes. Modern bourgeois society with its relations of production, of exchange and of property, a society that has conjured up such gigantic means of production and of exchange, is like the sorcerer, who is no longer able to control the powers of the nether world whom he has called up by his spells. For many a decade past the history of industry and commerce is but the history of the revolt of modern productive forces against modern conditions of production, against the property relations that are the conditions for the existence of the bourgeoisie and of its rule. It is enough to mention the commercial crises that by their periodical return put on its trial, each time more threateningly, the existence of the entire bourgeois society. In these crises a great part not only of the existing products, but also of the previously created productive forces, are periodically destroyed. In these crises there breaks out an epidemic that, in all earlier epochs, would have seemed an absurdity—the epidemic of over-production. Society suddenly finds itself put back into a state of momentary barbarism; it appears as if a famine, a universal war of devastation had cut off the supply of every means of subsistence; industry and commerce seem to be destroyed; and why? Because there is too much civilisation, too much means of subsistence, too much industry, too much commerce. The productive forces at the disposal of society no longer tend to further the development of the conditions of bourgeois property; on the contrary, they have become too powerful for these conditions, by which they are fettered, and so soon as they overcome these fetters, they bring disorder into the whole of bourgeois society, endanger the existence of bourgeois property. The conditions of bourgeois society are too narrow to comprise the wealth created by them. And how does the bourgeoisie get over these crises? On the one hand by enforced destruction of a mass of productive forces; on the other, by the conquest of new markets, and by the more thorough exploitation of the old ones. That is to say, by paving the way for more extensive and more destructive crises, and by diminishing the means whereby crises are prevented.

The weapons with which the bourgeoisie felled feudalism to the ground are now turned against the bourgeoisie itself.

But not only has the bourgeoisie forged the weapons that bring death to itself; it has also called into existence the men who are to wield those weapons—the modern working class—the proletarians.

In proportion as the bourgeoisie, *i.e.,* capital, is developed, in the same proportion is the proletariat, the modern working class, developed—a class of labourers, who live only so long as they find work, and who find work only so long as their labour increases capital. These labourers, who must sell themselves piecemeal, are a commodity, like every other article of commerce, and are consequently exposed to all the vicissitudes of competition, to all the fluctuations of the market.

Owing to the extensive use of machinery and to division of labour, the work of the proletarians has lost all individual character, and, consequently, all charm for the workman. He becomes an appendage of the machine, and it is only the most simple, most monotonous, and most easily acquired knack, that is required of him. Hence, the cost of production of a workman is restricted, almost entirely, to the means of subsistence that he requires for his maintenance, and for the propagation of his race. But the price of a commodity, and therefore also of labour, is equal to its cost of production. In proportion, therefore, as the repulsiveness of the work increases, the wage decreases. Nay more, in proportion as the use of machinery and division of labour increases, in the same proportion the burden of toil also increases, whether by prolongation of the working hours, by increase of the work exacted in a given time or by increased speed of the machinery, etc.

Modern industry has converted the little workshop of the patriarchal master into the great factory of the industrial capitalist. Masses of labourers, crowded into the factory, are organised like soldiers. As privates of the industrial army they are placed under the command of a perfect hierarchy of officers and sergeants. Not only are they slaves of the bourgeois class, and of the bourgeois State; they are daily and hourly enslaved by the machine, by the overlooker, and, above all, by the individual bourgeois manufacturer himself. The more openly this despotism proclaims gain to be its end and aim, the more petty, the more hateful and the more embittering it is.

The less the skill and exertion of strength implied in manual labour, in other words, the more modern industry becomes developed, the more is the labour of men superseded by that of women. Differences of age and sex have no longer any distinctive social validity for the working class. All are instruments of labour, more or less expensive to use, according to their age and sex.

No sooner is the exploitation of the labourer by the manufac- 40
turer, so far, at an end, and he receives his wages in cash, than he is set upon by the other portions of the bourgeoisie, the landlord, the shopkeeper, the pawnbroker, etc.

The lower strata of the middle class—the small tradespeople, shopkeepers, and retired tradesmen generally, the handicraftsmen and peasants—all these sink gradually into the proletariat, partly because their diminutive capital does not suffice for the scale on which Modern Industry is carried on, and is swamped in the competition with the large capitalists, partly because their specialised skill is rendered worthless by new methods of production. Thus the proletariat is recruited from all classes of the population.

The proletariat goes through various stages of development. With its birth begins its struggle with the bourgeoisie. At first the contest is carried on by individual labourers, then by the workpeople of a factory, then by the operatives of one trade, in one locality, against the individual bourgeois who directly exploits them. They direct their attacks not against the bourgeois conditions of production, but against the instruments of production themselves; they destroy imported wares that compete with their labour, they smash to pieces machinery, they set factories ablaze, they seek to restore by force the vanished status of the workman of the Middle Ages.

At this stage the labourers still form an incoherent mass scattered over the whole country, and broken up by their mutual competition. If anywhere they unite to form more compact bodies, this is not yet the consequence of their own active union, but of the union of the bourgeoisie, which class, in order to attain its own political ends, is compelled to set the whole proletariat in motion, and is moreover yet, for a time, able to do so. At this stage, therefore, the proletarians do not fight their enemies, but the enemies of their enemies, the remnants of absolute monarchy, the landowners, the non-industrial bourgeois, the petty bourgeoisie. Thus the whole historical movement is concentrated in the hands of the bourgeoisie; every victory so obtained is a victory for the bourgeoisie.

But with the development of industry the proletariat not only increases in number; it becomes concentrated in greater masses, its strength grows, and it feels that strength more. The various interests and conditions of life within the ranks of the proletariat are more and more equalised, in proportion as machinery obliterates all distinctions of labour, and nearly everywhere reduces wages to the same low level. The growing competition among the bourgeois, and the resulting commercial crises, make the wages of the workers ever more fluctuating. The unceasing improvement of machinery, ever more rapidly developing, makes their livelihood more and more precarious; the collisions between individual workmen and individual bourgeois take more and more the character of collisions between two classes. Thereupon the workers begin to form combinations (Trades' Unions) against the bourgeois; they club together in order to keep up the rate of wages; they found permanent associations in order to make provision beforehand for these occasional revolts. Here and there the contest breaks out into riots.

Now and then the workers are victorious, but only for a time. The real fruit of their battles lies, not in the immediate result, but in the ever-expanding union of the workers. This union is helped on by the improved means of communication that are created by modern industry and that place the workers of different localities in contact with one another. It was just this contact that was needed to centralise the numerous local struggles, all of the same character, into one national struggle between classes. But every class struggle is a political struggle. And that union, to attain which the burghers of the Middle Ages, with their miserable highways, required centuries, the modern proletarians, thanks to railways, achieve in a few years.

This organisation of the proletarians into a class, and consequently into a political party, is continually being upset again by the competition between the workers themselves. But it ever rises up again, stronger, firmer, mightier. It compels legislative recognition of particular interests of the workers, by taking advantage of the divisions among the bourgeoisie itself. Thus the ten-hours' bill in England was carried.

Altogether collisions between the classes of the old society further, in many ways, the course of development of the proletariat. The bourgeoisie finds itself involved in a constant battle. At first with the aristocracy; later on, with those portions of the bourgeoisie itself, whose interests have become antagonistic to the progress of industry; at all times, with the bourgeoisie of foreign countries. In all these battles it sees itself compelled to appeal to the proletariat, to ask for its help, and thus, to drag it into the political arena. The bourgeoisie itself, therefore, supplies the proletariat with its own elements of political and general education, in other words, it furnishes the proletariat with weapons for fighting the bourgeoisie.

Further, as we have already seen, entire sections of the ruling classes are, by the advance of industry, precipitated into the proletariat, or are at least threatened in their conditions of existence. These also supply the proletariat with fresh elements of enlightenment and progress.

Finally, in times when the class struggle nears the decisive hour, the process of dissolution going on within the ruling class, in fact within the whole range of old society, assumes such a violent, glaring character, that a small section of the ruling class cuts itself adrift, and joins the revolutionary class, the class that holds the future in its hands. Just as, therefore, at an earlier period, a section of the nobility went over to the bourgeoisie, so now a portion of the bourgeoisie goes over to the proletariat, and in particular, a portion of the bourgeois ideologists, who have raised themselves to the level of comprehending theoretically the historical movement as a whole.

Of all the classes that stand face to face with the bourgeoisie 50
today, the proletariat alone is a really revolutionary class. The other classes decay and finally disappear in the face of Modern Industry; the proletariat is its special and essential product.

The lower middle class, the small manufacturer, the shopkeeper, the artisan, the peasant, all these fight against the bourgeoisie, to save from extinction their existence as fractions of the middle class.

They are therefore not revolutionary, but conservative. Nay more, they are reactionary, for they try to roll back the wheel of history. If by chance they are revolutionary, they are so only in view of their impending transfer into the proletariat, they thus defend not their present, but their future interests, they desert their own standpoint to place themselves at that of the proletariat.

The "dangerous class," the social scum, that passively rotting mass thrown off by the lowest layers of old society may, here and there, be swept into the movement by a proletarian revolution; its conditions of life, however, prepare it far more for the part of a bribed tool of reactionary intrigue.

In the conditions of the proletariat, those of old society at large are already virtually swamped. The proletarian is without property; his relation to his wife and children has no longer anything in common with the bourgeois family relations; modern industrial labour, modern subjection to capital, the same in England as in France, in America as in Germany, has stripped him of every trace of national character. Law, morality, religion, are to him so many bourgeois prejudices, behind which lurk in ambush just as many bourgeois interests.

All the preceding classes that got the upper hand, sought to fortify their already acquired status by subjecting society at large to their conditions of appropriation. The proletarians cannot become masters of the productive forces of society, except by abolishing their own previous mode of appropriation, and thereby also every other previous mode of appropriation. They have nothing of their own to secure and to fortify; their mission is to destroy all previous securities for, and insurances of, individual property.

All previous historical movements were movements of minorities, or in the interest of minorities. The proletarian movement is the self-conscious, independent movement of the immense majority, in the interest of the immense majority. The proletariat, the lowest stratum of our present society, cannot stir, cannot raise itself up, without the whole super-incumbent strata of official society being sprung into the air.

Though not in substance, yet in form, the struggle of the proletariat with the bourgeoisie is at first a national struggle.

The proletariat of each country must, of course, first of all settle matters with its own bourgeoisie.

In depicting the most general phases of the development of the proletariat, we traced the more or less veiled civil war, raging within existing society, up to the point where that war breaks out into open revolution, and where the violent overthrow of the bourgeoisie lays the foundation for the sway of the proletariat.

Hitherto, every form of society has been based, as we have already seen, on the antagonism of oppressing and oppressed classes. But in order to oppress a class, certain conditions must be assured to it under which it can, at least, continue its slavish existence. The serf, in the period of serfdom, raised himself to membership in the commune, just as the petty bourgeois, under the yoke of feudal absolutism, managed to develop into a bourgeois. The modern labourer, on the contrary, instead of rising with the progress of industry, sinks deeper and deeper below the conditions of existence of his own class. He becomes a pauper, and pauperism develops more rapidly than population and wealth. And here it becomes evident, that the bourgeoisie is unfit any longer to be the ruling class in society, and to impose its conditions of existence upon society as an over-riding law. It is unfit to rule because it is incompetent to assure an existence to its slave within his slavery, because it cannot help letting him sink into such a state, that it has to feed him, instead of being fed by him. Society can no longer live under this bourgeoisie, in other words, its existence is no longer compatible with society.

The essential condition for the existence, and for the sway of the bourgeois class, is the formation and augmentation of capital; the condition for capital is wage-labour. Wage-labour rests exclusively on competition between the labourers. The advance of industry, whose involuntary promoter is the bourgeoisie, replaces the isolation of the labourers, due to competition, by their revolutionary combination, due to association. The development of Modern Industry, therefore, cuts from under its feet the very foundation on which the bourgeoisie produces and appropriates products. What the bourgeoisie, therefore, produces, above all, is its own grave-diggers. Its fall and the victory of the proletariat are equally inevitable.

Social Responsibility of Business and Labor

Milton Friedman [b. 1912]

The view has been gaining widespread acceptance that corporate officials and labor leaders have a "social responsibility" that goes beyond serving the interest of their stockholders or their members. This view shows a fundamental misconception of the character and nature of a free economy. In such an economy, there is one and only one social responsibility of business—to use its resources and engage in activities designed to increase its profits so long as it stays within the rules of the game, which is to say, engages in open and free competition, without deception or fraud. Similarly, the "social responsibility" of labor leaders is to serve the interests of the members of their unions. It is the responsibility of the rest of us to establish a framework of law such that an individual in pursuing his own interest is, to quote Adam Smith again, "led by an invisible hand to promote an end which was no part of his intention. Nor is it always the worse for the society that it was no part of it. By pursuing his own interest, he frequently promotes that of the society more effectually than when he really intends to promote it. I have never known much good done by those who affected to trade for the public good."[1]

Few trends could so thoroughly undermine the very foundations of our free society as the acceptance by corporate officials of a social responsibility other than to make as much money for their stockholders as possible. This is a fundamentally subversive doctrine. If businessmen do have a social responsibility other than making maximum profits for stockholders, how are they to know what it is? Can self-selected private individuals decide what the social interest is? Can they decide how great a burden they are justified in

[1] Adam Smith, *The Wealth of Nations* (1776), Bk. IV, chapter ii, p. 421 (Cannan, ed., London, 1930).

placing on themselves or their stockholders to serve that social interest? Is it tolerable that these public functions of taxation, expenditure, and control be exercised by the people who happen at the moment to be in charge of particular enterprises, chosen for those posts by strictly private groups? If businessmen are civil servants rather than the employees of their stockholders, then in a democracy they will, sooner or later, be chosen by the public techniques of election and appointment.

And long before this occurs, their decision-making power will have been taken away from them. A dramatic illustration was the cancellation of a steel price increase by U.S. Steel in April 1962 through the medium of a public display of anger by President Kennedy and threats of reprisals on levels ranging from antitrust suits to examination of the tax reports of steel executives. This was a striking episode because of the public display of the vast powers concentrated in Washington. We were all made aware of how much of the power needed for a police state was already available. It illustrates the present point as well. If the price of steel is a public decision, as the doctrine of social responsibility declares, then it cannot be permitted to be made privately.

The particular aspect of the doctrine which this example illustrates, and which has been most prominent recently, is an alleged social responsibility of business and labor to keep prices and wage rates down in order to avoid price inflation. Suppose that at a time when there was upward pressure on prices—ultimately of course reflecting an increase in the stock of money—every businessman and labor leader were to accept this responsibility and suppose all could succeed in keeping any price from rising, so we had voluntary price and wage control without open inflation. What would be the result? Clearly product shortages, labor shortages, gray markets, black markets. If prices are not allowed to ration goods and workers, there must be some other means to do so. Can the alternative rationing schemes be private? Perhaps for a time in a small and unimportant area. But if the goods involved are many and important, there will necessarily be pressure, and probably irresistible pressure, for governmental rationing of goods, a governmental wage policy, and governmental measures for allocating and distributing labor.

Price controls, whether legal or voluntary, if effectively enforced would eventually lead to the destruction of the free-enterprise system and its replacement by a centrally controlled system. And it would not even be effective in preventing inflation. History offers ample evidence that what determines the average level of prices and wages is the amount of money in the economy and not the greediness of businessmen or of workers. Governments ask for the self-restraint of business and labor because of their inability to manage their own affairs—which includes the control of money—and the natural human tendency to pass the buck.

One topic in the area of social responsibility that I feel duty-bound to touch on, because it affects my own personal interests, has been the claim that business should contribute to the support of charitable activities and especially to universities. Such giving by corporations is an inappropriate use of corporate funds in a free-enterprise society.

The corporation is an instrument of the stockholders who own it. If the corporation makes a contribution, it prevents the individual stockholder from himself deciding how he should dispose of his funds. With the corporation tax and the deductibility of contributions, stockholders may of course want the corporation to make a gift on their behalf, since this would enable them to make a larger gift. The best solution would be the abolition of the corporate tax. But so long as there is a corporate tax, there is no justification for permitting deductions for contributions to charitable and educational institutions. Such contributions should be made by the individuals who are the ultimate owners of property in our society.

People who urge extension of the deductibility of this kind of corporate contribution in the name of free enterprise are fundamentally working against their own interest. A major complaint made frequently against modern business is that it involves the separation of ownership and control—that the corporation has become a social institution that is a law unto itself, with irresponsible executives who do not serve the interests of their stockholders. This charge is not true. But the direction in which policy is now moving, of permitting corporations to make contributions for charitable purposes and allowing deductions for income tax, is a step in the direction of creating a true divorce between ownership and control and of undermining the basic nature and character of our society. It is a step away from an individualistic society and toward the corporate state.

Management Women and the New Facts of Life

Felice N. Schwartz [1925–1996]

The cost of employing women in management is greater than the cost of employing men. This is a jarring statement, partly because it is true, but mostly because it is something people are reluctant to talk about. A new study by one multinational corporation shows that the rate of turnover in management positions is 2½ times higher among top-performing women than it is among men. A large producer of consumer goods reports that one half of the women who take maternity leave return to their jobs late or not at all. And we know that women also have a greater tendency to plateau or to interrupt their careers in ways that limit their growth and development. But we have become so sensitive to charges of sexism and so afraid of confrontation, even litigation, that we rarely say what we know to be true. Unfortunately, our bottled-up awareness leaks out in misleading metaphors ("glass ceiling" is one notable example), veiled hostility, lowered expectations, distrust, and reluctant adherence to Equal Employment Opportunity requirements.

Career interruptions, plateauing, and turnover are expensive. The money corporations invest in recruitment, training, and development is less likely to produce top executives among women than among men, and the invaluable company experience that developing executives acquire at every level as they move up through management ranks is more often lost.

The studies just mentioned are only the first of many, I'm quite sure. Demographic realities are going to force corporations all across the country to analyze the cost of employing women in managerial positions, and what they will discover is that women cost more.

But here is another startling truth: The greater cost of employing women is not a function of inescapable gender differences. Women *are* different from men, but what increases their cost to the corporation is principally the clash of their perceptions, attitudes, and behavior with those of men, which is to say, with the policies and practices of male-led corporations.

It is terribly important that employers draw the right conclusions from the studies now being done. The studies will be useless—or worse, harmful—if all they teach us is that women are expensive to employ. What we need to learn is how to reduce that expense, how to stop throwing away the investments we make in talented women, how to become more responsive to the needs of the women that corporations *must* employ if they are to have the best and the brightest of all those now entering the work force.

The gender differences relevant to business fall into two categories: those related to maternity and those related to the differing traditions and expectations of the sexes. Maternity is biological rather than cultural. We can't alter it, but we can dramatically reduce its impact on the workplace and in many cases eliminate its negative effect on employee development. We can accomplish this by addressing the second set of differences, those between male and female socialization. Today, these differences exaggerate the real costs of maternity and can turn a relatively slight disruption in work schedule into a serious business problem and a career derailment for individual women. If we are to overcome the cost differential between male and female employees, we need to address the issues that arise when female socialization meets the male corporate culture and masculine rules of career development—issues of behavior and style, of expectation, of stereotypes and preconceptions, of sexual tension and harassment, of female mentoring, lateral mobility, relocation, compensation, and early identification of top performers.

The one immutable, enduring difference between men and women is maternity. Maternity is not simply childbirth but a continuum that begins with an awareness of the ticking of the biological clock, proceeds to the anticipation of motherhood, includes pregnancy, childbirth, physical recuperation, psychological adjustment, and continues on to nursing, bonding, and child rearing. Not all women choose to become mothers, of course, and among those who do, the process varies from case to case depending on the health of the mother and baby, the values of the parents, and the availability, cost, and quality of child care.

In past centuries, the biological fact of maternity shaped the traditional roles of the sexes. Women performed the home-centered functions that related to the bearing and nurturing of children. Men did the work that required great physical strength. Over time, however, family size contracted, the community assumed greater responsibility for the care and education of children, packaged foods and household technology reduced the work load in the home, and technology eliminated much of the need for muscle power at the workplace. Today, in the developed world, the only role still uniquely gender related is childbearing. Yet men and women are still socialized to perform their traditional roles.

Men and women may or may not have some innate psychological disposition toward these traditional roles—men to be aggressive, competitive, self-reliant, risk taking; women to be supportive, nurturing, intuitive, sensitive, communicative—but certainly both men and women are capable of the full range of behavior. Indeed, the male and female roles have already begun to expand and merge. In the decades ahead, as the socialization of boys and girls and the experience and expectations of young men and women grow steadily more androgynous, the differences in workplace behavior will continue to fade. At the moment, however, we are still plagued by disparities in perception and behavior that make the integration of men and women in the workplace unnecessarily difficult and expensive.

Let me illustrate with a few broadbrush generalizations. Of course, these are only stereotypes, but I think they help to exemplify the kinds of preconceptions that can muddy the corporate waters.

Men continue to perceive women as the rearers of their children, so they find it understandable, indeed appropriate, that women should renounce their careers to raise families. Edmund Pratt, CEO of Pfizer, once asked me in all sincerity, "Why would any woman choose to be a chief financial officer rather than a full-time mother?" By condoning and taking pleasure in women's traditional behavior, men reinforce it. Not only do they see parenting as fundamentally female, they see a career as fundamentally male—either an unbroken series of promotions and advancements toward CEOdom or stagnation and disappointment. This attitude serves to legitimize a woman's choice to extend maternity leave and even, for those who can afford it, to leave employment altogether for several years. By the same token, men who might want to take a leave after the birth of a child know that management will see such behavior as a lack of career commitment, even when company policy permits parental leave for men.

Women also bring counterproductive expectations and perceptions to the workplace. Ironically, although the feminist movement was an expression of women's quest for freedom from their homebased lives, most women were remarkably free already. They had many responsibilities, but they were autonomous and could be entrepreneurial in how and when they carried them out. And once their children grew up and left home, they were essentially free to do what they wanted with their lives. Women's traditional role also included freedom from responsibility for the financial support of their families. Many of us were socialized from girlhood to expect our husbands to take care of us, while our brothers were socialized from an equally early age to complete their educations, pursue careers, climb the ladder of success, and provide dependable financial support for their families. To the extent that this tradition of freedom lingers subliminally, women tend to bring to their employment a sense that they can choose to change jobs or careers at will, take time off, or reduce their hours.

Finally, women's traditional role encouraged particular attention to the quality and substance of what they did, specifically to the physical, psychological, and intellectual development of their children. This traditional focus may explain women's continuing tendency to search for more than monetary reward—intrinsic significance, social importance, meaning—in what they do. This too makes them more likely than men to leave the corporation in search of other values.

The misleading metaphor of the glass ceiling suggests an invisible barrier constructed by corporate leaders to impede the upward mobility of women beyond the middle levels. A more appropriate metaphor, I believe, is the kind of cross-sectional diagram used in geology. The barriers to women's leadership occur when potentially counterproductive layers of influence on women—maternity, tradition, socialization—meet management strata pervaded by the largely unconscious preconceptions, stereotypes, and expectations of men. Such interfaces do not exist for men and tend to be impermeable for women.

One result of these gender differences has been to convince some executives that women are simply not suited to top management. Other executives feel helpless. If they see even a few of their valued female employees fail to return to work from maternity leave on schedule or see one of their most promising women plateau in her career after the birth of a child, they begin to fear there is nothing they can do to infuse women with new energy and enthusiasm and persuade them to stay. At the same time, they know there is nothing they can do to stem the tide of women into management ranks.

Another result is to place every working woman on a continuum that runs from total dedication to career at one end to a balance between career and family at the other. What women discover is that the male corporate culture sees both extremes as unacceptable. Women who want the flexibility to balance their families and their careers are not adequately committed to the organization. Women who perform as aggressively and competitively as men are abrasive and unfeminine. But the fact is, business needs all the talented women it can get. Moreover, as I will explain, the women I call career-primary and those I call career-and-family each have particular value to the corporation.

Women in the corporation are about to move from a buyer's to a seller's market. The sudden, startling recognition that 80% of new entrants in the work force over the next decade will be women, minorities, and immigrants has stimulated a mushrooming incentive to "value diversity."

Women are no longer simply an enticing pool of occasional creative talent, a thorn in the side of the EEO officer, or a source of frustration to corporate leaders truly puzzled by the slowness of their upward trickle into executive positions. A real demographic change is taking place. The era of sudden population growth of the 1950s and 1960s is over. The birth rate has dropped about 40%, from a high of 25.3 live births per 1,000 population in 1957, at the peak of the baby boom, to a stable low of a little more than 15 per 1,000 over the last 16 years, and there is no indication of a return to a higher rate. The tidal wave of baby boomers that swelled the recruitment pool to overflowing seems to have been a one-time phenomenon. For 20 years, employers had the pick of a very large crop and were able to choose males almost exclusively for the executive track. But if future population remains fairly stable while the economy continues to expand, and if the new information society simultaneously creates a greater need for creative, educated managers, then the gap between supply and demand will grow dramatically and, with it, the competition for managerial talent.

The decrease in numbers has even greater implications if we look at the traditional source of corporate recruitment for leadership positions—white males from the top 10% of the country's best universities. Over the past decade, the increase in the number of women graduating from leading universities has been much greater than the increase in the total number of graduates, and these women are well represented in the top 10% of their classes.

The trend extends into business and professional programs as 20
well. In the old days, virtually all MBAs were male. I remember addressing a meeting at the Harvard Business School as recently as the mid-1970s and looking out at a sea of exclusively male faces. Today, about 25% of that audience would be women. The pool of male MBAs from which corporations have traditionally drawn their leaders has shrunk significantly.

Of course, this reduction does not have to mean a shortage of talent. The top 10% is at least as smart as it always was—smarter, probably, since it's now drawn from a broader segment of the population. But it now consists increasingly of women. Companies that are determined to recruit the same number of men as before will have to dig much deeper into the male pool, while their competitors will have the opportunity to pick the best people from both the male and female graduates.

Under these circumstances, there is no question that the management ranks of business will include increasing numbers of women. There remains, however, the question of how these women will succeed—how long they will stay, how high they will climb, how completely they will fulfill their promise and potential, and what kind of return the corporation will realize on its investment in their training and development.

There is ample business reason for finding ways to make sure that as many of these women as possible will succeed. The first step in this process is to recognize that women are not all alike. Like men, they are individuals with differing talents, priorities, and motivations. For the sake of simplicity, let me focus on the two women I referred to earlier, on what I call the career-primary woman and the career-and-family woman.

Like many men, some women put their careers first. They are ready to make the same trade-offs traditionally made by the men who seek leadership positions. They make a career decision to put in extra hours, to make sacrifices in their personal lives, to make the most of every opportunity for professional development. For women, of course, this decision also requires that they remain single or at least childless or, if they do have children, that they be satisfied to have others raise them. Some 90% of executive men but only 35% of executive women have children by the age of 40. The *automatic* association of all women with babies is clearly unjustified.

The secret to dealing with such women is to recognize them early, accept them, and clear artificial barriers from their path to the top. After all, the best of these women are among the best managerial talent you will ever see. And career-primary women have another important value to the company that men and other women lack. They can act as role models and mentors to younger women who put their careers first. Since upwardly mobile career-primary women still have few role models to motivate and inspire them, a company with women in its top echelon has a significant advantage in the competition for executive talent.

Men at the top of the organization—most of them over 55, with wives who tend to be traditional—often find career women "masculine" and difficult to accept as colleagues. Such men miss the point, which is not that these women are just like men but that they are just like the *best* men in the organization. And there is such a shortage of the best people that gender cannot be allowed to matter. It is clearly counterproductive to disparage in a woman with executive talent the very qualities that are most critical to the business and that might carry a man to the CEO's office.

Clearing a path to the top for career-primary women has four requirements:

1. Identify them early.
2. Give them the same opportunity you give to talented men to grow and develop and contribute to company profitability. Give them client and customer responsibility. Expect them to travel and relocate, to make the same commitment to the company as men aspiring to leadership positions.
3. Accept them as valued members of your management team. Include them in every kind of communication. Listen to them.
4. Recognize that the business environment is more difficult and stressful for them than for their male peers. They are always a minority, often the only woman. The male perception of talented, ambitious women is at best ambivalent, a mixture of admiration, resentment, confusion, competitiveness, attraction, skepticism, anxiety, pride, and animosity. Women can never feel secure about how they should dress and act, whether they should speak out or grin and bear it when they encounter discrimination, stereotyping, sexual harassment, and paternalism. Social interaction and travel with male colleagues and with male clients can be charged. As they move up, the normal increase in pressure and responsibility is compounded for women because they are women.

Stereotypical language and sexist day-to-day behavior do take their toll on women's career development. Few male executives realize how common it is to call women by their first names while men in the same group are greeted with surnames, how frequently female executives are assumed by men to be secretaries, how often women are excluded from all-male social events where business is being transacted. With notable exceptions, men are still generally more comfortable with other men, and as a result women miss many of the career and business opportunities that arise over lunch, on the golf course, or in the locker room.

The majority of women, however, are what I call career-and-family women, women who want to pursue serious careers while participating actively in the rearing of children. These women are a precious resource that has yet to be mined. Many of them are talented and creative. Most of them are willing to trade some career growth and compensation for freedom from the constant pressure to work long hours and weekends.

Most companies today are ambivalent at best about the career-and-family women in their management ranks. They would prefer that all employees were willing to give their all to the company. They believe it is in their best interests for all managers to compete for the top positions so the company will have the largest possible pool from which to draw its leaders.

"If you have both talent and motivation," many employers seem to say, "we want to move you up. If you haven't got that motivation, if you want less pressure and greater flexibility, then you can leave and make room for a new generation." These companies lose on two counts. First, they fail to amortize the investment they made in the early training and experience of management women who find themselves committed to family as well as to career. Second, they fail to recognize what these women could do for their middle management.

The ranks of middle managers are filled with people on their way up and people who have stalled. Many of them have simply reached their limits, achieved career growth commensurate with or exceeding their capabilities, and they cause problems because their performance is mediocre but they still want to move ahead. The career-and-family woman is willing to trade off the pressures and demands that go with promotion for the freedom to spend more time with her children. She's very smart, she's talented, she's committed to her career, and she's satisfied to stay at the middle level, at least during the early child-rearing years. Compare her with some of the people you have there now.

Consider a typical example, a woman who decides in college on a business career and enters management at age 22. For nine years, the company invests in her career as she gains experience and skills and steadily improves her performance. But at 31, just as the investment begins to pay off in earnest, she decides to have a baby. Can the company afford to let her go home, take another job, or go into business for herself? The common perception now is yes, the corporation can afford to lose her unless, after six or eight weeks or even three months of disability and maternity leave, she returns to work on a full-time schedule with the same vigor, commitment, and ambition that she showed before.

But what if she doesn't? What if she wants or needs to go on leave for six months or a year or, heaven forbid, five years? In this worst case scenario, she works full-time from age 22 to 31 and from 36 to 65—a total of 38 years as opposed to the typical male's 43 years. That's not a huge difference. Moreover, my typical example is willing to work part-time while her children are young, if only her employer will give her the opportunity. There are two rewards for companies responsive to this need: higher retention of their best people and greatly improved performance and satisfaction in their middle management.

The high-performing career-and-family woman can be a major 35
player in your company. She can give you a significant business advantage as the competition for able people escalates. Sometimes too, if you can hold on to her, she will switch gears in mid-life and reenter the competition for the top. The price you must pay to retain these women is threefold: you must plan for and manage maternity, you must provide the flexibility that will allow them to be maximally productive, and you must take an active role in helping to make family supports and high-quality, affordable child care available to all women.

The key to managing maternity is to recognize the value of high performing women and the urgent need to retain them and keep them productive. The first step must be a genuine partnership between the woman and her boss. I know this partnership can seem difficult to forge. One of my own senior executives came to me recently to discuss plans for her maternity leave and subsequent return to work. She knew she wanted to come back. I wanted to make certain that she would. Still, we had a somewhat awkward conversation, because I knew that no woman can predict with certainty when she will be able to return to work or under what conditions. Physical problems can lengthen her leave. So can a demanding infant, a difficult family or personal adjustment, or problems with child care.

I still don't know when this valuable executive will be back on the job full-time, and her absence creates some genuine problems for our organization. But I do know that I can't simply replace her years of experience with a new recruit. Since our conversation, I also know that she wants to come back, and that she *will* come back—part-time at first—unless I make it impossible for her by, for example, setting an arbitrary date for her full-time return or resignation. In turn, she knows that the organization wants and needs her and, more to the point, that it will be responsive to her needs in terms of working hours and child-care arrangements.

In having this kind of conversation it's important to ask concrete questions that will help to move the discussion from uncertainty and anxiety to some level of predictability. Questions can touch on everything from family income and energy level to child care arrangements and career commitment. Of course you want your star manager to return to work as soon as possible, but you want her to return permanently and productively. Her downtime on the job is a drain on her energies and a waste of your money.

For all the women who want to combine career and family—the women who want to participate actively in the rearing of their children and who also want to pursue their careers seriously—the key to retention is to provide the flexibility and family supports they need in order to function effectively.

Time spent in the office increases productivity if it is time well spent, but the fact that most women continue to take the primary responsibility for child care is a cause of distraction, diversion, anxiety, and absenteeism—to say nothing of the persistent guilt experienced by all working mothers. A great many women, perhaps most of all women who have always performed at the highest levels, are also frustrated by a sense that while their children are babies they cannot function at their best either at home or at work.

In its simplest form, flexibility is the freedom to take time off—a couple of hours, a day, a week—or to do some work at home and some at the office, an arrangement that communication technology makes increasingly feasible. At the complex end of the spectrum are alternative work schedules that permit the woman to work less than full-time and her employer to reap the benefits of her experience and, with careful planning, the top level of her abilities.

Part-time employment is the single greatest inducement to getting women back on the job expeditiously and the provision women themselves most desire. A part-time return to work enables them to maintain responsibility for critical aspects of their jobs, keeps them in touch with the changes constantly occurring at the workplace and in the job itself, reduces stress and fatigue, often eliminates the need for paid maternity leave by permitting a return to the office as soon as disability leave is over, and, not least, can greatly enhance company loyalty. The part-time solution works particularly well when a work load can be reduced for one individual in a department or when a full-time job can be broken down by skill levels and apportioned to two individuals at different levels of skill and pay.

I believe, however, that shared employment is the most promising and will be the most widespread form of flexible scheduling in the future. It is feasible at every level of the corporation except at the pinnacle, for both the short and the long term. It involves two people taking responsibility for one job.

Two red lights flash on as soon as most executives hear the words "job sharing": continuity and client-customer contact. The answer to the continuity question is to place responsibility entirely on the two individuals sharing the job to discuss everything that transpires—thoroughly, daily, and on their own time. The answer to the problem of client-customer contact is yes, job sharing requires reeducation and a period of adjustment. But as both client and supervisor will quickly come to appreciate, two contacts means that the customer has continuous access to the company's representative, without interruptions for vacation, travel, or sick leave. The two people holding the job can simply cover for each other, and the uninterrupted, full-time coverage they provide together can be a stipulation of their arrangement.

Flexibility is costly in numerous ways. It requires more supervisory time to coordinate and manage, more office space, and somewhat greater benefits costs (though these can be contained with flexible benefits plans, prorated benefits, and, in two-paycheck families, elimination of duplicate benefits). But the advantages of reduced turnover and the greater productivity that results from higher energy levels and greater focus can outweigh the costs.

A few hints:

* Provide flexibility selectively. I'm not suggesting private arrangements subject to the suspicion of favoritism but rather a policy that makes flexible work schedules available only to high performers.
* Make it clear that in most instances (but not all) the rates of advancement and pay will be appropriately lower for those who take time off or who work part-time than for those who work full-time. Most career-and-family women are entirely willing to make that trade-off.
* Discuss costs as well as benefits. Be willing to risk accusations of bias. Insist, for example, that half time is half of whatever time it takes to do the job, not merely half of 35 or 40 hours.

The woman who is eager to get home to her child has a powerful incentive to use her time effectively at the office and to carry with her reading and other work that can be done at home. The talented professional who wants to have it all can be a high performer by carefully ordering her priorities and by focusing on objectives rather than on the legendary 15-hour day. By the time professional women have their first babies—at an average age of 31—they have already had nine years to work long hours at a desk, to travel, and to relocate. In the case of high performers, the need for flexibility coincides with what has gradually become the goal-oriented nature of responsibility.

Family supports—in addition to maternity leave and flexibility—include the provision of parental leave for men, support for two-career and single-parent families during relocation, and flexible benefits. But the primary ingredient is child care. The capacity of working mothers to function effectively and without interruption depends on the availability of good, affordable child care. Now that women make up almost half the work force and the growing percentage of managers, the decision to become involved in the personal lives of employees is no longer a philosophical question but a practical one. To make matters worse, the quality of child care has almost no relation to technology, inventiveness, or profitability but is more or less a pure function of the quality of child care personnel and the ratio of adults to children. These costs are irreducible. Only by joining hands with government and the public sector can corporations hope to create the vast quantity and variety of child care that their employees need.

Until quite recently, the response of corporations to women has been largely symbolic and cosmetic, motivated in large part by the will to avoid litigation and legal penalties. In some cases, companies were also moved by a genuine sense of fairness and a vague discomfort and frustration at the absence of women above the middle of the corporate pyramid. The actions they took were mostly quick, easy, and highly visible—child care information services, a three-month parental leave available to men as well as women, a woman appointed to the board of directors.

When I first began to discuss these issues 26 years ago, I was 50
sometimes able to get an appointment with the assistant to the assistant in personnel, but it was only a courtesy. Over the past decade, I have met with the CEOs of many large corporations, and I've watched them become involved with ideas they had never previously thought much about. Until recently, however, the shelf life of that enhanced awareness was always short. Given pressing, short-term concerns, women were not a front-burner issue. In the

past few months, I have seen yet another change. Some CEOs and top management groups now take the initiative. They call and ask us to show them how to shift gears from a responsive to a proactive approach to recruiting, developing, and retaining women.

I think this change is more probably a response to business needs—to concern for the quality of future profits and managerial talent—than to uneasiness about legal requirements, sympathy with the demands of women and minorities, or the desire to do what is right and fair. The nature of such business motivation varies. Some companies want to move women to higher positions as role models for those below them and as beacons for talented young recruits. Some want to achieve a favorable image with employees, customers, clients, and stockholders. These are all legitimate motives. But I think the companies that stand to gain most are motivated as well by a desire to capture competitive advantage in an era when talent and competence will be in increasingly short supply. These companies are now ready to stop being defensive about their experience with women and to ask incisive questions without preconceptions.

Even so, incredibly, I don't know of more than one or two companies that have looked into their own records to study the absolutely critical issue of maternity leave—how many women took it, when and whether they returned, and how this behavior correlated with their rank, tenure, age, and performance. The unique drawback to the employment of women is the physical reality of maternity and the particular socializing influence maternity has had. Yet to make women equal to men in the workplace we have chosen on the whole not to discuss this single most significant difference between them. Unless we do, we cannot evaluate the cost of recruiting, developing, and moving women up.

Now that interest is replacing indifference, there are four steps every company can take to examine its own experience with women:

1. Gather quantitative data on the company's experience with management-level women regarding turnover rates, occurrence of and return from maternity leave, and organizational level attained in relation to tenure and performance.

2. Correlate this data with factors such as age, marital status, and presence and age of children, and attempt to identify and analyze why women respond the way they do.
3. Gather qualitative data on the experience of women in your company and on how women are perceived by both sexes.
4. Conduct a cost-benefit analysis of the return on your investment in high-performing women. Factor in the cost to the company of women's negative reactions to negative experience, as well as the probable cost of corrective measures and policies. If women's value to your company is greater than the cost to recruit, train, and develop them—and of course I believe it will be—then you will want to do everything you can to retain them.

We have come a tremendous distance since the days when the prevailing male wisdom saw women as lacking the kind of intelligence that would allow them to succeed in business. For decades, even women themselves have harbored an unspoken belief that they couldn't make it because they couldn't be just like men, and nothing else would do. But now that women have shown themselves the equal of men in every area of organizational activity, now that they have demonstrated that they can be stars in every field of endeavor, now we can all venture to examine the fact that women and men are different.

On balance, employing women is more costly than employing 55
men. Women can acknowledge this fact today because they know that their value to employers exceeds the additional cost and because they know that changing attitudes can reduce the additional cost dramatically. Women in management are no longer an idiosyncrasy of the arts and education. They have always matched men in natural ability. Within a very few years, they will equal men in numbers as well in every area of economic activity.

The demographic motivation to recruit and develop women is compelling. But an older question remains: Is society better for the change? Women's exit from the home and entry into the work force has certainly created problems—an urgent need for good, affordable child care; troubling questions about the kind of parenting children need; the costs and difficulties of diversity in the workplace; the stress and fatigue of combining work and family responsibilities. Wouldn't we all be happier if we could turn back the clock to an age when men were in the workplace and women in the home, when male and female roles were clearly differentiated and complementary?

Nostalgia, anxiety, and discouragement will urge many to say yes, but my answer is emphatically no. Two fundamental benefits that were unattainable in the past are now within our reach. For the individual, freedom of choice—in this case the freedom to choose career, family, or a combination of the two. For the corporation, access to the most gifted individuals in the country. These benefits are neither self-indulgent nor insubstantial. Freedom of choice and self-realization are too deeply American to be cast aside for some wistful vision of the past. And access to our most talented human resources is not a luxury in this age of explosive international competition but rather the barest minimum that prudence and national self-preservation require.

Win-Win Flexibility

Karen Kornbluh [b. 1963]

Introduction

Today fully 70 percent of families with children are headed by two working parents or by an unmarried working parent. The "traditional family" of the breadwinner and homemaker has been replaced by the "juggler family," in which no one is home full-time. Two-parent families are working 10 more hours a week than in 1979 (Bernstein and Kornbluh).

To be decent parents, caregivers, and members of their communities, workers now need greater flexibility than they once did. Yet good part-time or flex-time jobs remain rare. Whereas companies have embraced flexibility in virtually every other aspect of their businesses (inventory control, production schedules, financing), full-time workers' schedules remain largely inflexible. Employers often demand workers be available around the clock. Moreover, many employees have no right to a minimum number of sick or vacation days; almost two-thirds of all workers—and an even larger percentage of low-income parents—lack the ability to take a day off to care for a family member (Lovell). The Family and Medical Leave Act (FMLA) of 1993 finally guaranteed that workers at large companies could take a leave of absence for the birth or adoption of a baby, or for the illness of a family member. Yet that guaranteed leave is unpaid.

Many businesses are finding ways to give their most valued employees flexibility but, all too often, workers who need flexibility find themselves shunted into part-time, temporary, on-call, or contract jobs with reduced wages and career opportunities—and, often, no benefits. A full quarter of American workers are in these jobs. Only 15 percent of women and 12 percent of men in such jobs receive health insurance from their employers (Wenger). A number of European countries provide workers the right to a part-time schedule and all have enacted legislation to implement a European Union directive to prohibit discrimination against part-time workers.

In America, employers are required to accommodate the needs of employees with disabilities—even if that means providing a part-time or flexible schedule. Employers may also provide religious accommodations for employees by offering a part-time or flexible schedule. At the same time, employers have no obligation to allow parents or employees caring for sick relatives to work part-time or flexible schedules, even if the cost to the employer would be inconsequential.

In the 21st Century global economy, America needs a new approach that allows businesses to gain flexibility in staffing without sacrificing their competitiveness and enables workers to gain control over their work-lives without sacrificing their economic security. This win-win flexibility arrangement will not be the same in every company, nor even for each employee working within the same organization. Each case will be different. But flexibility will not come for all employees without some education, prodding, and leadership. So, employers and employees must be required to come to the table to work out a solution that benefits everyone. American businesses must be educated on strategies for giving employees flexibility without sacrificing productivity or morale. And businesses should be recognized and rewarded when they do so.

America is a nation that continually rises to the occasion. At the dawn of a new century, we face many challenges. One of these is helping families to raise our next generation in an increasingly demanding global economy. This is a challenge America must meet with imagination and determination.

Background: The Need for Workplace Flexibility

Between 1970 and 2000, the percentage of mothers in the workforce rose from 38 to 67 percent (Smolensky and Gootman). Moreover, the number of hours worked by dual-income families has increased dramatically. Couples with children worked a full 60 hours a week in 1979. By 2000 they were working 70 hours a week (Bernstein and Kornbluh). And more parents than ever are working long hours. In 2000, nearly 1 out of every 8 couples with children was putting in 100 hours a week or more on the job, compared to only 1 out of 12 families in 1970 (Jacobs and Gerson).

In addition to working parents, there are over 44.4 million Americans who provide care to another adult, often an older relative. Fifty-nine percent of these caregivers either work or have worked while providing care ("Caregiving").

In a 2002 report by the Families and Work Institute, 45 percent of employees reported that work and family responsibilities interfered with each other "a lot" or "some" and 67 percent of employed parents report that they do not have enough time with their children (Galinksy, Bond, and Hill).

Over half of workers today have no control over scheduling 10
alternative start and end times at work (Galinksy, Bond, and Hill). According to a recent study by the Institute for Women's Policy Research, 49 percent of workers—over 59 million Americans—lack basic paid sick days for themselves. And almost two-thirds of all workers—and an even larger percentage of low-income parents—lack the ability to take a day off to care for a family member (Lovell). Thirteen percent of non-poor workers with caregiving responsibilities lack paid vacation leave, while 28 percent of poor caregivers lack any paid vacation time (Heymann). Research has shown that flexible arrangements and benefits tend to be more accessible in larger and more profitable firms, and then to the most valued professional and managerial workers in those firms (Golden). Parents with young children and working welfare recipients—the workers who need access to paid leave the most—are the least likely to have these benefits, according to research from the Urban Institute (Ross Phillips).

In the US, only 5 percent of workers have access to a job that provides paid parental leave. The Family and Medical Leave Act grants the right to 12 weeks of unpaid leave for the birth or adoption of a child or for the serious illness of the worker or a worker's family member. But the law does not apply to employees who work in companies with fewer than 50 people, employees who have worked for less than a year at their place of employment, or employees who work fewer than 1,250 hours a year. Consequently, only 45 percent of parents working in the private sector are eligible to take even this unpaid time off (Smolensky and Gootman).

Workers often buy flexibility by sacrificing job security, benefits, and pay. Part-time workers are less likely to have employer-provided health insurance or pensions and their hourly wages are lower. One study in 2002 found that 43 percent of employed parents said that using flexibility would jeopardize their advancement (Galinksy, Bond, and Hill).

Children, in particular, pay a heavy price for workplace inflexibility (Waters Boots 2004). Almost 60 percent of child care arrangements are of poor or mediocre quality (Smolensky and Gootman). Children in low-income families are even less likely to be in good or excellent care settings. Full-day child care easily costs $4,000 to $10,000 per year—approaching the price of college tuition at a public university. As a result of the unaffordable and low quality nature of child care in this country, a disturbing number of today's children are left home alone: Over 3.3 million children age 6–12 are home alone after school each day (Vandivere et al).

Many enlightened businesses are showing the way forward to a 21st Century flexible workplace. Currently, however, businesses have little incentive to provide families with the flexibility they need. We need to level the playing field and remove the competitive disadvantages for all businesses that do provide workplace flexibility.

This should be a popular priority. A recent poll found that 77 percent of likely voters feel that it is difficult for families to earn enough and still have time to be with their families. Eighty-four percent of voters agree that children are being shortchanged when their parents have to work long hours. . . .

Proposal: Win-Win Flexibility

A win-win approach in the US to flexibility . . . might function as follows. It would be "soft touch" at first—requiring a process and giving business an out if it would be costly to implement—

with a high-profile public education campaign on the importance of workplace flexibility to American business, American families, and American society. A survey at the end of the second year would determine whether a stricter approach is needed.

Employees would have the right to make a formal request to their employers for flexibility in the number of hours worked, the times worked, and/or the ability to work from home. Examples of such flexibility would include part-time, annualized hours, compressed hours, flex-time, job-sharing, shift working, staggered hours, and telecommuting.

The employee would be required to make a written application providing details on the change in work, the effect on the employer, and solutions to any problems caused to the employer: The employer would be required to meet with the employee and give the employee a decision on the request within two weeks, as well as provide an opportunity for an internal appeal within one month from the initial request.

The employee request would be granted unless the employer demonstrated it would require significant difficulty or expense entailing more than ordinary costs, decreased job efficiency, impairment of worker safety, infringement of other employees' rights, or conflict with another law or regulation.

The employer would be required to provide an employee 20
working a flexible schedule with the same hourly pay and proportionate health, pension, vacation, holiday, and FMLA benefits that the employee received before working flexibly and would be required thereafter to advance the employee at the same rate as full-time employees.

Who would be covered: Parents (including parents, legal guardians, foster parents) and other caregivers at first. Eventually all workers should be eligible in our flexible, 24×7 economy. During the initial period, it will be necessary to define non-parental "caregivers." One proposal is to define them as immediate relatives or other caregivers of "certified care recipients" (defined as those whom a doctor certifies as having three or more limitations that impede daily functioning—using diagnostic criteria such as Activities of Daily Living [ADL]/Instrumental Activities of Daily Living [IADL]—for at least 180 consecutive days). . . .

Public Education: Critical to the success of the proposal will be public education along the lines of the education that the government and business schools conducted in the 1980s about the need for American business to adopt higher quality standards to compete against Japanese business. A Malcolm Baldridge-like award should be created for companies that make flexibility win-win. A public education campaign conducted by the Department of Labor should encourage small businesses to adopt best practices of win-win flexibility. Tax credits could be used in the first year to reward early adopters.

[2005]

Works Cited

Bernstein, Jared, and Kornbluh, Karen. *Running Harder to Stay in Place: The Growth of Family Work Hours and Incomes.* Washington, DC: New America Foundation, 2005.

"Caregiving in the U.S." The National Alliance for Caregiving and AARP. 6 July 2005. <http://www.caregiving.org/data/04finalreport.pdf>.

Galinksy, Ellen, Bond, James, and Hill, E. Jeffrey. *Workplace Flexibility: What Is It? Who Has It? Who Wants It? Does It Make a Difference?* New York: Families and Work Institute, 2004.

Golden, Lonnie. *The Time Bandit: What U.S. Workers Surrender to Get Greater Flexibility in Work Schedules.* Washington, DC: Economic Policy Institute, 2000.

Heymann, Jody. *The Widening Gap: Why America's Working Families are in Jeopardy—and What Can Be Done About It.* New York: Basic, 2000.

Jacobs, Jerry, and Gerson, Kathleen. *The Time Divide: Work, Family and Gender Inequality.* Cambridge: Harvard UP, 2004.

Lovell, Vicky. *No Time to Be Sick: Why Everyone Suffers When Workers Don't Have Paid Sick Leave*. Washington, DC: Institute for Women's Policy Research, 2004.

Ross Phillips, Katherine. *Getting Time Off: Access to Leave among Working Parents*. Assessing the New Federalism, Washington, DC: Urban Institute, April 2004.

Smolensky, Eugene, and Jennifer A. Gootman, eds. *Working Families and Growing Kids: Caring for Children and Adolescents*. National Research Council and Institute of Medicine, Washington, DC: The National Academies P, 2003.

Vandivere, Sharon, Tout, Kathryn, Zaslow, Martha, Calkins, Julia, Capizzano, Jeffrey. *Unsupervised Time: Family and Child Factors Associated with Self-Care*. Assessing the New Federalism, Occasional Paper No. 71, Washington, DC: Urban Institute, Nov. 2003.

Waters Boots, Shelley. *The Way We Work: How Children and Their Families Fare in a 21st Century Workplace*. Washington, DC: New America Foundation, 2004.

Wenger, Jeffrey. *Share of Workers in 'Nonstandard' Jobs Declines*. Briefing Paper. Washington, DC: Economic Policy Institute, 2003.

Beyond the Information Revolution

Peter F. Drucker [1909–2005]

The truly revolutionary impact of the Information Revolution is just beginning to be felt. But it is not "information" that fuels this impact. It is not "artificial intelligence." It is not the effect of computers and data processing on decisionmaking, policymaking, or strategy. It is something that practically no one foresaw or, indeed, even talked about ten or fifteen years ago: *e-commerce*—that is, the explosive emergence of the Internet as a major, perhaps eventually *the* major, worldwide distribution channel for goods, for services, and, surprisingly, for managerial and professional jobs. This is profoundly changing economies, markets, and industry structures; products and services and their flow; consumer segmentation, consumer values, and consumer behavior; jobs and labor markets. But the impact may be even greater on societies and politics and, above all, on the way we see the world and ourselves in it.

At the same time, new and unexpected industries will no doubt emerge, and fast. One is already here: biotechnology. And another: fish farming. Within the next fifty years fish farming may change us from hunters and gatherers on the seas into "marine pastoralists"—just as a similar innovation some 10,000 years ago changed our ancestors from hunters and gatherers on the land into agriculturists and pastoralists.

It is likely that other new technologies will appear suddenly, leading to major new industries. What they may be is impossible even to guess at. But it is highly probable—indeed, nearly certain—that they will emerge, and fairly soon. And it is nearly certain that few of them—and few industries based on them—will come out of computer and information technology. Like biotechnology and fish farming, each will emerge from its own unique and unexpected technology.

Of course, these are only predictions. But they are made on the assumption that the Information Revolution will evolve as several earlier technology-based "revolutions" have evolved over the past 500 years, since Gutenberg's printing revolution, around 1455. In particular the assumption is that the Information Revolution will be like the Industrial Revolution of the late eighteenth and early nineteenth centuries. And that is indeed exactly how the Information Revolution has been during its first fifty years.

The Railroad

The Information Revolution is now at the point at which the In- 5
dustrial Revolution was in the early 1820s, about forty years after James Watt's improved steam engine (first installed in 1776) was first applied, in 1785, to an industrial operation—the spinning of cotton. And the steam engine was to the first Industrial Revolution what the computer has been to the Information Revolution—its trigger, but above all its symbol. Almost everybody today believes that nothing in economic history has ever moved as fast as, or had a greater impact than, the Information Revolution. But the Industrial Revolution moved at least as fast in the same time span, and had probably an equal impact if not a greater one. In short order it mechanized the great majority of manufacturing processes, beginning with the production of the most important industrial commodity of the eighteenth and early nineteenth centuries: textiles. Moore's Law asserts that the price of the Information Revolution's basic element, the microchip, drops by 50 percent every eighteen months. The same was true of the products whose manufacture was mechanized by the first Industrial Revolution. The price of cotton textiles fell by 90 percent in the fifty years spanning the start of the eighteenth century. The production of cotton textiles increased at least 150-fold in Britain alone in the same period. And although textiles were the most visible product of its early years, the Industrial Revolution mechanized the production of practically all other major goods, such as paper, glass, leather, and bricks. Its impact was by no means confined to consumer goods. The production of

iron and ironware—for example, wire—became mechanized and steam-driven as fast as did that of textiles, with the same effects on cost, price, and output. By the end of the Napoleonic Wars the making of guns was steam-driven throughout Europe; cannons were made ten to twenty times as fast as before, and their cost dropped by more than two thirds. By that time Eli Whitney had similarly mechanized the manufacture of muskets in America and had created the first mass-production industry.

These forty or fifty years gave rise to the factory and the "working class." Both were still so few in number in the mid-1820s, even in England, as to be statistically insignificant. But psychologically they had come to dominate (and soon would politically also). Before there were factories in America, Alexander Hamilton foresaw an industrialized country in his 1791 *Report on Manufactures*. A decade later, in 1803, a French economist, Jean-Baptiste Say, saw that the Industrial Revolution had changed economics by creating the "entrepreneur."

The social consequences went far beyond factory and working class. As the historian Paul Johnson has pointed out, in *A History of the American People* (1997), it was the explosive growth of the steam-engine-based textile industry that revived slavery. Considered to be practically dead by the Founders of the American Republic, slavery roared back to life as the cotton gin—soon steam-driven—created a huge demand for low-cost labor and made breeding slaves America's most profitable industry for some decades.

The Industrial Revolution also had a great impact on the family. The nuclear family had long been the unit of production. On the farm and in the artisan's workshop husband, wife, and children worked together. The factory, almost for the first time in history, took worker and work out of the home and moved them into the workplace, leaving family members behind—whether spouses of adult factory workers or, especially in the early stages, parents of child factory workers.

Indeed, the "crisis of the family" did not begin after the Second World War. It began with the Industrial Revolution—and was in fact a stock concern of those who opposed the Industrial Revolution and the factory system. (The best description of the divorce of work and family, and of its effect on both, is probably Charles Dickens's 1854 novel *Hard Times*.)

But despite all these effects, the Industrial Revolution in its first half century only mechanized the production of goods that had been in existence all along. It tremendously increased output and tremendously decreased cost. It created both consumers and consumer products. But the products themselves had been around all along. And products made in the new factories differed from traditional products only in that they were uniform, with fewer defects than existed in products made by any but the top craftsmen of earlier periods.

There was only one important exception, one new product, in those first fifty years: the steamboat, first made practical by Robert Fulton in 1807. It had little impact until thirty or forty years later. In fact, until almost the end of the nineteenth century more freight was carried on the world's oceans by sailing vessels than by steamships.

Then, in 1829, came the railroad, a product truly without precedent, and it forever changed economy, society, and politics.

In retrospect it is difficult to imagine why the invention of the railroad took so long. Rails to move carts had been around in coal mines for a very long time. What could be more obvious than to put a steam engine on a cart to drive it, rather than have it pushed by people or pulled by horses? But the railroad did not emerge from the cart in the mines. It was developed quite independently. And it was not intended to carry freight. On the contrary, for a long time it was seen only as a way to carry people. Railroads became freight carriers thirty years later, in America. (In fact, as late as the 1870s and 1880s the British engineers who were hired to build the railroads of newly Westernized Japan designed them to carry passengers—and to this day Japanese railroads are not equipped to carry freight.) But until the first railroad actually began to operate, it was virtually unanticipated.

Within five years, however, the Western world was engulfed by the biggest boom history had ever seen—the railroad boom. Punctuated by the most spectacular busts in economic history, the boom continued in Europe for thirty years, until the late 1850s, by which time most of today's major railroads had been built. In the United States it continued for another thirty years, and in outlying areas—Argentina, Brazil, Asian Russia, China—until the First World War.

The railroad was the truly revolutionary element of the Industrial Revolution, for not only did it create a new economic dimension but also it rapidly changed what I would call the *mental geography*. For the first time in history human beings had true mobility. For the first time the horizons of ordinary people expanded. Contemporaries immediately realized that a fundamental change in mentality had occurred. (A good account of this can be found in what is surely the best portrayal of the Industrial Revolution's society in transition, George Eliot's 1871 novel *Middlemarch*.) As the great French historian Fernand Braudel pointed out in his last major work, *The Identity of France* (1986), it was the railroad that made France into one nation and one culture. It had previously been a congeries of self-contained regions, held together only politically. And the role of the railroad in creating the American West is, of course, a commonplace in U.S. history.

Routinization

Like the Industrial Revolution two centuries ago, the Information Revolution so far—that is, since the first computers, in the mid-1940s—has only transformed processes that were here all along. In fact, the real impact of the Information Revolution has not been in the form of "information" at all. Almost none of the effects of information envisaged forty years ago have actually happened. For instance, there has been practically no change in the way major decisions are made in business or government. But the Information Revolution has routinized traditional *processes* in an untold number of areas.

The software for tuning a piano converts a process that traditionally took three hours into one that takes twenty minutes. There is software for payrolls, for inventory control, for delivery schedules, and for all the other routine processes of a business. Drawing the inside arrangements of a major building (heating, water supply, sewerage, and so on) such as a prison or a hospital formerly took, say, twenty-five highly skilled draftsmen up to fifty days; now there is a program that enables one draftsman to do the job in a couple of days, at a tiny fraction of the cost. There is software to help people do their tax returns and software that teaches hospital residents how to take out a gall bladder. The people who now speculate in the stock market online do exactly what their predecessors in the 1920s did while spending hours each day in a brokerage office. The processes have not been changed at all. They have been routinized, step by step, with a tremendous saving in time and, often, in cost.

The psychological impact of the Information Revolution, like that of the Industrial Revolution, has been enormous. It has perhaps been greatest on the way in which young children learn. Beginning at age four (and often earlier), children now rapidly develop computer skills, soon surpassing their elders; computers are their toys and their learning tools. Fifty years hence we may well conclude that there was no "crisis of American education" in the closing years of the twentieth century—there was only a growing incongruence between the way twentieth-century schools taught and the way late-twentieth-century children learned. Something similar happened in the sixteenth-century university, a hundred years after the invention of the printing press and movable type.

But as to the way we work, the Information Revolution has so far simply routinized what was done all along. The only exception is the CD-ROM, invented around twenty years ago to present operas, university courses, a writer's oeuvre, in an entirely new way. Like the steamboat, the CD-ROM has not immediately caught on.

The Meaning of E-Commerce

E-commerce is to the Information Revolution what the railroad 20
was to the Industrial Revolution—a totally new, totally unprecedented, totally unexpected development. And like the railroad 170 years ago, e-commerce is creating a new and distinct boom, rapidly changing the economy, society, and politics.

One example: A mid-sized company in America's industrial Midwest, founded in the 1920s and now run by the grandchildren of the founder, used to have some 60 percent of the market in inexpensive dinnerware for fast-food eateries, school and office cafeterias, and hospitals within a hundred-mile radius of its factory. China is heavy and breaks easily, so cheap china is traditionally sold within a small area. Almost overnight this company lost more than half of its market. One of its customers, a hospital cafeteria where someone went "surfing" on the Internet, discovered a European manufacturer that offered china of apparently better quality at a lower price and shipped cheaply by air. Within a few months the main customers in the area shifted to the European supplier. Few of them, it seems, realize—let alone care—that the stuff comes from Europe.

In the new mental geography created by the railroad, humanity mastered distance. In the mental geography of e-commerce, distance has been eliminated. There is only one economy and only one market.

One consequence of this is that every business must become globally competitive, even if it manufactures or sells only within a local or regional market. The competition is not local anymore—in fact, it knows no boundaries. Every company has to become transnational in the way it is run. Yet the traditional multinational may well become obsolete. It manufactures and distributes in a number of distinct geographies, in which it is a *local* company. But in e-commerce there are neither local companies nor distinct geographies. Where to manufacture, where to sell, and how to sell will remain important business decisions. But in another twenty years they may no longer determine what a company does, how it does it, and where it does it.

At the same time, it is not yet clear what kinds of goods and services will be bought and sold through e-commerce and what kinds will turn out to be unsuitable for it. This has been true whenever a new distribution channel has arisen. Why, for instance, did the railroad change both the mental and the economic geography of the West, whereas the steamboat—with its equal impact on world trade and passenger traffic—did neither? Why was there no "steamboat boom"?

Equally unclear has been the impact of more-recent changes in distribution channels—in the shift, for instance, from the local grocery store to the supermarket, from the individual supermarket to the supermarket chain, and from the supermarket chain to Wal-Mart and other discount chains. It is already clear that the shift to e-commerce will be just as eclectic and unexpected.

Here are a few examples. Twenty-five years ago it was generally believed that within a few decades the printed word would be dispatched electronically to individual subscribers' computer screens. Subscribers would then either read text on their computer screens or download it and print it out. This was the assumption that underlay the CD-ROM. Thus any number of newspapers and magazines, by no means only in the United States, established themselves online; few, so far, have become gold mines. But anyone who twenty years ago predicted the business of Amazon.com and barnesandnoble.com—that is, that books would be sold on the Internet but delivered in their heavy, printed form—would have been laughed off the podium. Yet Amazon.com and barnesandnoble.com are in exactly that business, and they are in it worldwide. The first order for the U.S. edition of my most recent book, *Management Challenges for the 21st Century* (1999), came to Amazon.com, and it came from Argentina.

Another example: Ten years ago one of the world's leading automobile companies made a thorough study of the expected impact on automobile sales of the then emerging Internet. It concluded that the Internet would become a major distribution channel for used cars, but that customers would still want to see new cars, to touch them, to test-drive them. In actuality, at least so far, most used cars are still being bought not over the Internet but in a dealer's lot. However, as many as half of all new cars sold (excluding luxury cars) may now actually be "bought" over the Internet. Dealers only deliver cars that customers have chosen well before they enter the dealership. What does this mean for the future of the local automobile dealership, the twentieth century's most profitable small business?

Another example: Traders in the American stock-market boom of 1998 and 1999 increasingly buy and sell online. But investors seem to be shifting away from buying electronically. The major U.S. investment vehicle is mutual funds. And whereas almost half of all mutual funds a few years ago were bought electronically, it is estimated that the figure will drop to 35 percent next year and to 20 percent by 2005. This is the opposite of what "everybody expected" ten or fifteen years ago.

The fastest-growing e-commerce in the United States is in an area where there was no "commerce" until now—in jobs for professionals and managers. Almost half of the world's largest companies now recruit through Web sites, and some two and a half million managerial and professional people (two thirds of them not even engineers or computer professionals) have their résumés on the Internet and solicit job offers over it. The result is a completely new labor market.

This illustrates another important effect of e-commerce. New distribution channels change who the customers are. They change not only *how* customers buy but also *what* they buy. They change consumer behavior, savings patterns, industry structure—in short, the entire economy. This is what is now happening, and not only in the United States but increasingly in the rest of the developed world, and in a good many emerging countries, including mainland China.

Luther, Machiavelli, and the Salmon

The railroad made the Industrial Revolution accomplished fact. What had been revolution became establishment. And the boom it triggered lasted almost a hundred years. The technology of the steam engine did not end with the railroad. It led in the 1880s and 1890s to the steam turbine, and in the 1920s and 1930s to the last magnificent American steam locomotives, so beloved by railroad buffs. But the technology centered on the steam engine and in manufacturing operations ceased to be central. Instead the dynamics of the technology shifted to totally new industries that emerged almost immediately after the railroad was invented, not one of which had anything to do with steam or steam engines. The electric telegraph and photography were first, in the 1830s, followed soon thereafter by optics and farm equipment. The new and different fertilizer industry, which began in the late 1830s, in short order transformed agriculture. Public health became a major and central growth industry, with quarantine, vaccination, the supply of pure water, and sewers, which for the first time in history made the city a more healthful habitat than the countryside. At the same time came the first anesthetics.

With these major new technologies came major new social institutions: the modern postal service, the daily paper, investment banking, and commercial banking, to name just a few. Not one of them had much to do with the steam engine or with the technology of the Industrial Revolution in general. It was these new industries and institutions that by 1850 had come to dominate the industrial and economic landscape of the developed countries.

This is very similar to what happened in the printing revolution—the first of the technological revolutions that created the modern world. In the fifty years after 1455, when Gutenberg had perfected the printing press and movable type he had been working on for years, the printing revolution swept Europe and completely changed its economy and its psychology. But the books printed during the first fifty years, the ones called incunabula, contained largely the same texts that monks, in their scriptoria, had for centuries laboriously copied by hand: religious tracts and whatever remained of the writings of antiquity. Some 7,000 titles were published in those first fifty years, in 35,000 editions. At least 6,700 of these were traditional titles. In other words, in its first fifty years printing made available—and increasingly cheap—traditional information and communication products. But then, some sixty years after Gutenberg, came Luther's German Bible—thousands and thousands of copies sold almost immediately at an unbelievably low price. With Luther's Bible the new printing technology ushered in a new society. It ushered in Protestantism, which conquered half of Europe and, within another twenty years, forced the Catholic Church to reform itself in the other half. Luther used the new medium of print deliberately to restore religion to the center of individual life and of society. And this unleashed a century and a half of religious reform, religious revolt, religious wars.

At the very same time, however, that Luther used print with the avowed intention of restoring Christianity, Machiavelli wrote and published *The Prince* (1513), the first Western book in more than a thousand years that contained not one biblical quotation and no reference to the writers of antiquity. In no time at all *The Prince* became the "other best seller" of the sixteenth century, and its most notorious but also most influential book. In short order there was a wealth of purely secular works, what we today call literature: novels and books in science, history, politics, and, soon, economics. It was not long before the first purely secular art form arose, in England—the modern theater. Brand-new social institutions also arose: the Jesuit order, the Spanish infantry, the first modern navy, and, finally, the sovereign national state. In other words, the printing revolution followed the same trajectory as did the Industrial Revolution, which began 300 years later, and as does the Information Revolution today.

What the new industries and institutions will be, no one can say yet. No one in the 1520s anticipated secular literature, let alone the secular theater. No one in the 1820s anticipated the electric telegraph, or public health, or photography.

The one thing (to say it again) that is highly probable, if not nearly certain, is that the next twenty years will see the emergence of a number of new industries. At the same time, it is nearly certain that few of them will come out of information technology, the computer, data processing, or the Internet. This is indicated by all historical precedents. But it is true also of the new industries that are already rapidly emerging. Biotechnology, as mentioned, is already here. So is fish farming.

Twenty-five years ago salmon was a delicacy. The typical convention dinner gave a choice between chicken and beef. Today salmon is a commodity, and is the other choice on the convention menu. Most salmon today is not caught at sea or in a river but grown on a fish farm. The same is increasingly true of trout. Soon, apparently, it will be true of a number of other fish. Flounder, for instance, which is to seafood what pork is to meat, is just going into oceanic mass production. This will no doubt lead to the genetic development of new and different fish, just as the domestication of sheep, cows, and chickens led to the development of new breeds among them.

But probably a dozen or so technologies are at the stage where biotechnology was twenty-five years ago—that is, ready to emerge.

There is also a *service* waiting to be born: insurance against the risks of foreign-exchange exposure. Now that every business is part of the global economy, such insurance is as badly needed as was insurance against physical risks (fire, flood) in the early stages of the Industrial Revolution, when traditional insurance emerged. All the knowledge needed for foreign-exchange insurance is available; only the institution itself is still lacking.

The next two or three decades are likely to see even greater 40
technological change than has occurred in the decades since the emergence of the computer, and also even greater change in industry structures, in the economic landscape, and probably in the social landscape as well.

The Gentleman Versus the Technologist

The new industries that emerged after the railroad owed little technologically to the steam engine or to the Industrial Revolution in general. They were not its "children after the flesh"—but they were its "children after the spirit." They were possible only because of the mind-set that the Industrial Revolution had created and the skills it had developed. This was a mind-set that accepted—indeed, eagerly welcomed—invention and innovation. It was a mind-set that accepted, and eagerly welcomed, new products and new services.

It also created the social values that made possible the new industries. Above all, it created the "technologist." Social and financial success long eluded the first major American technologist, Eli Whitney, whose cotton gin, in 1793, was as central to the triumph of the Industrial Revolution as was the steam engine. But a generation later the technologist—still self-taught—had become the American folk hero and was both socially accepted and financially rewarded. Samuel Morse, the inventor of the telegraph, may have been the first example; Thomas Edison became the most prominent. In Europe the "businessman" long remained a social inferior, but the university-trained engineer had by 1830 or 1840 become a respected "professional."

By the 1850s England was losing its predominance and beginning to be overtaken as an industrial economy, first by the United States and then by Germany. It is generally accepted that neither economics nor technology was the major reason. The main cause was social. Economically, and especially financially, England remained the great power until the First World War. Technologically it held its own throughout the nineteenth century. Synthetic dyestuffs, the first products of the modern chemical industry, were invented in England, and so was the steam turbine. But England did not accept the technologist socially. He never became a "gentleman." The English built first-rate engineering schools in India but almost none at home. No other country so honored the "scientist"—and, indeed, Britain retained leadership in physics throughout the nineteenth century, from James Clerk Maxwell and Michael Faraday all the way to Ernest Rutherford. But the technologist remained a "tradesman." (Dickens, for instance, showed open contempt for the upstart ironmaster in his 1853 novel *Bleak House*.)

Nor did England develop the venture capitalist, who has the means and the mentality to finance the unexpected and unproved. A French invention, first portrayed in Balzac's monumental *La Comédie humaine*, in the 1840s, the venture capitalist was institutionalized in the United States by J. P. Morgan and, simultaneously, in Germany and Japan by the universal bank. But England, although it invented and developed the commercial bank to finance trade, had no institution to finance industry until two German refugees, S. G. Warburg and Henry Grunfeld, started an entrepreneurial bank in London, just before the Second World War.

What might be needed to prevent the United States from becoming the England of the twenty-first century? I am convinced that a drastic change in the social mind-set is required—just as leadership in the industrial economy after the railroad required the drastic change from "tradesman" to "technologist" or "engineer." 45

What we call the Information Revolution is actually a Knowledge Revolution. What has made it possible to routinize processes is not machinery; the computer is only the trigger. Software is the reorganization of traditional work, based on centuries of experience, through the application of knowledge and especially of systematic, logical analysis. The key is not electronics; it is cognitive science. This means that the key to maintaining leadership in the economy and the technology that are about to emerge is likely to be the social position of knowledge professionals and social acceptance of their values. For them to remain traditional "employees" and be treated as such would be tantamount to England's treating its technologists as tradesmen—and likely to have similar consequences.

Today, however, we are trying to straddle the fence—to maintain the traditional mind-set, in which capital is the key resource and the financier is the boss, while bribing knowledge workers to be content to remain employees by giving them bonuses and stock options. But this, if it can work at all, can work only as long as the emerging industries enjoy a stock-market boom, as the Internet companies have been doing. The next major industries are likely to behave far more like traditional industries—that is, to grow slowly, painfully, laboriously.

The early industries of the Industrial Revolution—cotton textiles, iron, the railroads—were boom industries that created millionaires overnight, like Balzac's venture bankers and like Dickens's ironmaster, who in a few years grew from a lowly domestic servant into a "captain of industry." The industries that emerged after 1830 also created millionaires. But they took twenty years to do so, and it was twenty years of hard work, of struggle, of disappointments and failures, of thrift. This is likely to be true of the industries that will emerge from now on. It is already true of biotechnology.

Bribing the knowledge workers on whom these industries depend will therefore simply not work. The key knowledge workers in these businesses will surely continue to expect to share financially in the fruits of their labor. But the financial fruits are likely to take much longer to ripen, if they ripen at all. And then, probably within ten years or so, running a business with (short-term) "shareholder value" as its first—if not its only—goal and justification will have become counterproductive. Increasingly, performance in these new knowledge-based industries will come to depend on running the institution so as to attract, hold, and motivate knowledge workers. When this can no longer be done by satisfying knowledge workers' greed, as we are now trying to do, it will have to be done by satisfying their values, and by giving them social recognition and social power. It will have to be done by turning them from subordinates into fellow executives, and from employees, however well paid, into partners.

Globalization: The Super-Story

Thomas L. Friedman [b. 1953]

I am a big believer in the idea of the super-story, the notion that we all carry around with us a big lens, a big framework, through which we look at the world, order events, and decide what is important and what is not. The events of 9/11 did not happen in a vacuum. They happened in the context of a new international system—a system that cannot explain everything but *can* explain and connect more things in more places on more days than anything else. That new international system is called globalization. It came together in the late 1980s and replaced the previous international system, the cold war system, which had reigned since the end of World War II. This new system is the lens, the super-story, through which I viewed the events of 9/11.

I define globalization as the inexorable integration of markets, transportation systems, and communication systems to a degree never witnessed before—in a way that is enabling corporations, countries, and individuals to reach around the world farther, faster, deeper, and cheaper than ever before, and in a way that is enabling the world to reach into corporations, countries, and individuals farther, faster, deeper, and cheaper than ever before.

Several important features of this globalization system differ from those of the cold war system in ways that are quite relevant for understanding the events of 9/11. I examined them in detail in my previous book, *The Lexus and the Olive Tree*, and want to simply highlight them here.

The cold war system was characterized by one overarching feature—and that was *division*. That world was a divided-up, chopped-up place, and whether you were a country or a company, your threats and opportunities in the cold war system tended to grow out of who you were divided from. Appropriately, this cold war system was symbolized by a single word—*wall*, the Berlin Wall.

The globalization system is different. It also has one overarching feature—and that is *integration*. The world has become an increasingly interwoven place, and today, whether you are a company or a country, your threats and opportunities increasingly derive from who you are connected to. This globalization system is also characterized by a single word—*web*, the World Wide Web. So in the broadest sense we have gone from an international system built around division and walls to a system increasingly built around integration and webs. In the cold war we reached for the hotline, which was a symbol that we were divided but at least two people were in charge—the leaders of the United States and the Soviet Union. In the globalization system we reach for the Internet, which is a symbol that we are all connected and nobody is quite in charge.

Everyone in the world is directly or indirectly affected by this new system, but not everyone benefits from it, not by a long shot, which is why the more it becomes diffused, the more it also produces a backlash by people who feel overwhelmed by it, homogenized by it, or unable to keep pace with its demands.

The other key difference between the cold war system and the globalization system is how power is structured within them. The cold war system was built primarily around nation-states. You acted on the world in that system through your state. The cold war was a drama of states confronting states, balancing states, and aligning with states. And, as a system, the cold war was balanced at the center by two superstates, two superpowers: The United States and the Soviet Union.

The globalization system, by contrast, is built around three balances, which overlap and affect one another. The first is the traditional balance of power between nation-states. In the globalization system, the United States is now the sole and dominant superpower and all other nations are subordinate to it to one degree or another. The shifting balance of power between the United States and other states, or simply between other states, still very much matters for the stability of this system. And it can still explain a lot of the news you read on the front page of the paper, whether it is the news of

China balancing Russia, Iran balancing Iraq, or India confronting Pakistan.

The second important power balance in the globalization system is between nation-states and global markets. These global markets are made up of millions of investors moving money around the world with the click of a mouse. I call them the Electronic Herd, and this herd gathers in key global financial centers—such as Wall Street, Hong Kong, London, and Frankfurt—which I call the Supermarkets. The attitudes and actions of the Electronic Herd and the Supermarkets can have a huge impact on nation-states today, even to the point of triggering the downfall of governments. Who ousted Suharto in Indonesia in 1998? It wasn't another state, it was the Supermarkets, by withdrawing their support for, and confidence in, the Indonesian economy. You also will not understand the front page of the newspaper today unless you bring the Supermarkets into your analysis. Because the United States can destroy you by dropping bombs, but the Supermarkets can destroy you by downgrading your bonds. In other words, the United States is the dominant player in maintaining the globalization game board, but it is hardly alone in influencing the moves on that game board.

The third balance that you have to pay attention to—the one that is really the newest of all and the most relevant to the events of 9/11—is the balance between individuals and nation-states. Be- 10
cause globalization has brought down many of the walls that limited the movement and reach of people, and because it has simultaneously wired the world into networks, it gives more power to *individuals* to influence both markets and nation-states than at any other time in history. Whether by enabling people to use the Internet to communicate instantly at almost no cost over vast distances, or by enabling them to use the Web to transfer money or obtain weapons designs that normally would have been controlled by states, or by enabling them to go into a hardware store now and buy a five-hundred-dollar global positioning device, connected to a satellite, that can direct a hijacked airplane—globalization can be an incredible force-multiplier for individuals. Individuals can increasingly act on the world stage directly, unmediated by a state.

So you have today not only a superpower, not only Supermarkets, but also what I call "super-empowered individuals." Some of these super-empowered individuals are quite angry, some of them quite wonderful—but all of them are now able to act much more directly and much more powerfully on the world stage.

Osama bin Laden declared war on the United States in the late 1990s. After he organized the bombing of two American embassies in Africa, the U.S. Air Force retaliated with a cruise missile attack on his bases in Afghanistan as though he were another nation-state. Think about that: on one day in 1998, the United States fired 75 cruise missiles at bin Laden. The United States fired 75 cruise missiles, at $1 million apiece, at a person! That was the first battle in history between a superpower and a super-empowered angry man. September 11 was just the second such battle.

Jody Williams won the Nobel Peace Prize in 1997 for helping to build an international coalition to bring about a treaty outlawing land mines. Although nearly 120 governments endorsed the treaty, it was opposed by Russia, China, and the United States. When Jody Williams was asked, "How did you do that? How did you organize one thousand different citizens' groups and nongovernmental organizations on five continents to forge a treaty that was opposed by the major powers?" she had a very brief answer: "E-mail." Jody Williams used e-mail and the networked world to super-empower herself.

Nation-states, and the American superpower in particular, are still hugely important today, but so too now are Supermarkets and super-empowered individuals. You will never understand the globalization system, or the front page of the morning paper—or 9/11—unless you see each as a complex interaction between all three of these actors: states bumping up against states, states bumping up against Supermarkets, and Supermarkets and states bumping up against super-empowered individuals—many of whom, unfortunately, are super-empowered angry men.

What Are 'Class' and 'Inequality'?

Jeremy Seabrook [b. 1939]

All societies are stratified, in one way or another, in hierarchies of power and wealth. The few egalitarian exceptions, indigenous and tribal peoples, have been destroyed or degraded by contact with the modern world. Privilege has many methods of self-preservation, not least physical force, but sometimes through a mystical appeal to the special intellectual or spiritual powers the privileged claim to possess. Some societies are built on slavery, most upon the oppression of those who perform the most vital labor of that society. Throughout history, there have been struggles of the oppressed against their "superiors," although even when the "natural" order has been overthrown, it has rarely been long before new powerful groups established their own supremacy, their own lineage, their own religion or power over others.

At the time of the Industrial Revolution social classes became more sharply antagonistic, as older mystiques legitimating social stratification decayed, and the rich confronted the poor in stark antagonism. Social class, in its contemporary understanding, was defined primarily in Europe. The United States, with its egalitarian origins in reaction against the feudal order of Europe, saw itself as liberated from archaic categories of aristocracy and the lower orders. It was only later that the profound inequalities of slavery were addressed, and while the idea of class remained foreign to the U.S. tradition, institutionalized social injustice has persisted. Today this is discussed in terms of "inequality" rather than of opposing social classes. The modern idea of class was born in Europe, became an obsession in Britain, and was denied in the United States.

Global Inequality

According to the United Nations *Human Development Report*,[1] the world's richest 20 percent receive 86 percent of the world's gross product; the middle 60 percent, 13 percent; while the poorest 20 percent receive one percent. The ratio between the incomes of the top and bottom fifth of humanity is seventy-four to one. In 1960 it was thirty to one.

But there is another story, which perhaps helps to explain why these often quoted, extreme inequalities are not only tolerated by the peoples of the world, but regarded as part of the natural order of things; why, in other words, there is so little pressure to resist the continuously growing economic injustice in the world.

Datamonitor UK also notes that there are nearly 4 million people (that is, 8 percent of the population over sixteen years of age) who have liquid assets of between $45,000 (£30,000) and $300,000 (£200,000).[2] The numbers in this group have been growing by 12 percent a year for the past five years. Their wealth consists of cash or shares, before the value of any property or pension funds they hold is taken into account.

A survey based on fieldwork from the Office for National Statistics found that at the end of 1999, 26 percent of the British population was living in poverty, measured in terms of low income and multiple deprivation of necessities. This pattern is repeated (with minor variations) in all industrialized countries.

Global Rich

There exists a global rich class, made up of inheritors of wealth, but increasingly of celebrities; entrepreneurs; the makers of spectacular fortunes; the new rich of Information Technology, life sciences, and . . . other recent technological windfalls; sports and media stars; musicians; and show people. There is also a fast-growing and powerful global middle class. This serves, in one way or another, the process of the creation of surplus value, or profit, often for big transnational corporations and the bureaucracies that support them. These people are a significant force in the world. Their role is twofold. They offer a model to the aspiring poor, and they help police poverty; for privilege, even modest privilege, may expand

* 1.3 billion people lack access to clean water: 1.2 billion live on less than a dollar a day: 840 million are malnourished.
* More than 20,000 people die each day from hunger-related diseases.
* The assets of the world's 200 richest individuals more than doubled between 1994 and 1998 to over $1 trillion.
* The richest three people in the world have assets greater than the combined output of the 48 poorest countries.
* In the 1990s, 55 countries experienced real per capita income decrease.
* There are around 7 million millionaires in the world, half of them in the United States.
* 12 of the 20 richest people in the world are Americans.
* Independent market analysis research from Datamonitor in Britain,[2] states that the number of millionaries in Britain is growing at the rate of 17 percent a year; and by 2001 there were 74,000 millionaires.
* Data from the UK's Office for National Statistics stated that 1999–2000 saw the highest gap between rich and poor yet recorded. The poorest fifth of households had 6 percent of national income after tax, while the share held by the top fifth rose from 44 to 45 percent.

and grow only if the gap between rich and poor is maintained, or increased, as is the case in almost every country in the world.

Inequality is an abstraction. Its great advantage to the rich is that it replaces earlier concepts of class. These were embodied in real living figures of flesh and blood and their relationship to each other. Inequality is a statistical term in which the participants appear only as victims or beneficiaries. If human beings have any part to play in remedies for inequality, these will be highly qualified experts and professionals. Ordinary people are absent from inequality; in class relationships the people are omnipresent.

Growing Inequality

The U.N. *Human Development Report* tells only part of the story, for the 60 percent in the middle who receive the 13 percent of income are by no means a homogeneous group. Their inclusion as a single entity is misleading, for it implies that only the bottom 20 percent are poor—those living on less than a dollar a day. But *three billion* people live on less than two dollars a day and far more than that on less than five dollars a day. So the figures that lump together 60 percent need to be broken down to give a clearer picture, not only of the extremes—which are shocking enough—but also of the inequalities hidden by the bulging middle.

These figures are widely published, accessible, and in whatever form they are presented, they lead to the same conclusion. Growing inequality is continuously monitored by international institutions and by academic establishments within countries. There is no attempt to conceal or justify this process. It is just the way things are.

This acceptance of inequality is at odds with a world which constantly advertises its miracles of technology, its mastery of the secrets of nature, its capacity for transforming the lives of the people. The global economy creates the impression of a busy, restless, can-do culture sweeping with irresistible force across the face of the earth. Nothing, it seems, can withstand the impact of the communications revolution, the conquest of space, breakthroughs in medicine, the mapping of the human genome, and all the other promises of emancipation for humanity. Why are governments and international institutions apparently impotent when confronted by the widening divide between rich and poor? In a world where everything is possible, why should this central issue present such a difficult problem?

Why do the poor accept an arbitrary withholding from them of the necessities of life, when the rich take for themselves a disproportionate share of the wealth of the world? This question requires an understanding of the history—and continuing existence—of class relationships and their reconfiguration in the wake of globalization. For social classes have not been eliminated by the treacherous continuum of inequality, but have been remade, often in ways which make them obscure to the participants. The story (and it is a story) is a simple one; yet it consists of layers of complexity and *complicatedness*, which sometimes make it difficult to follow the thread.

Why Class Became Crucial

Class stratification means the division of society into unequal strata or groups. The differences between them express social relationships and constitute the social identity of the members of each group. Some mobility between classes is usually possible. Caste, on the other hand, ascribes a position to people usually through birth, and it is more difficult for individuals to move beyond the inherited position in the caste hierarchy. There are elements of both class and caste in most societies.

Discussions of class in industrial society have been colored by philosopher Karl Marx, who reduced class interests to two—the owners of capital and those who have nothing but their labor power to sell. It is the objective of the former to make profit out of the surplus value produced by the workers. The relationship is exploitative, antagonistic, and according to Marx, highly unstable. It must lead to conflict, which will end either in the triumph of the workers or in the ruin of the contending classes—the famous choice between socialism and barbarism.

The word *class*, meaning the economic and social position 15
of groups of people, is of fairly recent origin. Its present-day use dates from the mid-eighteenth century. Its roots are in the Latin *classis*, referring to the six orders the Romans were divided into for the purposes of taxation. Before the idea of class became significant in the West, concepts of *rank* and *station* described the social position of individuals. In Britain, the word *order*—dating from around 1300—indicated the collective position of groups of people.

In the medieval world, society was divided into *estates*. They comprised three legal classifications—the nobility, the clergy, and the common people. Class came into usage in France, partly as a consequence of the work of the *Encyclopedistes*, a group of eighteenth-century French intellectuals who attempted to assemble all the knowledge available to the modern world. This led them to systematic classification of plants, animals, and minerals, and phenomena of the natural world. It was then a short step to apply the methodology to the social and economic position of individuals in society. In Britain, the philanthropist Jonas Hanway was the first to refer to the "lower classes of people" in 1772. The economist Adam Smith, in his *Wealth of Nations* (1776), used the word class in a general sense, but when he spoke of the division of labor, with its different functions, he spoke of "the ranks and conditions" of people in society.

The concept of *class* fitted in with changes brought about by industrial society, and it gained wide currency with early industrialism in the first half of the nineteenth century. The medieval idea of estates had suggested an organic relationship. Classes, although mutually dependent, were also antagonistic; it was Marx who elevated this clash into his fateful theory of irreconcilable interests between *bourgeoisie* and *proletariat*. Marx specifically stated that class was an expression of a relationship to the means of production—the capitalists who owned the mills, mines, and factories and the workers who had nothing but their labor power to sell.

The origins of the word proletariat are in the Latin *proletarii*. This referred to the poorest classes, those whose only resources lay in their offspring. The word found its way into French in the eighteenth century but occurred in its modern sense in English only in 1853, when it was used disparagingly of the lowest classes.

Bourgeois has a more complicated history. From Latin *burgus* and German *Burg*, meaning a town under the protection of a castle, it came to mean citizen in medieval France, as opposed to peasant or noble. The word was used in France to indicate the mercantile middle class (those involved in trade and commerce) from the seventeenth century. Before the revolution, the nobility used the word as a term of contempt towards those whose money they certainly did not despise. Both words—*bourgeois* and *proletarian*—still have an alien sound to English speakers.

The 20 Richest People in the World, 2000

Lists are produced each year of the wealthiest people; each list has a slightly different order but the same names crop up with astonishing regularity.

	Value (US$ Billions)	Country	Age	Source of Wealth
1. Gates, Bill	58.7	US	45	Microsoft
2. Buffett, Warren	32.3	US	70	investments
3. Allen, Paul	30.4	US	48	Microsoft
4. Ellison, Larry	26.0	US	56	Oracle computers
5. Albrecht, Theo & Karf	25.0	Germany	—	supermarkets
6. Prince Alaweed Bin Talal	20.0	Saudi Arabia	44	investments
7. Walton, Jim	18.8	US	53	Wal-Mart
8. Walton, John	18.7	US	55	Wal-Mart
9. Walton, Robson	18.6	US	57	Wal-Mart
10. Walton, Alice	18.5	US	52	Wal-Mart
11. Walton, Helen	18.5	US	81	Wal-Mart
12. Quandt, Joanna	17.8	Germany	74	BMW
13. Ballmer, Steve	16.6	US	45	Microsoft
14. Thomson, Kenneth	16.4	Canada	77	publishing
15. Bettencourt, Liliane	15.6	France	75	L'Oréal
16. Anachutz, Philip	15.3	Sweden	75	Ikea
18. { Redstone, Sumner	12.6	US	78	Viacom
Li Ka Ly	12.6	Hong Kong	73	diversified
20. Kirch, Leo	12.0	Germany	74	media

Forbes 500.

In Britain, definitions of class continued to be influenced by older ideas of rank, despite the social upheaval of industrialization. The lower orders, the laboring classes, and the middling ranks of society existed alongside the aristocracy and gentry. As the stratification of industrial society became more rigid, these definitions settled into the now familiar classification of upper, middle, and working *class.*

The discrepancy in these categories was pointed out by philosopher and social critic Raymond Williams.[3] He wrote, "Most people in Britain think of themselves as 'middle class' or 'working class.' But the first point to make is that these are not true alternatives. The alternatives to 'middle' are 'lower' and 'upper'; the alternative to 'working' is 'independent' or 'propertied.' The wonderful muddle we are now in springs mainly from this confusion, that one term has a primarily social, the other a primarily economic reference."

"Middle" suggests simply a position in society. "Working" suggests a function. This helps, perhaps, to explain why a working class has become virtually invisible in the contemporary Western world. In the United States in particular, but increasingly in Europe also, this is a category in which people decreasingly recognize themselves. U.S. politicians regularly refer to the middle classes and sometimes to working people, but mention of a working class is said to turn people off.

The idea of a growing middle class expresses a relationship not so much to the means of production, as to *other people*. It introduces an element of *status*, which derives from sociologist Max Weber's efforts to define more clearly the complexity of expanding industrial society towards the end of the nineteenth century, a time when the wider range of economic possibilities blurred the easy classification of capitalists and workers. For Weber, class is multidimensional, and includes both the relationship to the means of production and to the means of consumption. Class becomes more diffuse and complex.

In the United States, the idea of working class, although it figured in politics, was virtually absent from academic discussion until the Great Depression in the mid-twentieth century. It is a paradox that the most advanced capitalist society dispensed with categories which Marx and most European commentators regarded as vital to discussion of social relationships in industrial societies. Status replaced class as the key indicator on the continuum of rich and poor in the United States. Status was acquired through power rather than power through status: The American belief that anyone can rise from humble origins to become President of the United States continued to exercise a powerful hold over the imagination even when it had clearly become myth (most U.S. Presidents have come from wealthy, often highly privileged backgrounds).

Even so, the United States promised freedoms that would wipe 25
out European hierarchies. It offered greater opportunities to get rich and to consume than were available to the majority in Europe. In the United States, moreover, the proportion of people in the industrial sector never reached levels seen in early industrial Britain. The growth of middle-class occupations stifled the emergence of a dominant working-class consciousness.

Rich As Rockefeller

In the period since the Second World War, the positional aspect of status has supplanted the functional aspect of class for many (former working-class) people in Europe as well as in the United States. Sociologist Vance Packard suggested people were ceasing to identify themselves as members of this or that social class, but were creating a new sense of belonging through objects of consumption.[4] Communities of shared tastes and lifestyles were being defined against those of different (lower or higher) patterns of expenditure. Status, in contemporary society, is close to station in preindustrial hierarchies, with the important difference that station implies socially fixed positions, while status-oriented society is extremely mobile. The jackpot winner, the singer with the hit record, the TV star, and the successful entrepreneur can surround themselves with the trappings of luxury as fast as they can buy them.

The United States and the Mystery of the Disappearing Working Class

The working class has been believed, ever since Marx, to be inseparable from working-class organization. From the relative weakness of such movements in the United States (although of course there were many activists and struggles) it has been concluded that the working class scarcely exists. In a country marked by continuous diversity of migration, other struggles and identities have taken priority—people have seen themselves as black, Jewish, Irish, Italian, Hispanic before they see themselves as working class. In 2001, more than 30.5 million Americans were born outside the country—more than 11 percent of the population. The ideology of the Americanization of immigrants has been a more powerful unifying force than perceptions of class, especially to those who saw the United States as a destination, a haven from poverty and persecution elsewhere.

In preindustrial society, it was acknowledged that "birth" or "breeding" distinguished those at the top of the social pyramid. The upper classes were separated from the "lower orders" by the "middling rank" of society. In status-conscious societies, objects of conspicuous consumption are identified with forms of honor, which formerly clustered around other characteristics—inherited position, property, military prowess. The contemporary iconography of high status is more open—anyone who can afford it can go through the obligatory shopping list of ornate villas with tight security, champagne and caviar, diamonds, yachts, Rolls Royce cars, Armani suits, and accessories bearing the "correct" brand-name.

Before industrialization, social belonging was a function simply of position in society. It was only with the Industrial Revolution that a working class—or proletariat, as Marx called it—emerged. The fact that the *function* of this class is its principal characteristic suggests that industrial labor was a profoundly disruptive force. It was destined not only to disturb social hierarchies which had persisted since the feudal times of the Middle Ages (c800–1300) but also to overshadow the antagonism which had grown between the old aristocracy of landed classes and the class of entrepreneurs who were, by the end of the eighteenth century, knocking at the doors of political power and privilege.

Forever Feudal

Feudalism was essentially a caste system and is significant because it still characterizes many agrarian societies in the world. It lays the groundwork for the structures of class, caste, and hierarchies that exist today. To find out about it, we step back in time to the Middle Ages in England.

The word *feudal* comes from the same root as the German 30
word *Viehl*, meaning cattle, reflecting an earlier nomadic society in which cattle were the principal source of wealth. The king stood at the apex above a strongly hierarchical system of landed dependency. Lords obtained land for past services (mainly military) and in expectation of similar future loyalty. The *vassal* was the personal follower of his immediate lord. Lords granted land to their vassals not in ownership, but in *usufruct*, which means they had access to the produce of that land. This was granted originally on a personal basis, but eventually became hereditary. The land held by a vassal was the expression of an invisible bond to his superior. Lords had power to hold their own courts, a power derived ultimately from the king. This secular hierarchy was paralleled by a religious one of bishops and priests and monks—the second "estate" of the three great estates that constituted medieval society.

Feudalism was eroded in the late Middle Ages by the growth of towns and the rise of a money-based rather than a land-based economy. It became impracticable for lords to retain knights in their service waiting for the call of war. The knights commuted their military obligations for money; and eventually money replaced land as a symbol of power. Similarly, the emancipation of *villeins* (*serfs* or tied peasants cultivating a lord's land) grew, and tenure by service gave way to tenure by rent—the lord's fields were tilled by hired laborers.

The Black Death wiped out surplus labor; it became impossible legally to bind labor to the soil. Villeins escaped from their own lords to become laborers for hire. Lords became landlords, and villeins landless laborers. Although birth remained the principal determinant of status, the growth of mercantilism—merchants and trading—and manufacturing led to a steady accession of the particularly talented into higher ranks of society, usually by means of royal and political patronage. But until the industrial era, the sense of hierarchy persisted: the superior, middle, and lower ranks in society.

Privilege Prevails

Privilege in every society spins myths to legitimize its power or its monopoly over resources. Ruling castes or classes perpetuate themselves by a mystical appeal to antiquity, lineage, divine sanction, or breeding, which justify their right to rule. Historian Walter Bagehot[5] claimed that the nobility preserves a country from too great a worship of money and that reverence for rank is less base than reverence for money. In 1835, after the passage of the 1832 Reform Bill, British Prime Minister Benjamin Disraeli wrote, "For nearly five centuries the hereditary Peerage . . . has formed an active and powerful branch of our legislature. . . . No statesman can doubt that the peculiar character of the hereditary branch of our legislature has mainly contributed to the stability of our institutions, and to the order and prosperous security which that stability has produced. Nor can we forget that the hereditary principle has at all times secured a senate for this country inferior in intelligence to no political assembly on record. . . ."[6] He refers to "an ancient people, who have made inheritance the pervading principle of their social polity, who are proud of their old families and fond of their old laws."

An idealized version of hierarchical relationships reinforced the British idea of its own past; this took root, paradoxically, in the psyche of the industrial bourgeoisie, who made their fortunes out of manufacture. Historian Martin Wiener[7] speaks of the "consolidation of a 'gentrified' bourgeois culture, particularly the rooting of pseudo-aristocratic attitudes and values in upper-middle class educated opinion." Wiener sees this as harmful to economic efficiency and a cause of the relative economic decline of Britain. However that may be, it is remarkable that whatever the disdain for financial gain on the part of the old nobility, they managed to salvage a great deal of their material advantage, as well as their power and honor, in the generations after the Industrial Revolution.

In the end, the interests of the nobility merged with those of the new moneyed middle class; a compromise born of expediency, especially when confronted by a rising working class. The heritage of the old rich was maintained by the wealth of the new, a marriage of convenience.

In our time, this has yielded to a more overt stratification by 35
money, exemplified by pop stars and sports heroes—people like Madonna or Magic Johnson—where money and talent create a new class of celebrities, which is honored and admired—and plays a significant role in reconciling the poor to their status. These people have, in some measure, replaced the aristocracy and monarchy. The decline in reverence for the royal family in Britain reflects this change: Positions derived from birth no longer inspire the respect commanded by wealth from the intensive marketing of talent, youth, and glamour. The Spice Girls pop group, five women who answered a newspaper advertisement in the early 1990s, had personal fortunes by 2001 of at least $33 million (£22 million) each. This rise of exceptional individuals is of course familiar in the United States, where people were founding their own plutocratic—wealth makes them powerful—dynasties, while British entrepreneurs aped the aristocracy.

Not that the old ruling class has become impoverished. Among the richest people in the world, the Queen of England, the Sultan of Brunei, and the King of Saudi Arabia are still present, along with Bill Gates and other representatives of spectacular contemporary enterprise. The wealth of the Duke of Westminster amounts to $5.6 billion (£3.75 billion). If the private assets of the Queen are included, she is probably among the twenty richest people in the world.

The Rich List, compiled each year by the London *Sunday Times,* recorded an increase between 1999 and 2000 of almost $47 billion (£31 billion) in the wealth of the thousand richest people in Britain. Of these, "only" 258 inherited their millions, compared with two-thirds in 1989. Whether wealth is old or new is rather academic in a world in which inequality is growing so spectacularly.

Notes

1. *United Nations Development Report,* UNDP/OUP 2000.
2. Datamonitor, United Kingdom, 2001.
3. *The Long Revolution,* Raymond Williams, Chatto and Windus, 1961.
4. *The Status Seekers,* Vance Packard, 1959, Bedford/St Martin's Press, 1995.
5. *The English Constitution,* Walter Bagehot, 1904 (cited in *The English Ruling Class,* W. L. Guttsman, Weidenfeld and Nicholson, 1969).
6. "A Vindication of the English Constitution" in *Whigs and Whiggism: Political Writings,* Benjamin Disraeli, London, 1913.
7. *English Culture and the Decline of the Industrial Spirit 1850–1980,* Martin Wiener, Penguin, 1985.

Where I Lived, and What I Lived For

Henry David Thoreau [1817–1862]

I went to the woods because I wished to live deliberately, to front only the essential facts of life, and see if I could not learn what it had to teach, and not, when I came to die, discover that I had not lived. I did not wish to live what was not life, living is so dear; nor did I wish to practice resignation, unless it was quite necessary. I wanted to live deep and suck out all the marrow of life, to live so sturdily and Spartan-like as to put to rout all that was not life, to cut a broad swath and shave close, to drive life into a corner, and reduce it to its lowest terms, and, if it proved to be mean, why then to get the whole and genuine meanness of it, and publish its meanness to the world; or if it were sublime, to know it by experience, and be able to give a true account of it in my next excursion. For most men, it appears to me, are in a strange uncertainty about it, whether it is of the devil or of God, and have *somewhat hastily* concluded that it is the chief end of man here to "glorify God and enjoy him forever."

Still we live meanly, like ants; though the fable tells us that we were long ago changed into men; like pygmies we fight with cranes; it is error upon error, and clout upon clout, and our best virtue has for its occasion a superfluous and evitable wretchedness. Our life is frittered away by detail. An honest man has hardly need to count more than his ten fingers, or in extreme cases he may add his ten toes, and lump the rest. Simplicity, simplicity, simplicity! I say, let your affairs be as two or three, and not a hundred or a thousand; instead of a million count half a dozen, and keep your accounts on your thumb-nail. In the midst of this chopping sea of civilized life, such are the clouds and storms and quick-sands and thousand-and-one items to be allowed for, that a man has to live, if he would not founder and go to the bottom and not make his port at all, by dead reckoning, and he must be a great calculator indeed who succeeds. Simplify, simplify. Instead of three meals a day, if it be necessary eat but one; instead of a hundred dishes, five; and reduce other things in proportion. Our life is like a German Confederacy, made of up petty states, with its boundary forever fluctuating, so that even a German cannot tell you how it is bounded at any moment. The nation itself, with all its so-called internal improvements, which, by the way are all external and superficial, is just such an unwieldy and overgrown establishment, cluttered with furniture and tripped up by its own traps, ruined by luxury and heedless expense, by want of calculation and a worthy aim, as the million households in the lands; and the only cure for it, as for them, is in a rigid economy, a stern and more than Spartan simplicity of life and elevation of purpose. It lives too fast. Men think that it is essential that the *Nation* have commerce, and export ice, and talk through a telegraph, and ride thirty miles an hour, without a doubt, whether *they* do or not; but whether we should live like baboons or like men, is a little uncertain. If we do not get our sleepers, and forge rails, and devote days and nights to the work, but go to tinkering upon our *lives* to improve *them*, who will build railroads? And if railroads are not built, how shall we get to heaven in season? But if we stay at home and mind our business, who will want railroads? We do not ride on the railroad; it rides upon us. Did you ever think what those sleepers are that underlie the railroad? Each one is a man, an Irishman, or a Yankee man. The rails are laid on them, and they are covered with sand, and the cars run smoothly over them. They are sound sleepers, I assure you. And every few years a new lot is laid down and run over, so that, if some have the pleasure of riding on a rail, others have the misfortune to be ridden upon. And when they run over a man that is walking in his sleep, a supernumerary sleeper in the wrong position, and wake him up, they suddenly stop the cars, and make a hue and cry about it, as if this were an exception. I am glad to know that it takes a gang of men for every five miles to keep the sleepers down and level in their beds as it is, for this is a sign that they may sometimes get up again.

Why should we live with such hurry and waste of life? We are determined to be starved before we are hungry. Men say that a stitch in time saves nine, and so they take a thousand stitches to-day to save nine tomorrow. As for *work*, we haven't any of any consequence. We have the Saint Vitus' dance, and cannot possibly keep our heads still. If I should only give a few pulls at the parish bell-rope, as for a fire, that is, without setting the bell, there is hardly a man on his farm in the outskirts of Concord, notwithstanding that press of engagements which was his excuse so many times this morning, nor a boy, nor a woman, I might almost say, but would foresake all and follow that sound, not mainly to save property from the flames, but, if we will confess the truth, much more to see it burn, since burn it must, and we, be it known, did not set it on fire—or to see it put out, and have a hand in it, if that is done as handsomely; yes, even if it were the parish church itself. Hardly a man takes a half-hour's nap after dinner, but when he wakes he holds up his head and asks, "What's the news?" as if the rest of mankind had stood his sentinels. Some give directions to be waked every half-hour, doubtless for no other purpose; and then, to pay for it, they tell what they have dreamed. After a night's sleep the news is as indispensable as the breakfast. "Pray tell me anything new that has happened to a man anywhere on this globe"—and he reads it over his coffee and rolls, that a man has had his eyes gouged out this morning on the Wachito River; never dreaming the while that he lives in the dark unfathomed mammoth cave of this world, and has but the rudiment of an eye himself.

For my part, I could easily do without the post-office. I think that there are very few important communications made through it. To speak critically, I never received more than one or two letters in my life—I wrote this some years ago—that were worth the postage. The penny-post is, commonly, an institution through which you seriously offer a man that penny for his thoughts which is so often safely offered in jest. And I am sure that I never read any memorable news in a newspaper. If we read of one man robbed, or murdered, or killed by accident, or one house burned, or one vessel wrecked or one steamboat blown up, or one cow run over on the Western Railroad, or one mad dog killed, or one lot of grasshoppers in the winter—we never need read of another. One is enough. If you are acquainted with the principle, what do you care for a myriad instances and applications? To a philosopher all news, as it is called, is gossip, and they who edit and read it are old women over their tea. Yet not a few are greedy after this gossip. There was such a rush, as I hear, the other day at one of the offices to learn the foreign news by the last arrival, that several large squares of plate glass belonging to the establishment were broken by the pressure—news which I seriously think a ready wit might write a twelvemonth, or twelve years, beforehand with sufficient accuracy. As for Spain, for instance, if you know how to throw in Don Carlos and the Infanta, and Don Pedro and Seville and Granada, from time to time in the right proportions—they may have changed the names a little since I saw the papers—and serve up a bullfight when other entertainments fail, it will be true to the letter, and give us as good an idea of the exact state or ruin of things in Spain as the most succinct and lucid reports under this head in the newspapers; and as for England, almost the last significant scrap of news from that quarter was the revolution of 1649; and if you have learned the history of her crops for an average year, you never need attend to that thing again, unless your speculations are of a merely pecuniary character. If one may judge who rarely looks into the newspapers, nothing new does ever happen in foreign parts, a French revolution not excepted.

What news! how much more important to know what that is which was never old! "Kieou-he-yu (great dignitary of the state of Wei) sent a man to Khoung-tseu to know his news. Khoung-tseu caused the messenger to be seated near him, and questioned him in these terms: What is your master doing? The messenger answered with respect: My master desires to diminish the number of his faults, but he cannot come to the end of them. The messenger being gone, the philosopher remarked: What a worthy messenger! What a worthy messenger!" The preacher, instead of vexing the ears of drowsy farmers on their day of rest at the end of the week—for Sunday is the fit conclusion of an ill-spent week, and not the fresh and brave beginning of a new one—with this one other draggle-tail of a sermon, should shout with thundering voice, "Pause! Avast! Why so seeming fast, but deadly slow?"

Shams and delusions are esteemed for soundless truths, while reality is fabulous. If men would steadily observe realities only, and not allow themselves to be deluded, life, to compare it with such things as we know, would be like a fairy tale and the Arabian Nights' Entertainments. If we respected only what is inevitable and has a right to be, music and poetry would resound along the streets. When we are unhurried and wise, we perceive that only great and worthy things have any permanent and absolute existence, that petty fears and petty pleasures are but the shadow of the reality. This is always exhilarating and sublime. By closing the eyes and slumbering, and consenting to be deceived by shows, men establish and confirm their daily life of routine and habit everywhere, which still is built on purely illusory foundations. Children, who play life, discern its true law and relations more clearly than men, who fail to live it worthily, but who think that they are wiser by experience, that is, by failure. I have read in a Hindoo book, that "there was a king's son, who, being expelled in infancy from his native city, was brought up by a forester, and, growing up to maturity in that state, imagined himself to belong to the barbarous race with which he lived. One of his father's ministers having discovered him, revealed to him what he was, and the misconception of his character was removed, and he knew himself to be a prince. So soul," continues the Hindoo philosopher, "from the circumstances in which it is placed, mistakes its own character, until the truth is revealed to it by some holy teacher and then it knows itself to be *Brahme*." I perceive that we inhabitants of New England live this mean life that we do because our vision does not penetrate the surface of things. We think that that *is* which *appears* to be. If a man should walk through this town and see only the reality, where, think you, would the "Milldam" go to? If he should give us an account of the realities he beheld there, we should not recognize the place in his description. Look at the meetinghouse, or a courthouse, or a jail, or a shop, or a dwelling-house, and say what that thing really is before a true gaze, and they would all go to pieces in your account of them. Men esteem truth remote, in the outskirts of the system, behind the farthest star, before Adam and after the last man. In eternity there is indeed something true and sublime. But all these times and places and occasions are now and here. God himself culminates in the present moment, and will never be more divine in the lapse of all the ages. And we are enabled to apprehend at all what is sublime and noble only by the perpetual instilling and drenching of the reality that surrounds us. The universe constantly and obediently answers to our conceptions; whether we travel fast or slow, the track is laid for us. Let us spend our lives in conceiving then. The poet or the artist never yet had so fair and noble a design but some of his posterity at least could accomplish it.

Let us spend one day as deliberately as Nature, and not be thrown off the track by every nutshell and mosquito's wing that falls on the rails. Let us rise early and fast, or breakfast, gently and without perturbation; let company come and let company go, let the bells ring and the children cry—determined to make a day of it. Why should we knock under and go with the stream? Let us not be upset and overwhelmed in that terrible rapid and whirlpool called a dinner, situated in the meridian shallows. Weather this danger and you are safe, for the rest of the way is downhill. With unrelaxed nerves, with morning vigor, sail by it, looking another way, tied to the mast like Ulysses. If the engine whistles, let it whistle till it is hoarse for its pains. If the bell rings, why should we run? We will consider what kind of music they are like. Let us settle ourselves and work and wedge our feet downward through the mud and slush of opinion, and prejudice, and tradition, and delusion, and appearance, that alluvion which covers the globe, through Paris and London, through New York and Boston and Concord, through Church and State, through poetry and philosophy and religion, till we come to a hard bottom and rocks in place, which we can call *reality*, and say, This is, and no mistake; and then begin, having *a point d'appui*, below freshet and frost and fire, a place where you might found a wall or a state, or set a lamppost safely, or perhaps a gauge, not a Nilometer, but a Realometer, that future ages might know how deep a freshet of shams and appearances had gathered from time to time. If you stand right fronting and face to face to a fact, you will see the sun glimmer on both its surfaces, as if it were a cimeter, and feel its sweet edge dividing you through the heart and marrow, and so you will happily conclude your mortal career. Be it life or death, we crave only reality. If we are really dying, let us hear the rattle in our throats and feel cold in the extremities; if we are alive, let us go about our business.

Time is but the stream I go afishing in. I drink at it; but while I drink I see the sandy bottom and detect how shallow it is. Its thin current slides away but eternity remains. I would drink deeper; fish in the sky, whose bottom is pebbly with stars. I cannot count one. I know not the first letter of the alphabet. I have always been regretting that I was not as wise as the day I was born. The intellect is a cleaver; it discerns and rifts its way into the secret of things. I do not wish to be any more busy with my hands than is necessary. My head is hands and feet. I feel all my best faculties concentrated in it. My instinct tells me that my head is an organ for burrowing, as some creatures use their snout and fore paws, and with it I would mine and burrow my way through these hills. I think that the richest vein is somewhere hereabouts; so by the divining-rod and thin rising vapors, I judge; and here I will begin to mine.

[1854]

Class

Sherman Alexie

Sherman Alexie (1966–) was born on a Spokane Indian Reservation in Wellprint, Washington. His mother was Spokane while his father Coeur d'Alene. Though his life began with medical difficulties, he learned to read at three and became a star high school athlete. He graduated from Washington State University-Pullman in American Studies. In addition to writing, he has participated in the Museum of Tolerance project; appeared on the Lehrer News Hour (with President Clinton); recorded albums; performed as a standup comedian; and written and produced a film. He was awarded a Washington State Arts Commission Poetry Fellowship in 1991, and the National Endowment for the Arts Poetry Fellowship in 1992. Other awards include the PEN/Hemingway Award, the Lila Wallace Reader's Digest Writers' Award, the Before Columbus Foundation's American Book Award, and The Filmmakers Trophy. His works include The Lone Ranger and Tonto Fistfight in Heaven *(1994),* Reservation Blues *(1996), and* The First Indian on the Moon *(2004).*

She wanted to know if I was Catholic.

I was completely unprepared to respond with any degree of clarity to such a dangerous question. After all, we had been talking about the shrimp appetizers (which were covered with an ambitious pesto sauce) and where they fit, in terms of quality, in our very separate histories of shrimp appetizers in particular and seafood appetizers in general. I'd just been describing to her how cayenne and lobster seemed to be mortal enemies, one of the more secular and inane culinary observations I'd ever made, when she'd focused her blue eyes on me, really looked at me for the first time in the one minute and thirty-five seconds we'd known each other, and asked me if I was Catholic.

How do you answer a question like that, especially when you've just met the woman at one of those house parties where you'd expected to know everybody in attendance but had gradually come to realize that you knew only the host couple, and then only well enough to ask about the welfare of the two kids (a boy and a girl or two boys) you thought they parented? As far as I could tell, there were no priests, ministers, or pastors milling about, so I had no easy visual aids in guessing at the dominant denomination in the room. If there'd been a Jesuit priest, Hasidic rabbi, or Tibetan monk drinking a pale ale over by the saltwater aquarium, I might have known the best response, the clever, scintillating answer that would have compelled her to take me home with her for a long night of safe and casual sex.

"Well," she asked again, with a musical lilt in her voice. "Are you Catholic?"

Her left eye was a significantly darker blue than the right.

"Your eyes," I said, trying to change the subject. "They're different."

"I'm blind in this one," she said, pointing to the left eye.

"Oh, I'm sorry," I said, mortified by my lack of decorum.

"Why? It was my big brother who stabbed me with the pencil. He didn't mean it, though."

She told the story as if she'd only skinned a knee or received a slight concussion, as if the injury had been temporary.

"He was aiming for my little sister's eye," she added. "But she ducked. She was always more athletic than me."

"Where's your sister now?"

"She's dead. Car wreck. Bang, bang, bang."

So much pain for such a white woman. I wondered how often a man can say the wrong thing during the course of a particular conversation.

"What about your brother?" I asked, praying that he had not been driving the car that killed her sister.

"He's right over there," she said and pointed at a handsome man, taller than everybody else in the room, who was sitting on the carpeted stairs with a woman whose red hair I'd been admiring all evening. Though engaged in what appeared to be a passionate conversation, the brother sensed his sister's attention and looked up. Both of his eyes were the same shade of blue as her good eye.

"He's the one who did it," she said and tapped her blind eye.

In response, the brother smiled and tapped his left eye. He could see perfectly.

"You cruel bastard," she mouthed at him, though she made it sound like an affectionate nickname, like a tender legacy from childhood.

"You cruel bastard," she repeated. Her brother could obviously read her lips because he laughed again, loud enough for me to hear him over the din of the party, and hugged the redhead in a tender but formal way that indicated they'd made love only three or four times in their young relationship.

"Your brother," I said, trying to compliment her by complimenting the family genetics. "He's good-looking."

"He's okay," she said.

"He's got your eyes."

"Only one of them, remember," she said and moved one step closer to me. "Now, quit trying to change the subject. Tell me. Are you Catholic or are you not Catholic?"

"Baptized," I said. "But not confirmed."

"That's very ambiguous."

"I read somewhere that many women think ambiguity is sexy."

"Not me. I like men who are very specific."

"You don't like mystery?"

"I always know who did it," she said and moved so close that I could smell the red wine and dinner mints on her breath.

I took a step back.

"Don't be afraid," she said. "I'm not drunk. And I just chewed on a few Altoids because I thought I might be kissing somebody very soon."

She could read minds. She was also drunk enough that her brother had already pocketed the keys to her Lexus.

"Who is this somebody you're going to be kissing?" I asked. "And why just somebody? That sounds very ambiguous to me."

"And very sexy," she said and touched my hand. Blond, maybe thirty-five, and taller than me, she was the tenth most attractive white woman in the room. I always approached the tenth most attractive white woman at any gathering. I didn't have enough looks, charm, intelligence, or money to approach anybody more attractive than that, and I didn't have enough character to approach the less attractive. Crassly speaking, I'd always made sure to play ball only with my equals.

"You're Indian," she said, stretching the word into three syllables and nearly a fourth.

"Do you like that?"

"I like your hair," she said, touching the black braids that hung down past my chest. I'd been growing the braids since I'd graduated from law school. My hair impressed jurors but irritated judges. Perfect.

"I like your hair, too," I said and brushed a pale strand away from her forehead. I counted three blemishes and one mole on her face. I wanted to kiss the tips of her fingers. Women expected kisses on the parts of their bodies hidden by clothes, the private places, but were often surprised when I paid more attention to their public features: hands, hairline, the soft skin around their eyes.

"You're beautiful," I said.

"No, I'm not," she said. "I'm just pretty. But pretty is good enough."

I still didn't know her name, but I could have guessed at it. Her generation of white women usually carried two-syllable names, like Becky, Erin, and Wendy, or monosyllabic nicknames that lacked any adornment. Peg, Deb, or Sam. Efficient names, quick-in-the-shower names, just-brush-it-and-go names. Her mother and her mother's friends would be known by more ornate monikers, and if she had daughters, they would be named after their grandmothers. The country was filling up with little white girls named Rebecca, Elizabeth, and Willamena.

"Sara," I guessed. "Your name is Sara."

"With or without an *h*?" she asked.

"Without," I said, pleased with my psychic ability.

"Actually, it's neither. My name is Susan. Susan McDermott. Without the *h*."

"I'm Edgar Eagle Runner," I said, though my driver's license still read Edgar Joseph.

"Eagle Runner," she repeated, feeling the shape of my name fill her mouth, then roll past her tongue, teeth, and lips.

"Susan," I said.

"Eagle Runner," she whispered. "What kind of Indian are you?"

"Spokane."

"Never heard of it."

"We're a small tribe. Salmon people."

"The salmon are disappearing," she said.

"Yes," I said. "Yes, they are."

Susan McDermott and I were married in a small ceremony seven months later in St. Therese Catholic Church in Madrona, a gentrified neighborhood ten minutes from downtown Seattle. She'd been baptized at St. Therese as a toddler by a Jesuit who many years later went hiking on Mount Rainier and vanished. Father David or Joseph or Father Something Biblical. She didn't remember anything about him, neither the color of his hair nor the exact shape of his theology, but she thought that his disappearance was a metaphor for her love life.

"One day, many years ago," she said, "my heart walked into the snow and vanished. But then you found it and gave it heat."

"Is that a simile or a metaphor?" I asked.

"It might be an analogy," she said.

Our vows were witnessed by three dozen of Susan's best friends, along with most of her coworkers at the architecture firm, but Susan's handsome brother and parents stayed away as a protest against my pigmentation.

"I can understand fucking him," her brother had said upon hearing the news of our engagement. "But why do you want to share a checking account?"

He was so practical.

Half of the partners and all of my fellow associates from the law firm showed up to watch me tie the knot.

Velma, my dark-skinned mother, was overjoyed by my choice of mate. She'd always wanted me to marry a white woman and beget half-breed children who would marry white people who would beget quarter-bloods, and so on and so on, until simple mathematics killed the Indian in us.

When asked, my mother told white people she was Spanish, not Mexican, not Hispanic, not Chicana, and certainly not Spokane

Indian with a little bit of Aztec thrown in for spice, even though she was all of these things.

As for me, I'd told any number of white women that I was part Aztec and I'd told a few that I was completely Aztec. That gave me some mystery, some ethnic weight, a history of glorious color and mass executions. Strangely enough, there were aphrodisiacal benefits to claiming to be descended from ritual cannibals. In any event, pretending to be an Aztec warrior was a lot more impressive than revealing I was just some bright kid who'd fought his way off the Spokane Indian Reservation in Washington State and was now a corporate lawyer in Seattle who pretended to have a lot more money that he did.

I'd emptied my meager savings account to pay for the wedding and reception, refusing to allow Susan to help, though she made twice what I did. I was living paycheck to paycheck, a bizarre circumstance for a man whose monthly wage exceeded his mother's yearly income as a social worker in the small city of Spokane, Washington.

My mother was an Indian woman who taught drunk white people not to drink, stoned whites not to smoke, and abusive whites not to throw the punch. A simple and honorable job. She was very good at it and I loved her. She wore a black dress to the wedding, nearly funeral wear, but brightened it with a salmon-colored scarf and matching shoes.

I counted seventeen white women at the wedding. On an average day, Susan would have been the fourth or fifth most attractive. On this, her wedding day, dressed in an ivory gown with plunging neckline, she was easily the most beautiful white woman in the chapel; she was more serene, sexy, and spiritual than the wooden Mary hanging on the west wall or the stained-glassed Mary filling up one of the windows.

Susan's niece, an eighteen-year-old, served as her maid of honor. She modeled teen wear for Nordstrom's. I tried not to stare at her. My best man was one of the partners in the law firm where I worked.

"Hey, Runner," he had said just before the ceremony began. "I love you, man."

I'd hugged him, feeling guilty. My friendship with him was strictly professional.

During the ceremony, he cried. I couldn't believe it. I'm not one of those men who believe tears are a sign of weakness. On the contrary, I believe it's entirely appropriate, even attractive, for a man to cry under certain circumstances, but my wedding was not tear-worthy. In fact, there was a decided lack of emotion during the ceremony, mostly due to the absence of Susan's immediate family.

My mother was the only member of my family sitting in the pews, but that didn't bother or surprise me. She was the only one I had invited.

The ceremony itself was short and simple, because Susan believed brevity was always more elegant, and more sexy, than excess. I agreed with her.

"I will," she said.

"I will," I said.

We did.

▲

During the first two years of our marriage, we attended thirty-seven cocktail parties, eighteen weddings, one divorce, seven Christmas parties, two New Year's Eve parties, three New Year's Day parties, nine birthday parties—only one of them for a child under the age of eighteen—six opera performances, nine literary readings, twelve museum openings, one museum closing, three ballets, including a revival of *Swan Lake* in New York City, one spouse-swapping party we left before we took off our coats, and thirty-two films, including most of those nominated for Oscars and two or three that had screened at the Sundance Film Festival.

I attended business lunches Monday through Friday, and occasionally on Saturdays, while Susan kept her Friday lunches free so she could carry on an affair with an architect named Harry. She'd begun the affair a few days after our first anniversary and it had gone on for seven months before she'd voluntarily quit him, never having known that I'd known about the tryst, that I'd discovered his love letters hidden in a shoe box at the bottom of her walk-in closet.

I hadn't been snooping on her when I'd found the letters and I didn't bother to read any of them past the salutation that began each. "My love, my love, my love," they'd read, three times, always three times, like a chant, like a prayer. Brokenhearted, betrayed, I'd kept the letters sacred by carefully placing them back, intact and unread, in the shoe box and sliding the box back into its hiding place.

I suppose I could have exacted revenge on her by sleeping with one or more of her friends or coworkers. I'd received any number of subtle offers to do such a thing, but I didn't want to embarrass her. Personal pain should never be made public. Instead, in quiet retaliation, I patronized prostitutes whenever I traveled out of town. Miami, Los Angeles, Boston. Chicago, Minneapolis, Houston.

In San Francisco for a deposition hearing, I called the first service listed in the Yellow Pages.

"A-1 Escorts," said the woman. A husky voice, somehow menacing. I'm sure her children hated the sound of it, even as I found myself aroused by its timbre.

"A-1 Escorts," she said again when I did not speak.

"Oh," I said. "Hi. Hello. Uh, I'm looking for some company this evening."

"Where you at?"

"The Prescott."

"Nice place."

"Yeah, they have whirlpool bathtubs."

"Water sports will cost you extra."

"Oh, no, no, no. I'm, uh, rather traditional."

"Okay, Mr. Traditional, what are you looking for?"

I'd slept with seventeen prostitutes, all of them blond and blue-eyed. Twelve of them had been busty while the other five had been small-breasted. Eight of them had claimed to be college students; one of them even had a chemistry textbook in her backpack.

"Do you employ any Indian women?" I asked.

"Indian? Like with the dot in the forehead?"

"No, no, that's East Indian. From India. I'm looking for American Indian. You know, like Tonto."

"We don't have any boys."

"Oh, no, I mean, I want an Indian woman."

There was a long silence on the other end. Was she looking through some kind of catalogue? Searching her inventory for the perfect woman for me? Was she calling other escort companies, looking for a referral? I wanted to hang up the phone. I'd never had intercourse with an Indian woman.

"Yeah, we got somebody. She's a pro."

"What do you mean by pro?"

"She used to work pornos."

"Pornos?"

"Dirty movies? X-rated? You got them right there on the pay-per-view in your room, buddy."

"What's her name?"

"She calls herself Tawny Feather."

"You're kidding."

"I never kid."

I wondered what kind of Indian woman would call herself Tawny Feather. Sexually speaking, Indian women and men are simultaneously promiscuous and modest. That's a contradiction, but it also happens to be the truth. I just couldn't imagine an Indian woman who would star in pornographic movies.

"Well, you want a date or not?" asked the husky-voiced woman.

"How much?"

"How much you got?"

"How much you want?"

"Two hundred."

"Sold," I said.

"What room?"

"1216."

"Who should she ask for?"

"Geronimo."

"Ha, ha," she said and hung up the phone.

Less than an hour later, there was a knock on the door. I peered through the peephole and saw her.

Tawny Feather.

She wore a conservative tan suit and a string of fake pearls. Dream-catcher earrings, turquoise rings, a stainless-steel eagle pinned to her lapel. Good camouflage. Professional but eccentric. She looked like a woman on her way to or from a meeting. She looked like a woman with an Individualized Retirement Account.

She was also a white woman wearing a black wig over her short blond hair.

"You're not Indian," I said when I opened the door.

She looked me up and down.

"No, I'm not," she said. "But you are."

"Mostly."

"Well," she said as she stepped into the room and kissed my neck. "Then you can mostly pretend I'm Indian."

She stayed all night, which cost me another five hundred dollars, and ordered eggs and toast for breakfast, which cost me another twenty.

"You're the last one," I said as she prepared to leave.

"The last what?"

"My last prostitute."

"The last one today?" she asked. "Or the last one this month? What kind of time period are we talking about here?"

She swore she was an English major.

"The last one forever," I said.

She smiled, convinced that I was lying and/or fooling myself, having heard these same words from any number of customers. She knew that she and her coworkers were drugs for men like me.

"Sure I am," she said.

"No, really," I said. "I promise."

She laughed.

"Son," she said, though she was ten years younger than me. "You don't have to make me any damn promises."

She took off her black wig and handed it to me.

"You keep it," she said and gave me a free good-bye kiss.

▲

Exactly three years after our wedding, Susan gave birth to our first child, a boy. He weighed eight pounds, seven ounces, and was twenty-two inches long. A big baby. His hair was black and his eyes were a strange gray. He died ten minutes after leaving Susan's body.

▲

After our child died, Susan and I quit having sex. Or rather, she stopped wanting to have sex. I just want to tell the whole story. For months I pressured, coerced, seduced, and emotionally blackmailed her into sleeping with me. At first, I assumed she'd been engaged in another affair with another architect named Harry, but my private detective found only evidence of her grief: crying jags in public rest rooms, aimless wandering in the children's departments of Nordstrom's and the Bon Marche, and visits to a therapist I'd never heard about.

She wasn't touching anybody else but me. Our lives moved on.

After a year of reluctant sex, I believed her orgasms were mostly due to my refusal to quit touching her until she did come, the arduous culmination of my physical endeavors rather than the result of any emotional investment she might have had in fulfillment. And then, one night, while I was still inside her, moving my hips in rhythm with hers, I looked into her eyes, her blue eyes, and saw that her good eye held no more light in it than her dead eye. She wasn't literally blind, of course. She'd just stopped seeing me. I was startled by the sudden epiphany that she'd been faking her orgasms all along, certainly since our child had died, and probably since the first time we'd made love.

"What?" she asked, a huge question to ask and answer at any time in our lives. Her hands never left their usual place at the small of my back.

"I'm sorry," I told her, and I was sorry, and left her naked and alone in bed while I quickly dressed and went out for a drink.

I don't drink alcohol, never have, mostly because I don't want to maintain and confirm any of my ethnic stereotypes, let alone the most prevalent one, but also because my long-lost father, a half-breed, is still missing somewhere in the bottom of a tequila bottle. I had always wondered if he was a drunk because he was Indian or because he was white or because he was both.

Personally, I like bottled water, with gas, as the Europeans like to say. If I drink enough of that bubbly water in the right environment, I can get drunk. After a long night of Perrier or Pellegrino, I can still wake up with a vicious hangover. Obviously, I place entirely too much faith in the power of metaphor.

When I went out carousing with my fellow lawyers, I ended up in fancy hotel lounges, private clubs, and golf course cigar rooms, the places where the alcoholics adhere to a rigid dress code, but after leaving my marriage bed I wanted to drink in a place free from lawyers and their dress codes, from emotional obligations and beautiful white women, even the kind of white woman who might be the tenth most attractive in any room in the world.

I chose Chuck's, a dive near the corner of Virginia and First.

I'd driven by the place any number of times, had seen the Indians who loitered outside. I assumed it was an Indian bar, one of those establishments where the clientele, through chance and design, is mostly indigenous. I'd heard about these kinds of places. They are supposed to exist in every city.

"What can I get you?" asked the bartender when I sat on the stool closest to the door. She was an Indian woman with scars on her face and knuckles. A fighter. She was a woman who had once been pretty but had grown up in a place where pretty was punished. Now, twenty pounds overweight, on her way to forty pounds more, she was most likely saving money for a complete move to a city yet to be determined.

"Hey, handsome," she asked again as I stared blankly at her oft-broken nose. I decided that her face resembled most of the furniture in the bar: dark, stained by unknown insults, and in a continual state of repair. "What the fuck would you like to drink?"

"Water," I said, surprised that the word "fuck" could sound so friendly.

"Water?"

"Yeah, water."

She filled a glass from the tap behind her and plunked it down in front of me.

"A dollar," she said.

"For tap water?"

"For space rental."

I handed her a five-dollar bill.

"Keep the change," I said and took a big drink.

"Cool. Next time, you get a clean glass," she said and waited for my reaction.

I swallowed hard, kept my dinner down, and smiled.

"I don't need to know what's coming next," I said. "I like mysteries."

"What kind of mysteries?"

"Hard-boiled. The kind where the dog gets run over, the hero gets punched in the head, and the bad guy gets eaten by sharks."

"Not me," she said. "I got too much blood in my life already. I like romances."

I wondered if she wanted to sleep with me.

"You want something else," she said, "just shout it out. I'll hear you."

She moved to the other end of the bar where an old Indian man sipped at a cup of coffee. They talked and laughed. Surprisingly jealous of their camaraderie, I turned away and looked around the bar. It was a small place, maybe fifty feet long by twenty feet wide, with one pinball machine, one pool table, and two bathrooms. I supposed the place would be packed on a weekend.

As it was, on a cold Thursday, there were only five Indians in the bar, other than the bartender, her old friend, and me.

Two obese Indian women shared a table in the back, an Indian couple danced in front of a broken jukebox, and one large and muscular Indian guy played pool by himself. In his white T-shirt, blue-jean jacket, tight jeans, and cowboy boots, he looked like Chief

Broom from *One Flew Over the Cuckoo's Nest*. I decided he could have killed me with a flick of one finger.

He looked up from his pool cue when he felt my eyes on him.

"What the fuck are you looking at?" he asked. His eyes were darker than the eight ball. I had no idea that "fuck" could be such a dangerous word.

"Nothing," I said.

Still holding his cue stick, he walked a few paces closer to me. I was afraid, very afraid.

"Nothing?" he asked. "Do I look like nothing to you?"

"No, no, that's not what I meant. I mean, I was just watching you play pool. That's all."

He stared at me, studied me like an owl might study a field mouse.

"You just keep your eyes to yourself," he said and turned back to his game.

I thought I was safe. I looked down to the bartender, who was shaking her head at me.

"Because I just, I just want to know," sputtered the big Indian. "I just want to know who the hell you think you are."

Furious, he shouted, a primal sort of noise, as he threw the cue stick against the wall. He rushed at me and lifted me by the collar.

"Who are you?" he shouted. "Who the fuck are you?"

"I'm nobody," I said, wet with fear. "Nobody. Nobody."

"Put him down, Junior," said the bartender.

Junior and I both turned to look at her. She held a pistol down by her hip, not as a threat, but more like a promise. Junior studied the bartender's face, estimated the level of her commitment, and dropped me back onto the stool.

He took a few steps back, pointed at me.

"I'm sick of little shits like you," he said. "Fucking urban Indians in your fancy fucking clothes. Fuck you. Fuck you."

I looked down and saw my denim jacket and polo shirt, the khakis and brown leather loafers. I looked like a Gap ad.

"I ever see you again," Junior said. "I'm going to dislocate your hips."

I flinched. Junior obviously had some working knowledge of human anatomy and the most effective means of creating pain therein. He saw my fear, examined its corners and edges, and decided it was large enough.

"Jesus," he said. "I don't know why I'm even talking to you. What are you going to do? You fucking wimp. You're not worth my time. Why don't you get the fuck out of here? Why don't you just get in your BMW, that's what you drive, enit? Why don't you get in your fucking BMW and get out of here before I change my mind, before I pop out one of your eyes with a fucking spoon, all right?"

I didn't drive a BMW; I drove a Saab.

"Yeah, fuck you," Junior said, thoroughly enjoying himself now. "Just drive back to your fucking mansion on Mercer Island or Edmonds or whatever white fucking neighborhood you live in. Drive back to your white wife. She's white, enit? Yeah, blond and blue-eyed, I bet. White, white. I bet her pussy hair is blond, too. Isn't it? Isn't it?"

I wanted to hate him.

"Go back to your mansion and read some fucking Teletubbies to your white fucking kids."

"What?" I asked.

"I said, go home to your white fucking kids."

"Fuck you," I said and completely surprised Junior. Good thing. He hesitated for a brief moment before he rushed at me again. His hesitation gave the bartender enough time to vault the bar and step in between Junior and me. I couldn't believe how fast she was.

She pressed the pistol tightly against Junior's forehead.

"Let it go, Junior," said the bartender.

"Why are you protecting him?" Junior asked.

"I don't give a shit about him," she said. "But I do care about you. You get into trouble again and you're going to jail forever. You know that."

Junior smiled.

"Sissy," he said to the bartender. "In another world, you and I are Romeo and Juliet."

"But we live in this world, Junior."

"Okay," said Sissy. "This is what's going to happen, Junior. You're going to walk over behind the bar, get yourself another Diet Pepsi, and mellow out. And Mr. Tap Water here is going to walk out the front door and never return. How does that sound to the both of you?"

"Make it two Pepsis," said Junior.

"Deal," said Sissy. "How about you, Polo?"

"Fuck him," I said.

Junior didn't move anything except his mouth.

"Sissy," he said. "How can you expect me to remain calm, how can you expect me to stay reasonable, when this guy so obviously wants to die?"

"I'll fight you," I said.

"What?" asked Sissy and Junior, both amazed.

"I'll fight you," I said again.

"All right, that's what I want to hear," said Junior. "Maybe you do have some balls. There's an alley out back."

"You don't want to do this," Sissy said to me.

"I'll meet you out there, Junior," I said.

Junior laughed and shook his head.

"Listen up, Tommy Hilfiger," he said. "I'm not stupid. I go out the back door and you're going to run out the front door. You don't have to make things so complicated. You want to leave, I'll let you leave. Just do it now, man."

"He's giving you a chance," Sissy said to me. "You better take it."

"No," I said. "I want to fight. I'll meet you out there. I promise."

Junior studied my eyes.

"You don't lie, do you?"

"I lie all the time," I said. "Most of the time. But I'm not lying now. I want to fight."

"All right, then, bring your best," he said and walked out the back door.

"Are you out of your mind?" Sissy asked. "Have you ever been in a fight?"

"I boxed a little in college."

"You boxed a little in college? You boxed a little in college? I can't believe this. Do you have any idea who Junior is?"

"No, why should I?"

"He's a pro."

"What? You mean, like a professional boxer?"

"No, man. A professional street fighter. No judges, no ring, no rules. The loser is the guy who don't get up."

"Isn't that illegal?"

"Illegal? Illegal? What, you think you're a lawyer now?"

"Actually, I am a lawyer."

Sissy laughed until tears ran down her face.

"Sweetheart," she said after she'd finally calmed down. "You need to leave. Please. Junior's got a wicked temper but he'll calm down soon enough. Hell, you come in a week from now and he'll probably buy you some water."

"Really?"

"No, not at all. I'm lying. You come in a week from now and Junior will break your thumbs."

She laughed again, laughed until she had to lean against the bar for support.

"Stop it," I said.

She kept laughing.

"Stop it," I shouted.

She kept laughing.

"Sweetheart," she said, trying to catch her breath. "I could kick your ass."

I shrugged off my denim jacket and marched for the back door. Sissy tried to stop me, but I pulled away from her and stepped into the alley.

Junior was surprised to see me. I felt a strange sense of pride. Without another word, I rushed at Junior, swinging at him with a wide right hook, with dreams of connecting with his jaw and knocking him out with one punch.

Deep in the heart of the heart of every Indian man's heart, he believes he is Crazy Horse.

My half-closed right hand whizzed over Junior's head as he expertly ducked under my wild punch and then rose, surely and accurately, with a left uppercut that carried with it the moon and half of every star in the universe.

▲

I woke up with my head in Sissy's lap. She was washing my face with a cold towel.

"Where are we?" I asked.

"In the storeroom," she said.

"Where is he?"

"Gone."

My face hurt.

"Am I missing any teeth?"

"No," said Sissy. "But your nose is broken."

"Are you sure?"

"Trust me."

I looked up at her. I decided she was still pretty and pretty was good enough. I grabbed her breast.

"Shit," she said and shoved me away.

I sprawled on the floor while she scrambled to her feet.

"What's wrong with you?" she asked. "What is wrong with you?"

"What do you mean? What?"

"Did you think, did you somehow get it into your crazy head that I was going to fuck you back here? On the goddamn floor in the goddamn dirt?"

I didn't know what to say.

"Jesus Christ, you really thought I was going to fuck you, didn't you?"

"Well, I mean, I just . . ."

"You just thought because I'm an ugly woman that I'd be easy."

"You're not ugly," I said.

"Do you think I'm impressed by this fighting bullshit? Do you think it makes you some kind of warrior or something?"

She could read minds.

"You did, didn't you? All of you Indian guys think you're Crazy Horse."

I struggled to my feet and walked over to the sink. I looked in the mirror and saw a bloody mess. I also noticed that one of my braids was missing.

"Junior cut it off," said Sissy. "And took it with him. You're lucky he liked you. Otherwise, he would have taken a toe. He's done that before."

I couldn't imagine what that would have meant to my life.

"Look at you," she said. "Do you think that's attractive? Is that who you want to be?"

I carefully washed my face. My nose was most certainly broken.

"I just want to know, man. What are you doing here? Why'd you come here?"

My left eye was swelling shut. I wouldn't be able to see out of it in the morning.

"I wanted to be with my people," I said.

"Your people?" asked Sissy. "Your people? We're not your people."

"We're Indians."

"Yeah, we're Indians. You, me, Junior. But we live in this world and you live in your world."

"I don't like my world."

"You pathetic bastard," she said, her eyes swelling with tears that had nothing to do with laughter. "You sorry, sorry piece of shit. Do you know how much I want to live in your world? Do you know how much Junior wants to live in your world?"

Of course I knew. For most of my life, I'd dreamed about the world where I currently resided.

"Junior and me," she said. "We have to worry about having enough to eat. What do you have to worry about? That you're lonely? That you have a mortgage? That your wife doesn't love you? Fuck you, fuck you. *I have to worry about having enough to eat.*"

She stormed out of the room, leaving me alone.

I stood there in the dark for a long time. When I walked out, the bar was nearly empty. Another bartender was cleaning glasses.

He didn't look at me. Sissy was gone. The front door was wide open. I stepped into the street and saw her sitting at the bus stop.

"I'm sorry," I said.

"Whatever."

"Can I give you a ride somewhere?"

"Do you really want to do that?" she asked.

"No," I said.

"Finally, you're being honest."

I stared at her. I wanted to say the exact right thing.

"Go home," she said. "Just go home."

I walked away, stopped halfway down the block.

"Do you have any kids?" I shouted back at her.

"Three," she said.

▲

Without changing my clothes, I crawled back into bed with Susan. Her skin was warm to the touch. The house ticked, ticked, ticked. In the morning, my pillow would be soaked with my blood.

"Where did you go?" Susan asked me.

"I was gone," I said. "But now I'm back."

Laid-Back Labor

Stephen J. Dubner
And Steven D. Levitt

How did the repetitive household tasks our parents and grandparents tried to avoid become midlife leisure activities?

The $140 Homemade Scarf

During the late 19th century, piano manufacturing was one of New York City's largest industries. Every right-minded American family, it seemed, wanted to fill its home with music. The advent of the player piano—a music-making machine that required zero talent — drove the boom even further. By the 1920s, some 300,000 pianos were being sold in the United States each year, roughly two-thirds of them player pianos.

But a pair of newer technologies, the radio and the phonograph, soon began to drive the piano into a deep disfavor that continues to this day. Last year, Americans bought only 76,966 pianos. That's a decrease of 75 percent over a period in which the population more than doubled. As much as people may love music, most of them apparently don't feel the need to make it for themselves. According to Census Bureau statistics, only 7.3 percent of American adults have played a musical instrument in the past 12 months.

Compare this with the 17.5 percent of adults who currently engage in what the Census Bureau calls "cooking for fun." Or consider that 41 percent of households have flower gardens, 25 percent raise vegetables and 13 percent grow fruit trees — even though just 1 percent of Americans live on a farm today, down from 30 percent in 1920. On a more personal note: one of the authors of this column has a sister who runs a thriving *yarn store,* while the other is married to a knitting devotee who might buy $40 worth of yarn for a single scarf and then spend 10 hours knitting it. Even if her labor is valued at only $10 an hour, the scarf costs at least $140 — or roughly $100 more than a similar machine-made scarf might cost.

Isn't it puzzling that so many middle-aged Americans are spending so much of their time and money performing menial labors when they don't have to? Just as the radio and phonograph proved to be powerful substitutes for the piano, the forces of technology and capitalism have greatly eased the burden of feeding and clothing ourselves. So what's with all the knitting, gardening and "cooking for fun"? Why do some forms of menial labor survive as hobbies while others have been killed off? (For instance, we can't think of a single person who, since the invention of the washing machine, practices "laundry for fun.")

Economists have been trying for decades to measure how much leisure time people have and how they spend it, but there has been precious little consensus. This is in part because it's hard to say what constitutes leisure and in part because measurements of leisure over the years have not been very consistent.

Economists typically separate our daily activities into three categories: market work (which produces income), home production (unpaid chores) and pure leisure. How, then, are we to categorize knitting, gardening and cooking? While preparing meals at home can certainly be much cheaper than dining out and therefore viewed as home production, what about the "cooking for fun" factor?

In an attempt to address such gray areas, the economists Valerie A. Ramey and Neville Francis classified certain home activities as labor and others as leisure. In their recent paper "A Century of Work and Leisure," they employed a 1985 time-use survey in which people ranked their enjoyment of various activities on a scale of 0 to 10. Knitting, gardening and cooking were in the middle of the scale, with a 7.7, 7.1 and 6.6, respectively. These ranked well behind the three favorite activities — sex, playing sports and fishing (which scored 9.3, 9.2 and 9.1) — but firmly ahead of paying bills, cleaning the house and, yes, doing the laundry (5.2, 4.9 and 4.8).

But here's where it gets tricky. Ramey and Francis decided that anything at or above a 7.3 is leisure, while anything below is home production, (Knitting, therefore, makes the grade as leisure; gardening and cooking do not.) This leads them to calculate that we spend less time doing market work today than we did in 1900 but *more* time in home production. Men, it seems, have contributed mightily to this upsurge: in 1920, employed men spent only two or three hours a week on home production, but they averaged 11 hours by 1965 and 16 hours by 2004.

But how many of those home-production hours are in fact leisure hours? This, it seems, is the real question here: What makes a certain activity work for one person and leisure for another?

With no disrespect toward Ramey and Francis, how about this for an alternative definition: Whether or not you're getting paid, it's work if someone else tells you to do it and leisure if you choose to do it yourself. If you are the sort of person who likes to mow his own lawn even though you can afford to pay someone to do it, consider how you'd react if your neighbor offered to pay you the going rate to mow *his* lawn. The odds are that you wouldn't accept his job offer.

And so a great many people who can afford not to perform menial labor choose to do so, because — well, why? An evolutionary biologist might say that embedded in our genes is a drive to feed and clothe ourselves and tame our surroundings. An economist, meanwhile, might argue that we respond to incentives that go well beyond the financial; and that, mercifully, we are left free to choose which tasks we want to do ourselves.

Granted, these choices may say a good bit about who we are and where we come from. One of us, for instance (the economist, who lives in Chicago), grew up comfortably in a Midwestern city and has fond memories of visiting his grandparents' small farm. This author recently bought an indoor hydroponic plant grower. It cost about $150 and to date has produced approximately 14 cherry tomatoes — which, once you factor in the cost of seeds, electricity and even a nominal wage for the labor, puts the average price of a single tomato at roughly $20.

The other one of us (the journalist, who lives in New York) grew up on a small farm and was regularly engaged in all sorts of sowing, mucking and reaping. He, therefore, has little vestigial desire to grow his own food — but he *is* happy to spend hours shopping for and preparing a special dinner for family and friends. Such dinners, even if the labor were valued at only $10 an hour, are more expensive than a commensurate takeout meal.

Maybe someday the New York guy will get to cook a meal with some of the Chicago guy's cherry tomatoes. Add in another $32 for next-day shipping, and it might become one of the most expensive meals in recent memory — and, surely, worth every penny.

Social Class and the Hidden Curriculum of Work

Jean Anyon
(From: *Journal of Education,* Vol. 162, no. 1, Fall 1980.)

Scholars in political economy and the sociology of knowledge have recently argued that public schools in complex industrial societies like our own make available different types of educational experience and curriculum knowledge to students in different social classes. Bowles and Gintis[1] for example, have argued that students in different social-class backgrounds are rewarded for classroom behaviors that correspond to personality traits allegedly rewarded in the different occupational strata—the working classes for docility and obedience, the managerial classes for initiative and personal assertiveness. Basil Bernstein, Pierre Bourdieu, and Michael W. Apple focusing on school knowledge, have argued that knowledge and skills leading to social power and regard (medical, legal, managerial) are made available to the advantaged social groups but are withheld from the working classes to whom a more "practical" curriculum is offered (manual skills, clerical knowledge). While there has been considerable argumentation of these points regarding education in England, France, and North America, there has been little or no attempt to investigate these ideas empirically in elementary or secondary schools and classrooms in this country.[3]

This article offers tentative empirical support (and qualification) of the above arguments by providing illustrative examples of differences in student *work* in classrooms in contrasting social class communities. The examples were gathered *as* part of an ethnographical[4] study of curricular, pedagogical, and pupil evaluation practices in five elementary schools. The article attempts a theoretical contribution as well and assesses student work in the light of a theoretical approach to social-class analysis. . . It will be suggested that there is a "hidden curriculum" in schoolwork that has profound implications for the theory - and consequence - of everyday activity in education. . . .

The Sample of Schools

… The social-class designation of each of the five schools will be identified, and the income, occupation, and other relevant available social characteristics of the students and their parents will be described. The first three schools are in a medium-sized city district in northern New Jersey, and the other two are in a nearby New Jersey suburb.

The first two schools I will call *working class schools.* Most of the parents have blue-collar jobs. Less than a third of the fathers are skilled, while the majority are in unskilled or semiskilled jobs. During the period of the study (1978–1979), approximately 15 percent of the fathers were unemployed. The large majority (85 percent) of the families are white. The following occupations are typical: platform, storeroom, and stockroom workers; foundry-men, pipe welders, and boilermakers; semiskilled and unskilled assembly-line operatives; gas station attendants, auto mechanics, maintenance workers, and security guards. Less than 30 percent of the women work, some part-time and some full-time, on assembly lines, in storerooms and stockrooms, as waitresses, barmaids, or sales clerks. Of the fifth-grade parents, none of the wives of the skilled workers had jobs. Approximately 15 percent of the families in each school are at or below the federal "poverty" level;[5] most of the rest of the family incomes are at or below $12,000, except some of the skilled workers whose incomes are higher. The incomes of the majority of the families in these two schools (at or below $12,000) are typical of 38.6 percent of the families in the United States.[6]

The third school is called the *middle-class school*, although because of 5 neighborhood residence patterns, the population is a mixture of several social classes. The parents' occupations can be divided into three groups: a small group of blue-collar "rich," who are skilled, well-paid workers such as printers, carpenters, plumbers, and construction workers. The second group is composed of parents in working-class and middle-class white-collar jobs: women in office jobs, technicians, supervisors in industry, and parents employed by the city (such as firemen, policemen, and several of the school's teachers). The third group is composed of occupations such as personnel directors in local firms, accountants, "middle management," and a few small capitalists (owners of shops in the area). The children of several local doctors attend this school. Most family incomes are between $13,000 and $25,000, with a few higher. This income range is typical of 38.9 percent of the families in the United States.[7]

The fourth school has a parent population that is at the upper income level of the upper middle class and is predominantly professional. This school will be called the *affluent professional school.* Typical jobs are: cardiologist, interior designer, corporate lawyer or engineer, executive in advertising or television. There are some families who are not as affluent as the majority (the family of the superintendent of the district's schools, and the one or two families in which the fathers are skilled workers). In addition, a few of the families are more affluent than the majority and can be classified in the capitalist class (a partner in a prestigious Wall Street stock brokerage firm). Approximately 90 percent of the children in this school are white. Most family incomes are between $40,000 and $80,000. This income span represents approximately 7 percent of the families in the United States.[8]

In the fifth school the majority of the families belong to the capitalist class. This school will be called the *executive elite school* because most of the fathers are top executives (for example, presidents and vice-presidents) in major United States-based multinational corporations - for example, AT&T, RCA, Citibank, American Express, U.S. Steel. A sizable group of fathers are top executives in financial firms in Wall Street. There are also a number of fathers who list their occupations as "general counsel" to a particular corporation, and these corporations are also among the large multi-nationals. Many of the mothers do volunteer work in the Junior League, Junior Fortnightly, or other service groups; some are intricately involved in town politics; and some are themselves in well-paid occupations. There are no minority children in the school. Almost all the family incomes are over $100,000 with some in the $500,000 range. The incomes in this school represent less than 1 percent of the families in the United States.[9]

Since each of the five schools is only one instance of elementary education in a particular social class context, I will not generalize beyond the sample. However, the examples of schoolwork which follow will suggest characteristics of education in each social setting that appear to have theoretical and social significance and to be worth investigation in a larger number of schools.

The Working Class Schools

In the two working-class schools, work is following the steps of a procedure. The procedure is usually mechanical, involving rote behavior and very little decision making or choice. The teachers rarely explain why the work is being assigned, how it might connect to other assignments, or what the idea is that lies behind the procedure or gives it coherence and perhaps meaning or significance. Available textbooks are not always used, and the teachers often prepare their own dittos or put work examples on the board. Most of the rules regarding work are designations of what the children are to do; the rules are steps to follow. These steps are told to the children by the teachers and are often written on the board. The children are usually told to copy the steps as notes. These notes are to be studied. Work is often evaluated not according to whether it is right or wrong but according to whether the children followed the right steps.

The following examples illustrate these points. In math, when two-digit division was introduced, the teacher in one school gave a four-minute lecture on what the terms are called (which number is the divisor, dividend, quotient, and remainder). The children were told to copy these names in their notebooks. Then the teacher told them the steps to follow to do the problems, saying, "This is how you do them." The teacher listed the steps on the board, and they appeared several days later as a chart hung in the middle of the front wall: "Divide, Multiply, Subtract, Bring Down." The children often did examples of two-digit division. When the teacher went over the examples with them, he told them what the procedure was for each problem, rarely asking them to conceptualize or explain it themselves: "Three into twenty-two is seven; do your subtraction and one is left over." During the week that two-digit division was introduced (or at any other time), the investigator did not observe any discussion of the idea of grouping involved in division, any use of manipulables, or any attempt to relate two-digit division to any other mathematical process. Nor was there any attempt to relate the steps to an actual or possible thought process of the children. The observer did not hear the terms *dividend, quotient*, and so on, used again. The math teacher in the other working-class school followed similar procedures regarding two-digit division and at one point her class seemed confused. She said, "You're confusing yourselves. You're tensing up. Remember, when you do this, it's the same steps over and over again--and that's the way division always is." Several weeks later, after a test, a group of her children "still didn't get it," and she made no attempt to explain the concept of dividing things into groups or to give them manipulables for their own investigation. Rather, she went over the steps with them again and told them that they "needed more practice."

In other areas of math, work is also carrying out often unexplained fragmented procedures. For example, one of the teachers led the children through a series of steps to make a 1-inch grid on their paper *without* telling them that they were making a 1-inch grid or that it would be used to study scale. She said, "Take your ruler. Put it across the top. Make a mark at every number. Then move your ruler down to the bottom. No, put it across the bottom. Now make a mark on top of every number. Now draw a line from..." At this point a girl said that she had a faster way to do it and the teacher said, "No, you don't; you don't even know what I'm making yet. Do it this way or it's wrong." After they had made the lines up and down and across, the teacher told them she wanted them to make a figure by connecting some dots and to measure that, using the scale of 1 inch equals 1 mile. Then they were to cut it out. She said, "Don't cut it until I check it."

In both working-class schools, work in language arts is mechanics of punctuation (commas, periods, question marks, exclamation points), capitalization, and the four kinds of sentences. One teacher explained to me, "Simple punctuation is all they'll ever use." Regarding punctuation, either a teacher or a ditto stated the rules for where, for example, to put commas. The investigator heard no classroom discussion of the aural context of punctuation (which, of course, is what gives each mark its meaning). Nor did the investigator hear any statement or inference that placing a punctuation mark could be a decision-making process, depending, for example, on one's intended meaning. Rather, the children were told to follow the rules. Language arts did not involve creative writing. There were several writing assignments throughout the year but in each instance the children were given a ditto, and they wrote answers to questions on the sheet. For example, they wrote their "autobiography" by answering such questions as "Where were you born?" "What is your favorite animal?" on a sheet entitled "All About Me."

In one of the working-class schools, the class had a science period several times a week. On the three occasions observed, the children were not called upon to set up experiments or to give explanations for facts or concepts. Rather, on each occasion the teacher told them in his own words what the book said. The children copied the teacher's sentences from the board. Each day that preceded the day they were to do a science experiment, the teacher told them to copy the directions from the book for the procedure they would carry out the next day and to study the list at home that night. The day after each experiment, the teacher went over what they had "found" (they did the experiments as a class, and each was actually a class demonstration led by the teacher). Then the teacher wrote what they "found" on the board, and the children copied that in their notebooks. Once or twice a year there are science projects. The project is chosen and assigned by the teacher from a box of 3-by-5-inch cards. On the card the teacher has written the question to be answered, the books to use, and how much to write. Explaining the cards to the observer, the teacher said, "It tells them exactly what to do, or they couldn't do it."

Social studies in the working-class schools is also largely mechanical, rote work that was given little explanation or connection to larger contexts. In one school, for example, although there was a book available, social studies work was to copy the teacher's notes from the board. Several times a week for a period of several months the children copied these notes. The fifth grades in the district were to study United States history. The teacher used a booklet she had purchased called "The Fabulous Fifty States." Each day she put information from the booklet in outline form on the board and the children copied it. The type of information did not vary: the name of the state, its abbreviation, state capital, nickname of the state, its main products, main business, and a "Fabulous Fact" ("Idaho grew twenty-seven billion potatoes in one year. That's enough potatoes for each man, woman, and...") As the children finished copying the sentences, the teacher erased them and wrote more. Children would occasionally go to the front to pull down the wall map in order to locate the states they were copying, and the teacher did not dissuade them. But the observer never saw her refer to the map; nor did the observer ever hear her make other than perfunctory remarks concerning the information the children were copying. Occasionally the children colored in a ditto and cut it out to make a stand-up figure (representing, for example, a man roping a cow in the Southwest). These were referred to by the teacher as their social studies "projects."

Rote behavior was often called for in classroom work. When going over 15 math and language art skills sheets, for example, as the teacher asked for the answer to each problem, he fired the questions rapidly, staccato, and the scene reminded the observer of a sergeant drilling recruits: above all, the questions demanded that you stay at attention: "The next one? What do I put here? . . . Here? Give us the next." Or "How many commas in this sentence? Where do I put them . . . The next one?"

The four fifth grade teachers observed in the working-class schools attempted to control classroom time and space by making decisions without consulting the children and without explaining the basis for their decisions. The teacher's control thus often seemed capricious. Teachers, for instance, very often ignored the bells to switch classes - deciding among themselves to keep the children after the period was officially over to continue with the work or for disciplinary reasons or so they (the teachers) could stand in the hall and talk. There were no clocks in the rooms in either school, and the children often asked, "What period is this?" "When do we go to gym?" The children had no access to materials. These were handed out by teachers and closely guarded. Things in the room "belonged" to the teacher: "Bob, bring me my garbage can." The teachers continually gave the children orders. Only three times did the investigator hear a teacher in either working-class school preface a directive with an unsarcastic "please," or "let's" or "would you." Instead, the teachers said, "Shut up," "Shut your mouth," "Open your books," "Throw your gum away-if you want to rot your teeth, do it on your own time." Teachers made every effort to control the movement of the children, and often shouted, "'Why are you out of your seat??!!" If the children got permission to leave the room, they had to take a written pass with the date and time. . . .

Middle-Class School

In the middle-class school, work is getting the right answer. If one accumulates enough right answers, one gets a good grade. One must follow the directions in order to get the right answers, but the directions often call for some figuring, some choice, some decision making. For example, the children must often figure out by themselves what the directions ask them to do and how to get the answer: what do you do first, second, and perhaps third? Answers are usually found in books or by listening to the teacher. Answers are usually words, sentences, numbers, or facts and dates; one writes them on paper, and one should be neat. Answers must be given in the right order, and one cannot make them up.

The following activities are illustrative. Math involves some choice: one may do two-digit division the long way or the short way, and there are some math problems that can be done "in your head." When the teacher explains how to do two-digit division, there is recognition that a cognitive process is involved; she gives you several ways and says, "I want to make sure you understand what you're doing-so you get it right"; and, when they go over the homework, she asks the *children* to tell how they did the problem and what answer they got.

In social studies the daily work is to read the assigned pages in the textbook and to answer the teacher's questions. The questions are almost always designed to check on whether the students have read the assignment and understood it: who did so-and-so; what happened after that; when did it happen, where, and sometimes, why did it happen? The answers are in the book and in one's understanding of the book; the teacher's hints when one doesn't know the answers are to "read it again" or to look at the picture or at the rest of the paragraph. One is to search for the answer in the "context," in what is given.

Language arts is "simple grammar, what they need for everyday life." The language arts teacher says, "They should learn to speak properly, to write business letters and thank-you letters, and to understand what nouns and verbs and simple subjects are." Here, as well, actual work is to choose the right answers, to understand what is given. The teacher often says, "Please read the next sentence and then I'll question you about it." One teacher said in some exasperation to a boy who was fooling around in class, "If you don't know the answers to the questions I ask, then you can't stay in this *class!* [pause] You *never* know the answers to the questions I ask, and it's not fair to me-and certainly not to you!"

Most lessons are based on the textbook. This does not involve a critical perspective on what is given there. For example, a critical perspective in social studies is perceived as dangerous by these teachers because it may lead to controversial topics; the parents might complain. The children, however, are often curious especially in social studies. Their questions are tolerated and usually answered perfunctorily. But after a few minutes the teacher will say, "All right, we're not going any farther. Please open your social studies workbook." While the teachers spend a lot of time explaining and expanding on what the textbooks say, there is little attempt to analyze how or why things happen, or to give thought to how pieces of a culture, or, say, a system of numbers or elements of a language fit together or can be analyzed. What has happened in the past and what exists now may not be equitable or fair, but (shrug) that is the way things are and one does not confront such matters in school. For example, in social studies after a child is called on to read a passage about the pilgrims, the teacher summarizes the paragraph and then says, "So you can see how strict they were about everything." A child asks, "Why?" "Well, because they felt that if you weren't busy you'd get into trouble." Another child asks, "Is it true that they burned women at the stake?" The teacher says, "Yes, if a woman did anything strange, they hanged them. [*sic*] What would a woman do, do you think, to make them burn them? [*sic*] See if you can come up with better answers than my other [social studies] class." Several children offer suggestions, to which the teacher nods but does not comment. Then she says, "Okay, good," and calls on the next child to read.

Work tasks do not usually request creativity. Serious attention is rarely given in school work on *how* the children develop or express their own feelings and ideas, either linguistically or in graphic form. On the occasions when creativity or self-expression is requested, it is peripheral to the main activity or it is "enriched" or "for fun." During a lesson on what similes are, for example, the teacher explains what they are, puts several on the board, gives some other examples herself, and then asks the children if they can "make some up." She calls on three children who give similes, two of which are actually in the book they have open before them. The teacher does not comment on this and then asks several others to choose similes from the list of phrases in the book. Several do so correctly, and she says, "Oh good! You're picking them out! See how good we are?" Their homework is to pick out the rest of the similes from the list.

Creativity is not often requested in social studies and science projects, either. Social studies projects, for example, are given with directions to "find information on your topic" and write it up. The children are not supposed to copy but to "put it in your own words." Although a number of the projects subsequently went beyond the teacher's direction to find information and had quite expressive covers and inside illustrations, the teacher's evaluative comments had to do with the amount of information, whether they had "copied," and if their work was neat.

The style of control of the three fifth-grade teachers observed in this school varied from somewhat easygoing to strict, but in contrast to the working-class schools, the teachers' decisions were usually based on external rules and regulations--for example, on criteria that were known or available to the children. Thus, the teachers always honor the bells for changing classes, and they usually evaluate children's work by what is in the textbooks and answer booklets.

There is little excitement in schoolwork for the children, and the assignments are perceived as having little to do with their interests and feelings. As one child said, what you do is "store facts up in your head like cold storage - until you need it later for a test or your job." Thus, doing well is important because there are thought to be *other* likely rewards: a good job or college.[10]

Affluent Professional School

In the affluent professional school, work is creative activity carried out independently. The students are continually asked to express and apply ideas and concepts. Work involves individual thought and expressiveness, expansion and illustration of ideas, and choice of appropriate method and material. (The class is not considered an open classroom, and the principal explained that because of the large number of discipline problems in the fifth grade this year they did not departmentalize. The teacher who agreed to take part in the study said she is "more structured this year than she usually is.) The products of work in this class are often written stories, editorials and essays, or representations of ideas in mural, graph, or craft form. The products of work should not be like anybody else's and should show individuality. They should exhibit good design, and (this is important) they must also fit empirical reality. The relatively few rules to be followed regarding work are usually criteria for, or limits on, individual activity. One's product is usually evaluated for the quality of its expression and for the appropriateness of its conception to the task. In many cases, one's own satisfaction with the product is an important criterion for its evaluation. When right answers are called for, as in commercial materials like SRA (Science Research Associates) and math, it is important that the children decide on an answer as a result of thinking about the idea involved in what they're being asked to do. Teacher's hints are to "think about it some more."

The following activities are illustrative. The class takes home a sheet requesting each child's parents to fill in the number of cars they have, the number of television sets, refrigerators, games, or rooms in the house, and so on. Each child is to figure the average number of a type of possession owned by the fifth grade. Each child must compile the "data" from all the sheets. A calculator is available in the classroom to do the mechanics of finding the average. Some children decide to send sheets to the fourth-grade families for comparison. Their work should be "verified" by a classmate before it is handed in.

Each child and his or her family has made a geoboard. The teacher asks the class to get their geoboards from the side cabinet, to take a handful of rubber bands, and then to listen to what she would like them to do. She says, "I would like you to design a figure and then find the perimeter and area. When you have it, check with your neighbor. After you've done that, please transfer it to graph paper and tomorrow I'll ask you to make up a question about it for someone. When you hand it in, please let me know whose it is and who verified it. Then I have something else for you to do that's really fun. [pause] Find the average number of chocolate chips in three cookies. I'll give you three cookies, and you'll have to *eat* your way through, I'm afraid!" Then she goes around the room and gives help, suggestions, praise, and admonitions that they are getting noisy. They work sitting, or standing up at their desks, at benches in the back, or on the floor. A child hands the teacher his paper and she comments, "I'm not accepting this paper. Do a better design." To another child she says, "That's fantastic! But you'll never find the area. Why don't you draw a figure inside [the big one] and subtract to get the area?"

The school district requires the fifth grade to study ancient civilization (in particular, Egypt, Athens, and Sumer). In this classroom, the emphasis is on illustrating and re-creating the culture of the people of ancient times. The following are typical activities: the children made an 8mm film on Egypt, which one of the parents edited. A girl in the class wrote the script, and the class acted it out. They put the sound on themselves. They read stories of those days. They wrote essays and stories depicting the lives of the people and the societal and occupational divisions. They chose from a list of projects, all of which involved graphical presentations of ideas: for example. "Make a mural depicting the division of labor in Egyptian society."

Each wrote and exchanged a letter in hieroglyphics with a fifth grader in another class, and they also exchanged stories they wrote in cuneiform. They made a scroll and singed the edges so it looked authentic. They each chose an occupation and made an Egyptian plaque representing that occupation, simulating the appropriate Egyptian design. They carved their design on a cylinder of wax, pressed the wax into clay, and then baked the clay. Although one girl did not choose an occupation but carved instead a series of gods and slaves, the teacher said, "That's all right, Amber, it's beautiful." As they were working the teacher said, "Don't cut into your clay until you're satisfied with your design."

Social studies also involves almost daily presentation by the children of some event from the news. The teacher's questions ask the children to expand what they say, to give more details, and to be more specific. Occasionally she adds some remarks to help them see connections between events.

The emphasis on expressing and illustrating ideas in social studies is accompanied in language arts by an emphasis on creative writing. Each child wrote a rebus story for a first grader whom they had interviewed to see what kind of story the child liked best. They wrote editorials on pending decisions by the school board and radio plays, some of which were read over the school intercom from the office and one of which was performed in the auditorium. There is no language arts textbook because, the teacher said, "The principal wants us to be creative." There is not much grammar, but there is punctuation. One morning when the observer arrived, the class was doing a punctuation ditto. The teacher later apologized for using the ditto. "It's just for review," she said. "I don't teach punctuation that way. We use their language." The ditto had three unambiguous rules for where to put commas in a sentence. As the teacher was going around to help the children with the ditto, she repeated several times, "where you put commas depends on how you say the sentence; it depends on the situation and what you want to say. Several weeks later the observer saw another punctuation activity. The teacher had printed a five-paragraph story on an oak tag and then cut it into phrases. She read the whole story to the class from the book, then passed out the phrases. The group had to decide how the phrases could best be put together again. (They arranged the phrases on the floor.) The point was not to replicate the story, although that was not irrelevant, but to "decide what you think the best way is." Punctuation marks on cardboard pieces were then handed out, and the children discussed and then decided what mark was best at each place they thought one was needed. At the end of each paragraph the teacher asked, "Are you satisfied with the way the paragraphs are now? Read it to yourself and see how it sounds." Then she read the original story again, and they compared the two.

Describing her goals in science to the investigator, the teacher said, "We use ESS (Elementary Science Study). It's very good because it gives a hands-on experience--so they can make *sense* out of it. It doesn't matter whether it [what they find] is right or wrong. I bring them together and there's value in discussing their ideas."

The products of work in this class are often highly valued by the children and the teacher. In fact, this was the only school in which the investigator was not allowed to take original pieces of the children's work for her files. If the work was small enough, however, and was on paper, the investigator could duplicate it on the copying machine in the office.

The teacher's attempt to control the class involves constant negotiation. She does not give direct orders unless she is angry because the children have been too noisy. Normally, she tries to get them to foresee the consequences of their actions and to decide accordingly. For example, lining them up to go see a play written by the sixth graders, she says, "I presume you're lined up by someone with whom you want to sit. I hope you're lined up by someone you won't get in trouble with.". . .

One of the few rules governing the children's movement is that no more than three children may be out of the room at once. There is a school rule that anyone can go to the library at any time to get a book. In the fifth grade I observed, they sign their name on the chalkboard and leave. There are no passes. Finally, the children have a fair amount of officially sanctioned say over what happens in the class. For example, they often negotiate what work is to be done. If the teacher wants to move on to the next subject, but the children say they are not ready, they want to work on their present projects some *more*, she very often lets them do it.

Executive Elite School

In the executive elite school, work is developing one's analytical intellectual powers. Children are continually asked to reason through a problem, to produce intellectual products that are both logically sound and of top academic quality. A primary goal of thought is to conceptualize rules by which elements may fit together in systems and then to apply these rules in solving a problem. Schoolwork helps one to achieve, to excel, to prepare for life.

The following are illustrative. The math teacher teaches area and perimeter by having the children derive formulas for each. First she helps them, through discussion at the board, to arrive at A = W X L as a formula (not *the* formula) for area. After discussing several, she says, "Can anyone make up a formula for perimeter? Can you figure that out yourselves? [pause] Knowing what we know, can we think of a formula?" She works out three children's suggestions at the board, saying to two, "Yes, that's a good one," and then asks the class if they can think of any more. No one volunteers. To prod them, she says, "If you use rules and good reasoning, you get many ways. Chris, can you think up a formula?"

She discusses two-digit division with the children as a decision-making process. Presenting a new type of problem to them, she asks, "What's the *first* decision you'd make if presented with this kind of example? What is the first thing you'd *think?* Craig?" Craig says, "To find my first partial quotient." She responds, "Yes, that would be your first decision. How would you do that?" Craig explains, and then the teacher says, "OK, we'll see how that works for you." The class tries his way. Subsequently, she comments on the merits and shortcomings of several other children's decisions. Later, she tells the investigator that her goals in math are to develop their reasoning and mathematical thinking and that, unfortunately, "there's no time for manipulables."

While right answers are important in math, they are not "given" by the book or by the teacher but may be challenged by the children. Going over some problems in late September the teacher says, "Raise your hand if you do not agree." A child says, "I don't agree with sixty-four." The teacher responds, "OK, there's a question about sixty-four. [to class] Please check it. Owen, they're disagreeing with you. Kristen, they're checking yours." The teacher emphasized this repeatedly during September and October with statements like "Don't be afraid to say you disagree. In the last [math] class, somebody disagreed, and they were right. Before you disagree, check yours, and if you still think we're wrong, then we'll check it out." By Thanksgiving, the children did not often speak in terms of right and wrong math problems but of whether they agreed with the answer that had been given.

There are complicated math mimeos with many word problems. Whenever they go over the examples, they discuss how each child has set up the problem. The children must explain it precisely. On one occasion the teacher said, "I'm more--just as interested in *how* you set up the problem as in what answer you find. If you set up a problem in a good way, the answer is *easy* to find."

Social studies work is most often reading and discussion of concepts and independent research. There are only occasional artistic, expressive, or illustrative projects. Ancient Athens and Sumer are, rather, societies to analyze. The following questions are typical of those that guide the children's independent research. "What mistakes did Pericles make after the war?" "What mistakes did the citizens of Athens make?" "What are the elements of a civilization?" "How did Greece build an economic empire?" "Compare the way Athens chose its leaders with the way we choose ours." Occasionally the children are asked to make up sample questions for their social studies tests. On an occasion when the investigator was present, the social studies teacher rejected a child's question by saying, "That's just fact. If I asked you that question on a test, you'd complain it was just memory! Good questions ask for concepts."

In social studies--but also in reading, science, and health--the teachers initiate classroom discussions of current social issues and problems. These discussions occurred on every one of the investigator's visits, and a teacher told me, "These children's opinions are important - it's important that they learn to reason things through." The classroom discussions always struck the observer as quite realistic and analytical, dealing with concrete social issues like the following: "Why do workers strike?" "Is that right or wrong?" "Why do we have inflation, and what can be done to stop it?" "Why do companies put chemicals in food when the natural ingredients are available?" and so on. Usually the children did not have to be prodded to give their opinions. In fact, their statements and the interchanges between them struck the observer as quite sophisticated conceptually and verbally, and well-informed. Occasionally the teachers would prod with statements such as, "Even if you don't know [the answers], if you think logically about it, you can figure it out." And "I'm asking you [these] questions to help you think this through."

Language arts emphasizes language as a complex system, one that should be mastered. The children are asked to diagram sentences of complex grammatical construction, to memorize irregular verb conjugations (he lay, he has lain, and so on ...), and to use the proper participles, conjunctions, and interjections in their speech. The teacher (the same one who teaches social studies) told them, "It is not enough to get these right on tests; you must use what you learn [in grammar classes] in your written and oral work. I will grade you on that."

Most writing assignments are either research reports and essays for social studies or experiment analyses and write-ups for science. There is only an occasional story or other "creative writing" assignment. On the occasion observed by the investigator (the writing of a Halloween story), the points the teacher stressed in preparing the children to write involved the structural aspects of a story rather than the expression of feelings or other ideas. The teacher showed them a filmstrip, "The Seven Parts of a Story," and lectured them on plot development, mood setting, character development, consistency, and the use of a logical or appropriate ending. The stories they subsequently wrote were, in fact, well-structured, but many were also personal and expressive. The teacher's evaluative comments, however, did not refer to the expressiveness or artistry but were all directed toward whether they had "developed" the story well.

Language arts work also involved a large amount of practice in presentation of the self and in managing situations where the child was expected to be in charge. For example, there was a series of assignments in which each child had to be a "student teacher." The child had to plan a lesson in grammar, outlining, punctuation, or other language arts topic and explain the concept to the class. Each child was to prepare a worksheet or game and a homework assignment as well. After each presentation, the teacher and other children gave a critical appraisal of the "student teacher's" performance. Their criteria were: whether the student spoke clearly, whether the lesson was interesting, whether the student made any mistakes, and whether he or she kept control of the class. On an occasion when a child did not maintain control, the teacher said,

"When you're up there, you have authority and you have to use it. I'll back you up."

The executive elite school is the only school where bells do not demarcate the periods of time. The two fifth-grade teachers were very strict about changing classes on schedule, however, as specific plans for each session had been made. The teachers attempted to keep tight control over the children during lessons, and the children were sometimes flippant, boisterous, and occasionally rude. However, the children may be brought into line by reminding them that "It is up to you." "You must control yourself," "you are responsible for your work," you must "set your own priorities." One teacher told a child, "You are the only driver of your car-and only you can regulate your speed." A new teacher complained to the observer that she had thought "these children" would have more control.

While strict attention to the lesson at hand is required, the teachers make relatively little attempt to regulate the movement of the children at other times. For example, except for the kindergartners the children in this school do not have to wait for the bell to ring in the morning; they may go to their classroom when they arrive at school. Fifth graders often came early to read, to finish work, or to catch up. After the first two months of school, the fifth-grade teachers did not line the children up to change classes or to go to gym, and so on, but, when the children were ready and quiet, they were told they could go--sometimes without the teachers.

In the classroom, the children could get materials when they needed them and took what they needed from closets and from the teacher's desk. They were in charge of the office at lunchtime. During class they did not have to sign out or ask permission to leave the room; they just got up and left. Because of the pressure to get work done, however, they did not leave the room very often. The teachers were very polite to the children, and the investigator heard no sarcasm, no nasty remarks, and few direct orders. The teachers never called the children "honey" or "dear" but always called them by name. The teachers were expected to be available before school, after school, and for part of their lunchtime to provide extra help if needed.

The foregoing analysis of differences in schoolwork in contrasting social class contexts suggests the following conclusion: the "hidden curriculum" of schoolwork is tacit preparation for relating to the process of production in a particular way. Differing curricular, pedagogical, and pupil evaluation practices emphasize different cognitive and behavioral skills in each social setting and thus contribute to the development in the children of certain potential relationships to physical and symbolic capital,[11] to authority, and to the process of work. School experience, in the sample of schools discussed here, differed qualitatively by social class. These differences may not only contribute to the development in the children in each social class of certain types of economically significant relationships and not others but would thereby help to reproduce this system of relations in society. In the contribution to the reproduction of unequal social relations lies a theoretical meaning and social consequence of classroom practice.

The identification of different emphases in classrooms in a sample of contrasting social class contexts implies that further research should be conducted in a large number of schools to investigate the types of work tasks and interactions in each to see if they differ in the ways discussed here and to see if similar potential relationships are uncovered. Such research could have as a product the further elucidation of complex but not readily apparent connections between everyday activity in schools and classrooms and the unequal structure of economic relationships in which we work and live.

Notes

1. S. Bowles and H. Gintes, *Schooling in Capitalist America: Educational Reform and the Contradictions of Economic Life* (New York: Basic Books, 1976). [Author's note]
2. B. Bernstein, *Class, Codes and Control, Vol. 3. Towards a Theory of Educational Transmission*, 2d ed. (London: Routledge &

Kegan Paul, 1977); P. Bourdieu and J. Passeron, *Reproduction in Education, Society and Culture* (Beverly Hills, Calif.: Sage, 1977); M. W. Apple, *Ideology and Curriculum* (Boston: Routledge Kegan Paul, 1979). [Author's note]

3. But see, in a related vein, M.W. Apple and N. King, "What Do Schools Teach? "*Curriculum Inquiry* 6 (1977); 341–58; R. C. Rist, *The Urban School: A Factory for Failure* (Cambridge, Mass.: MIT Press, 1973). [Author's note]
4. *ethnographical*: Based on an anthropological study of cultures or subcultures-the "cultures" in this case being the five schools being observed.
5. The U.S. Bureau of the Census defines *poverty* for a nonfarm family of four as a yearly income of $6,191 a year or less. U.S. Bureau of the Census, *Statistical Abstract of the United States: 1978* (Washington, D. C.: U.S. Government Printing Office, 1978), p. 465 .table 754. [Author's note]
6. U.S. Bureau of the Census, "Money Income in 1977 of Families and Persons in the United States," *Current Population Reports* Series P-60, no. 118 (Washington, D.C.: U.S. Government Printing Office, 1978), p. 2 ,table A. [Author's note]
7. Ibid. [Author's note]
8. This figure is an estimate. According to the Bureau of the Census, only 2.6 percent of families in United States have money income of $50,000 or over. U.S. Bureau of the Census, *Current Population Reports* Series P-60. For figures on income at these higher levels, see J.D. Smith and S. Franklin, "The Concentration of Personal Wealth, 1922–1969," *American Economic Review* 64 (1974): 162–67. [Author's note]
9. Smith and Franklin, "The Concentration of Personal Wealth." [Author's note]
10. A dominant feeling expressed directly and indirectly by teachers in this school, was boredom with their work. They did, however, in contrast to the working-class schools,

almost always carry out lessons during class times. [Author's note]

11. *physical and symbolic capital*: Elsewhere Anyon defines *capital* as "property that is used to produce profit, interest, or rent": she defines *symbolic capital* as the knowledge and skills that "may yield social and cultural power."

Class in America: Myths and Realities (2000)

Gregory Mantsios

People in the United States don't like to talk about class. Or so it would seem. We don't speak about class privileges, or class oppression, or the class nature of society. These terms are not part of our everyday vocabulary, and in most circles they are associated with the language of the rhetorical fringe. Unlike people in most other parts of the world, we shrink from using words that classify along economic lines or that point to class distinctions: phrases like "working class," "upper class," and "ruling class" are rarely uttered by Americans.

For the most part, avoidance of class-laden vocabulary crosses class boundaries. There are few among the poor who speak of themselves as lower class; instead, they refer to their race, ethnic group, or geographic location. Workers are more likely to identify with their employer, industry, or occupational group than with other workers, or with the working class.[1]

Neither are those at the other end of the economic spectrum likely to use the word "class." In her study of thirty-eight wealthy and socially prominent women, Susan Ostrander asked participants if they considered themselves members of the upper class. One participant responded, "I hate to use the word 'class.' We are responsible, fortunate people, old families, the people who have something." Another said, "I hate [the term] upper class. It is so

[1] See Jay MacLead, *Ain't No Makin' It: Aspirations and Attainment in a Lower-Income Neighborhood* (Boulder, Colo.: Westview Press, 1995); Benjamin DeMott, *The Imperial Middle* (New York: Morrow, 1990); Ira Katznelson, *City Trenches: Urban Politics and Patterning of class in the United States* (New York: Pantheon Books, 1981); Charles W. Tucker, "A Comparative Analysis of Subjective Social Class: 1945–1963," *Social Forces*, no. 46, June 1968, pp. 508–514; Robert Nisbet, "The Decline and Fall of Social Class," *Pacific Sociological Review*, vol. 2, Spring 1959, pp, 11–17; and Oscar Glantz, "Class Consciousness and Political Solidarity," *American Sociological Review*, vol. 23, August 1958, pp. 375–382.

non-upper class to use it. I just call it 'all of us,' those who are wellborn."[2]

It is not that Americans, rich or poor, aren't keenly aware of class differences—those quoted above obviously are; it is that class is not in the domain of public discourse. Class is not discussed or debated in public because class identity has been stripped from popular culture. The institutions that shape mass culture and define the parameters of public debate have avoided class issues. In politics, in primary and secondary education, and in the mass media, formulating issues in terms of class is unacceptable, perhaps even un-American.

There are, however, two notable exceptions to this phenomenon. First, it is acceptable in the United States to talk about "the middle class." Interestingly enough, such references appear to be acceptable precisely because they mute class differences. References to the middle class by politicians, for example, are designed to encompass and attract the broadest possible constituency. Not only do references to the middle class gloss over differences, but these references also avoid any suggestion of conflict or exploitation.

This leads us to the second exception to the class-avoidance phenomenon. We are, on occasion, presented with glimpses of the upper class and the lower class (the language used is "the wealthy" and "the poor"). In the media, these presentations are designed to satisfy some real or imagined voyeuristic need of "the ordinary person." As curiosities, the ground-level view of street life and the inside look at the rich and the famous serve as unique models, one to avoid and one to aspire to. In either case, the two models are presented without causal relation to each other: one is not rich because the other is poor. Similarly, when social commentators or liberal politicians draw attention to the plight of the poor, they do

---

[2] Susan Ostander, "Upper-Class women: Class Consciousness as Conduct and Meaning," in G. William Domhoff, *Power Structure Research*, Beverly Hills, CA, Sage Productions, 1980, pp. 78–79. Also see, Stephen Birmingham, *America's Secret Aristocracy*, Boston, Little Brown, 1987.

so in a manner that obscures the class structure and denies class exploitation. Wealth and poverty are viewed as one of several natural and inevitable states of being: differences are only differences. One may even say differences are the American way, a reflection of American social diversity.

We are left with one of two possibilities: either talking about class and recognizing class distinctions are not relevant to U.S. society, or we mistakenly hold a set of beliefs that obscure the reality of class differences and their impact on people's lives.

Let us look at four common, albeit contradictory, beliefs about the United States.

Myth 1: The United States is fundamentally a classless society. Class distinctions are largely irrelevant today, and whatever differences do exist in economic standing are, for the most part, insignificant. Rich or poor, we are all equal in the eyes of the law, and such basic needs as health care and education are provided to all regardless of economic standing.

Myth 2: We are, essentially, a middle-class nation. Despite some variations in economic status, most Americans have achieved relative affluence in what is widely recognized as a consumer society.

Myth 3: We are all getting richer. The American public as a whole is steadily moving up the economic ladder, and each generation propels itself to greater economic well-being. Despite some fluctuations, the U.S. position in the global economy has brought previously unknown prosperity to most, if not all, North Americans.

Myth 4: Everyone has an equal chance to succeed. Success in the United States requires no more than hard work, sacrifice, and perseverance: "In America, anyone can become a millionaire; it's just a matter of being in the right place at the right time."

In trying to assess the legitimacy of these beliefs, we want to ask several important questions. Are there significant class differences among Americans? If these differences do exist, are they getting bigger or smaller, and do these differences have a significant impact on the way we live? Finally, does everyone in the United States really have an equal opportunity to succeed?

The Economic Spectrum

We will begin by looking at differences. An examination of available data reveals that variations in economic well-being are in fact immense. Consider the following:

* The wealthiest 20 percent of the American population holds 85 percent of the total household wealth in the country. That is, they own nearly seven-eighths of all the consumer durables (such as houses, cars, and stereos) and financial assets (such as stocks, bonds, property, and savings accounts).[3]
* Approximately 144,000 Americans, or 0.1 percent of the adult working population, earn more than $1 million annually, with many of these individuals earning over $10 million and some earning over $100 million annually. It would take the average American, earning $34,000 per year, more than 65 lifetimes to earn $100 million.[4]

Affluence and prosperity are clearly alive and well in certain segments of the United States population. However, this abundance is in contrast to the poverty and despair that is also prevalent in the United States. At the other end of the spectrum:

* A total of 13 percent of the American population—that is, one of every eight[5]—live below the government's official poverty line (calculated in 1999 at $8,500 for an individual and $17,028 for a family of four).[6] These

[3] Jared Bernstein, Lawrence Hishel, and John Schmitt, *The State of Working America: 1998–99*, ILR Press, Cornell University Press, 1998, p. 262.

[4] The number of individuals filing tax returns showing a gross adjusted income of $1 million or more in 1997 was 144, 459 (Internal Revenue Service, *Statistics of Income Bulletin, Summer 1999*, Washington, DC, 1999, p. 268). The total civilian employment in 1997 was 129,588,000 (U.S. Bureau of Labor Statistics, 1997).

[5] Joseph Dalaker, U.S. Bureau of the Census, "Current Population Reports," series pp. 60–207, *Poverty in the United States: 1998*. Washington, DC, U.S. Government Printing Office, 1999, p. v.

[6] "Preliminary Estimates of Weighted Average Poverty Thresholds in 1999," Department of Commerce, Bureau of Census, 2000.

poor include a significant number of homeless people—approximately two million Americans.

* Approximately one out of every five children in the United States under the age of eighteen lives in poverty.[7]

The contrast between rich and poor is sharp, and with nearly one-third of the American population living at one extreme or the other, it is difficult to argue that we live in a classless society. The income gap between rich and poor in the United States (measured as the percentage of total income held by the wealthiest 20 percent of the population versus the poorest 20 percent) is approximately 11 to 1, one of the highest ratios in the industrialized world. The ratio in Japan and Germany, by contrast, is 4 to 1.[8]

Reality 1: There are enormous differences in the economic status of American citizens. A sizable proportion of the U.S. population occupies opposite ends of the economic spectrum.

In the middle range of the economic spectrum:

* Sixty percent of the American population hold less than 4 percent of the nation's wealth.[9]
* While the real income of the top 1 percent of U.S. families skyrocketed by 89 percent during the economic growth period from 1977 to 1995, the income of the middle fifth of the population actually declined by 13 percent during that same period. [10] This led one prominent economist to describe economic growth as a "spectator sport for the majority of American families."[11]

---

[7] Ibid, p. v.

[8] See The Center on Budget and Policy Priorities, Economic Policy Institute, "Pulling Apart: State-by-State Analysis of Income Trends," January 2000, fact sheet; U.S. Department of Commerce, "Current Population Reports: Consumer Income," Washington, DC, 1993; The World Bank, "World Development Report: 1992," Washington, DC, International Bank for Reconstruction and Development, 1992; The World Bank "World Development Report 1999/2000," pp. 238–239.

[9] Jared Bernstein et al., op. cit., p. 262.

[10] Derived from Ibid, p. 95.

[11] Alan Blinder, quoted by Paul Krugman, in "Disparity and Despair," *U.S. News and World Report,* March 23, 1992, p. 54.

The level of inequality is sometimes difficult to comprehend fully with dollar figures and percentages. To help his students visualize the distribution of income, the well-known economist Paul Samuelson asked them to picture an income pyramid made of children's blocks, with each layer of blocks representing $1,000. If we were to construct Samuelson's pyramid today, the peak of the pyramid would be much higher than the Eiffel Tower, yet almost all of us would be within six feet of the ground.[12] In other words, the distribution of income is heavily skewed; a small minority of families take the lion's share of national income, and the remaining income is distributed among the vast majority of middle-income and low-income families. Keep in mind that Samuelson's pyramid represents the distribution of income, not wealth. The distribution of wealth is skewed even further.

Reality 2: The middle class in the United States holds a very small share of the nation's wealth, and its income—in constant dollars—is declining.

Lottery millionaires and celebrity salaries notwithstanding, evidence suggests that the level of inequality in the United States is getting higher. Census data show the gap between the rich and the poor to be the widest since the government began collecting information in 1947. Furthermore, the percentage of households earning between $25,000 and $75,000 has been falling steadily since 1969, while the percentage of households earning less than $25,000 has actually increased between 1989 and 1997.[13] And economic polarization is expected to increase over the next several decades.[14]

Reality 3: The middle class is shrinking in size, and the gap between rich and poor is bigger than it has ever been.

[12] Paul Samuelson, *Economics,* 10th ed., New York, McGraw-Hill, 1976, p. 84.

[13] "Money Income of Households, Families, and Persons in the United States: 1992," U.S. Department of Commerce, "Current Population Reports: Consumer Income" series P60–184, Washington, DC, 1993, p. B6. Also, Jared Bernstein et al., op, cit., p. 61.

[14] Paul Blumberg, *Inequality in an Age of Decline*, New York, Oxford University Press, 1980.

At last count, nearly 35 million Americans across the nation lived in unrelenting poverty.[15] Yet, as political scientist Michael Harrington once commented, "America has the best dressed poverty the world has ever known."[16] Clothing disguises much of the poverty in the United States, and this may explain, in part, its middle-class image. With increased mass marketing of "designer" clothing and with shifts in the nation's economy from blue-collar (and often better-paying) manufacturing jobs to white-collar and pink-collar jobs in the service sector, it is becoming increasingly difficult to distinguish class differences based on appearance.[17]

Beneath the surface, there is another reality. Let us look at some "typical" and not-so-typical lifestyles.

	American Profile No. 1
Name:	Harold S. Browning
Father:	manufacturer, industrialist
Mother:	prominent social figure in the community
Principal child-rearer:	governess
Primary education:	an exclusive private school on Manhattan's Upper East Side *Note*: a small well-respected primary school where teachers and administrators have a reputation for nurturing student creativity and for providing the finest educational preparation *Ambition:* "to become President"
Supplemental tutoring:	tutors in French and mathematics
Summer camp:	sleep-away camp in northern Connecticut

[15] U.S. Census Bureau, 1999, op. cit., p. v.

[16] Michael Harrington, *The Other America*, New York, Macmillan, 1962, p. 12–13.

[17] Stuart Ewen and Elizabeth Ewen, *Channels of Desire: Mass Images and the Shaping of American Consciousness,* New York, McGraw-Hill, 1982.

	Note: camp provides instruction in the creative arts, athletics, and the natural sciences
Secondary education:	a prestigious preparatory school in Westchester County *Note:* classmates included the sons of ambassadors, doctors, attorneys, television personalities, and well-known business leaders *After-school activities:* private riding lessons *Ambition:* "to take over my father's business" *High-school graduation gift:* BMW
Family activities:	theater, recitals, museums, summer vacations in Europe, occasional winter trips to the Caribbean *Note:* as members of and donors to the local art museum, the Brownings and their children attend private receptions and exhibit openings at the invitation of the museum director
Higher education:	an Ivy League liberal arts college in Massachusetts *Major:* economics and political science *After-class activities:* debating club, college newspaper, swim team *Ambition:* "to become a leader in business"
First full-time job (age 23):	assistant manager of operations, Browning Tool and Die, inc. (family enterprise)
Subsequent employment:	*3 years*—executive assistant to the president, Browning Tool and Die *Responsibilities included:* purchasing (materials and equipment), personnel, and distribution networks *4 years*—advertising manager, Lackheed Manufacturing (home appliances) *3 years*—director of marketing and sales, Comerex, Inc. (business machines)

Present employment (age 38):	executive vice president, SmithBond and Co. (digital instruments) *Typical daily activities:* review financial reports and computer printouts, dictate memoranda, lunch with clients, initiate conference calls, meet with assistants, plan business trips, meet with associates *Transportation to and from work:* chauffeured company limousine *Annual salary:* $315,000 *Ambition:* "to become chief executive officer of the firm, or one like it, within the next five to ten years"
Present residence:	eighteenth-floor condominium on Manhattan's Upper West Side, eleven rooms, including five spacious bedrooms and terrace overlooking river *Interior:* professionally designed and accented with elegant furnishings, valuable antiques, and expensive artwork *Note:* building management provides doorman and elevator attendant; family employs au pair for children and maid for other domestic chores
Second residence:	farm in northwestern Connecticut, used for weekend retreats and for horse breeding (investment/hobby) *Note:* to maintain the farm and cater to their needs when they are there, the Brownings employ a part-time maid, groundskeeper, and horse breeder

Harold Browning was born into a world of nurses, maids, and governesses. His world today is one of airplanes and limousines, five-star restaurants, and luxurious living accommodations. The life and lifestyle of Harold Browning is in sharp contrast to that of Bob Farrell.

American Profile No. 2

Name:	Bob Farrell
Father:	machinist
Mother:	retail clerk
Principal child-rearer:	mother and sitter
Primary education:	a medium-size public school in Queens, New York, characterized by large class size, outmoded physical facilities, and an educational philosophy emphasizing basic skills and student discipline *Ambition:* "to become President"
Supplemental tutoring:	none
Summer camp:	YMCA day camp *Note:* emphasis on team sports, arts and crafts
Secondary education:	large regional high school in Queens *Note:* classmates included the sons and daughters of carpenters, postal clerks, teachers, nurses, shopkeepers, mechanics, bus drivers, police officers, salespersons *After-school activities:* basketball and handball in school park *Ambition:* "to make it through college" *High-school graduation gift:* $500 savings bond
Family activities:	family gatherings around television set, bowling, an occasional trip to the movie theater, summer Sundays at the public beach
Higher education:	a two-year community college with a technical orientation *Major:* electrical technology *After-school activities:* employed as a part-time bagger in local supermarket *Ambition:* "to become an electrical engineer"

First full-time Job (age 19):	service-station attendant *Note:* continued to take college classes in the evening
Subsequent employment:	mail clerk at large insurance firm, manager trainee, large retail chain
Present employment (age 38):	assistant sales manager, building supply firm *Typical daily activities:* demonstrate products, write up product orders, handle customer complaints, check inventory *Transportation to and from work:* city subway *Annual salary:* $39,261 *Ambition:* "to open up my own business" *Additional income:* $6,100 in commissions from evening and weekend work as salesman in local men's clothing store
Present residence:	the Farrells own their own home in a working-class neighborhood in Queens

Bob Farrell and Harold Browning live very differently: the lifestyle of one is privileged; that of the other is not so privileged. The differences are class differences, and these differences have a profound impact on the way they live. They are differences between playing a game of handball in the park and taking riding lessons at a private stable; watching a movie on television and going to the theater; and taking the subway to work and being driven in a limousine. More important, the difference in class determines where they live, who their friends are, how well they are educated, what they do for a living, and what they come to expect from life.

Yet, as dissimilar as their lifestyles are, Harold Browning and Bob Farrell have some things in common. They live in the same city, they work long hours, and they are highly motivated. More important, they are both white males.

Let us look at someone else who works long and hard and is highly motivated. This person, however, is black and female.

American Profile No. 3

Name:	Cheryl Mitchell
Father:	janitor
Mother:	waitress
Principal child-rearer:	grandmother
Primary education:	large public school in Ocean Hill-Brownsville, Brooklyn, New York *Note:* rote teaching of basic skills and emphasis on conveying the importance of good attendance, good manners, and good work habits; school patrolled by security guards *Ambition:* "to be a teacher"
Supplemental tutoring:	none
Summer camp:	none
Secondary education:	large public school in Ocean Hill-Brownsville *Note:* classmates included sons and daughters of hairdressers, groundskeepers, painters, dressmakers, dishwashers, domestics *After-school activities:* domestic chores, part-time employment as babysitter and housekeeper *Ambition:* "to be a social worker" *High-school graduation gift:* corsage
Family activities:	church-sponsored socials
Higher education:	one semester of local community college *Note:* dropped out of school for financial reasons
First fill-time job (age 17):	counter clerk, local bakery
Subsequent employment:	file clerk with temporary service agency, supermarket checker
Present employment (age 38):	nurse's aide at a municipal hospital

	Typical daily activities: make up hospital beds, clean out bedpans, weigh patients and assist them to the bathroom, take temperature readings, pass out and collect food trays, feed patients who need help, bathe patients, and change dressings *Annual salary:* $14,024 *Ambition:* "to get out of the ghetto"
Present residence:	three-room apartment in the South Bronx, needs painting, has poor ventilation, is in a high-crime area *Note:* Cheryl Mitchell lives with her four-year-old son and her elderly mother

When we look at the lives of Cheryl Mitchell, Bob Farrell, and Harold Browning, we see lifestyles that are very different. We are not looking, however, at economic extremes. Cheryl Mitchell's income as a nurse's aide puts her above the government's official poverty line.[18] Below her on the income pyramid are 35 million poverty-stricken Americans. Far from being poor, Bob Farrell has an annual income as an assistant sales manager that puts him in the fifty-first percentile of the income distribution.[19] More than 50 percent of the U.S. population earns less money than Bob Farrell. And while Harold Browning's income puts him in a high-income bracket, he stands only a fraction of the way up Samuelson's income pyramid. Well above him are the 144,000 individuals whose annual salary exceeds $1 million. Yet Harold Browning spends more money on his horses than Cheryl Mitchell earns in a year.

Reality 4: Even ignoring the extreme poles of the economic spectrum, we find enormous class differences in the lifestyles among the haves, the have-nots, and the have-littles.

Class affects more than lifestyle and material well-being. It has a significant impact on our physical and mental well-being as well.

[18] This is based on the 1999 poverty threshold of $13,290 for a family of three.

[19] Based on a median income in 1998 of $38,885.

Researchers have found an inverse relationship between social class and health. Lower-class standing is correlated to higher rates of infant mortality, eye and ear disease, arthritis, physical disability, diabetes, nutritional deficiency, respiratory disease, mental illness, and heart disease.[20] In all areas of health, poor people do not share the same life chances as those in the social class above them. Furthermore, lower-class standing is correlated with a lower quality of treatment for illness and disease. The results of poor health and poor treatment are borne out in the life expectancy rates within each class. Researchers have found that the higher your class standing, the higher your life expectancy. Conversely, they have also found that within each age group, the lower one's class standing, the higher the death rate; in some age groups, the figures are as much as two and three times as high.[21]

Reality 5: From cradle to grave, class standing has a significant impact on our chances for survival.

The lower one's class standing, the more difficult it is to secure appropriate housing, the more time is spent on the routine tasks of everyday life, the greater is the percentage of income that goes to pay for food and other basic necessities, and the greater is the likelihood of crime victimization.[22] Class can predict chances for both survival and success.

---

[20] E. Pamuk, D. Makuc, K. Heck, C. Reuben, and K. Lochner, *Socioeconomic Status and Health Chartbook, Health, United States, 1998*, Hyattsville, MD, National Center for Health Statistics, 1998, pp. 145–159; Vincente Navarro "Class, Race, and Health Care in the United States," In Bersh Berberoglu, *Critical Pespectives in Sociology*, 2nd ed., Dubuque, IA, Kendall/Hunt, 1993, pp. 148–156; Melvin Krasner, *Poverty and Health in New York City*, United Hospital Fund of New York, 1989. See also U.S. Dept. of Health and Human Services, *Health Status of Minorities and Low Income Groups*, 1985; and Dan Hughes, Kay Johnson, Sara Rosenbaum, Elizabeth Butler, and Janet Simons, *The Health of America's Children*, The Children's Defense Fund, 1988.

[21] E. Pamuk et al., op. cit.; Kenneth Neubeck and Davita Glassberg, *Sociology: A Critical Approach*, New York, McGraw-Hill, 1996, pp. 436–438; Aaron Antonovsky, "Social Class, Life Expectancy, and Overall Mortality," in *The Impact of Social Class*, New York, Thomas Crowell, 1972, pp. 467–491. See also Harriet Duleep, "Measuring the Effect of Income on Adult Mortality Using Longitudinal Administrative Record Data," *Journal of Human Resources*, vol. 21, no. 2, Spring 1986.

[22] E. Pamuk et al., op. cit., fig. 20; Dennis W. Roncek, "Dangerous Places: Crime and Residential Environment," *Social Forces*, vol. 60, no. 1, September 1981, pp. 74–96.

School performance (grades and test scores) and educational attainment (level of schooling completed) also correlate strongly with economic class. Furthermore, despite some efforts to make testing fairer and schooling more accessible, current data suggest that the level of inequity is staying the same or getting worse.

In his study for the Carnegie Council on Children 15 years ago, Richard De Lone examined the test scores of over half a million students who took the College Board exams (SATs). His findings were consistent with earlier studies that showed a relationship between class and scores on standardized tests; his conclusion: "the higher the student's social status, the higher the probability that he or she will get higher grades."[23] Fifteen years after the release of the Carnegie report, College Board surveys reveal data that are no different; test scores still correlate strongly with family income.

Average Combined Scores by Income (400 to 1600 scale)[24]

Family Income	*Median Score*
More than $100,000	1130
$80,000 to $100,000	1082
$70,000 to $80,000	1058
$60,000 to $70,000	1043
$50,000 to $60,000	1030
$40,000 to $50,000	1011
$30,000 to $40,000	986
$20,000 to $30,000	954
$10,000 to $20,000	907
less than $10,000	871

These figures are based on the test results of 1,302,903 SAT takers in 1999.

[23] Richard De Lone, *Small Futures*, New York, Harcourt Brace Jovanovich, 1978, pp. 14–19.

[24] Derived from The College Entrance Examination Board, "1999, A Profile of College Bound Seniors: SAT Test Takers," *www.collegeboard.org/sat/cbsenior/yr1999/NAT/natbk499. html#income*

A little more than 20 years ago, researcher William Sewell showed a positive correlation between class and overall educational achievement. In comparing the top quartile (25%) of his sample to the bottom quartile, he found that students from upper-class families were twice as likely to obtain training beyond high school and four times as likely to attain a postgraduate degree. Sewell concluded: "Socioeconomic background . . . operates independently of academic ability at every stage in the process of educational attainment."[25]

Today, the pattern persists. There are, however, two significant changes. On the odds of getting into college have improved for the bottom quartile of the population, although they still remain relatively low compared to the top. On the other hand, the chances of completing a college degree have deteriorated markedly for the bottom quartile. Researchers estimate the chances of completing a four-year college degree (by age 24) to be 19 times as great for the top 25 percent of the population as it is for the bottom 25 percent. "Those from the bottom quartile of family income . . . are faring worse than they have at any time in the 23 years of published Current Population Survey data."[26]

Reality 6: Class standing has a significant impact on chances for educational attainment.

Class standing, and consequently life chances, are largely determined at birth. Although examples of individuals who have gone from rags to riches abound in the mass media, statistics on class mobility show these leaps to be extremely rare. In fact, dramatic advances in class standing are relatively few. One study showed that fewer than one in five men surpass the economic status of their fathers.[27] For those whose annual income is in six figures, economic success is due in large part to the wealth and privileges bestowed on them at birth. Over 66 percent of the consumer units with incomes of $100,000

---

[25] William H. Sewell, "Inequality of Opportunity for Higher Education," *American Sociological Review,* vol. 36, no. 5, 1971, pp. 793–809.

[26] The Mortenson Report on Public Policy Analysis of Opportunity for Postsecondary Education, "Postsecondary Education Opportunity," Iowa City, IA, September 1993, no. 16.

[27] De Lone, op. cit., pp. 14–19.

or more have some inherited assets. Of these units, over 86 percent reported that inheritances constituted a substantial portion of their total assets.[28]

Economist Harold Wachtel likens inheritance to a series of Monopoly games in which the winner of the first game refuses to relinquish his or her cash and commercial property for the second game. "After all," argues the winner, "I accumulated my wealth and income by my own wits." With such an arrangement, it is not difficult to predict the outcome of subsequent games.[29]

Reality 7: All Americans do not have an equal opportunity to succeed. Inheritance laws ensure a greater likelihood of success for the offspring of the wealthy.

---

[28] Howard Tuchman, *Economics of the Rich*, New York, Random House, 1973, p. 15.

[29] Howard Wachtel, *Labor and the Economy*, Orlando, FL, Academic Press, 1984, pp. 161–162.

Learning the Language

Perri Klass [b. 1958]

Perri Klass (1958–) was born to American parents in Trinidad and earned her M. D. from Harvard in 1986, going on to become a pediatrician. She has been writing and publishing widely while pursuing her medical career. Her fiction includes two novels, Recombinations *(1985) and* Other Women's Children *(1990), and a collection of short stories,* I Am Having an Adventure *(1986). She published a collection of autobiographical essays,* A Not Entirely Benign Procedure *(1987) about her experience in medical school. The following selection, "Learning the Language," is excerpted from that book. Klass is sensitive to uses of language and understands how language affects thinking. As you read this essay, think about other special groups who also use language in unique ways.*

"Mrs. Tolstoy is your basic LOL in NAD, admitted for a soft rule-out MI," the intern announces. I scribble that on my patient list. In other words, Mrs. Tolstoy is a Little Old Lady in No Apparent Distress who is in the hospital to make sure she hasn't had a heart attack (rule out a Myocardial Infarction). And we think it's unlikely that she has had a heart attack (a *soft* rule-out).

If I learned nothing else during my first three months of working in the hospital as a medical student, I learned endless jargon and abbreviations. I started out in a state of primeval innocence, in which I didn't even know that "s̄ CP, SOB, N/V" meant "without chest pain, shortness of breath, or nausea and vomiting." By the end I took the abbreviations so much for granted that I would complain to my mother the English professor, "And can you believe I had to put down *three* NG tubes last night?"

"You'll have to tell me what an NG tube is if you want me to sympathize properly," my mother said. NG, nasogastric—isn't it obvious?

I picked up not only the specific expressions but also the patterns of speech and the grammatical conventions; for example, you never say that a patient's blood pressure fell or that his cardiac enzymes rose. Instead, the patient is always the subject of the verb:

"He dropped his pressure." "He bumped his enzymes." This sort of construction probably reflects the profound irritation of the intern when the nurses come in the middle of the night to say that Mr. Dickinson has disturbingly low blood pressure. "Oh, he's gonna hurt me bad tonight," the intern might say, inevitably angry at Mr. Dickinson for dropping his pressure and creating a problem.

When chemotherapy fails to cure Mrs. Bacon's cancer, what we say is, "Mrs. Bacon failed chemotherapy."

"Well, we've already had one hit today, and we're up next, but at least we've got mostly stable players on our team." This means that our team (group of doctors and medical students) has already gotten one new admission today, and it is our turn again, so we'll get whoever is admitted next in emergency, but at least most of the patients we already have are fairly stable, that is, unlikely to drop their pressures or in any other way get suddenly sicker and hurt us bad. Baseball metaphor is pervasive. A no-hitter is a night without any new admissions. A player is always a patient—a nitrate player is a patient on nitrates, a unit player is a patient in the intensive care unit, and so on, until you reach the terminal player.

It is interesting to consider what it means to be winning, or doing well, in this perennial baseball game. When the intern hangs up the phone and announces, "I got a hit," that is not cause for congratulations. The team is not scoring points; rather, it is getting hit, being bombarded with new patients. The object of the game from the point of view of the doctors, considering the players for whom they are already responsible, is to get as few new hits as possible.

This special language contributes to a sense of closeness and professional spirit among people who are under a great deal of stress. As a medical student, I found it exciting to discover that I'd finally cracked the code, that I could understand what doctors said and wrote, and could use the same formulations myself. Some people seem to become enamored of the jargon for its own sake, perhaps because they are so deeply thrilled with the idea of medicine, with the idea of themselves as doctors.

I knew a medical student who was referred to by the interns on the team as Mr. Eponym because he was so infatuated with eponymous terminology, the more obscure the better. He never said "capillary pulsations" if he could say "Quincke's pulses." He would lovingly tell over the multinamed syndromes—Wolff-Parkinson-White, Lown-Ganong-Levine, Schönlein-Henoch—until the temptation to suggest Schleswig-Holstein or Stevenson-Kefauver or Baskin-Robbins became irresistible to his less reverent colleagues.

And there is the jargon that you don't ever want to hear yourself using. You know that your training is changing you, but there are certain changes you think would be going a little too far.

The resident was describing a man with devastating terminal pancreatic cancer. "Basically he's CTD," the resident concluded. I reminded myself that I had resolved not to be shy about asking when I didn't understand things. "CTD?" I asked timidly.

The resident smirked at me. "Circling The Drain."

The images are vivid and terrible. "What happened to Mrs. Melville?"

"Oh, she boxed last night." To box is to die, of course.

Then there are the more pompous locutions that can make the beginning medical student nervous about the effects of medical training. A friend of mine was told by his resident, "A pregnant woman with sickle-cell represents a failure of genetic counseling."

Mr. Eponym, who tried hard to talk like the doctors, once explained to me, "An infant is basically a brainstem preparation." The term "brainstem preparation," as used in neurological research, refers to an animal whose higher brain functions have been destroyed so that only the most primitive reflexes remain, like the sucking reflex, the startle reflex, and the rooting reflex.

And yet at other times the harshness dissipates into a strangely elusive euphemism. "As you know, this is a not entirely benign procedure," some doctor will say, and that will be understood to imply agony, risk of complications, and maybe even a significant mortality rate.

The more extreme forms aside, one most important function of medical jargon is to help doctors maintain some distance from their patients. By reformulating a patient's pain and problems into a language that the patient doesn't even speak, I suppose we are in some sense taking those pains and problems under our jurisdiction and also reducing their emotional impact. This linguistic separation between doctors and patients allows conversations to go on at the bedside that are unintelligible to the patient. "Naturally, we're worried about adeno-CA," the intern can say to the medical student, and lung cancer need never be mentioned.

I learned a new language this past summer. At times it thrills me to hear myself using it. It enables me to understand my colleagues, to communicate effectively in the hospital. Yet I am uncomfortably aware that I will never again notice the peculiarities and even atrocities of medical language as keenly as I did this summer. There may be specific expressions I manage to avoid, but even as I remark them, promising myself I will never use them, I find that this language is becoming my professional speech. It no longer sounds strange in my ears—or coming from my mouth. And I am afraid that as with any new language, to use it properly you must absorb not only the vocabulary but also the structure, the logic, the attitudes. At first you may notice these new and alien assumptions every time you put together a sentence, but with time and increased fluency you stop being aware of them at all. And as you lose that awareness, for better or for worse, you move closer and closer to being a doctor instead of just talking like one.

How to Lie with Statistics

Darrell Huff [1913–2001]

"The average Yaleman, Class of '24," *Time* magazine reported last year after reading something in the New York *Sun*, a newspaper published in those days, "makes $25,111 a year."

Well, good for him!

But, come to think of it, what does this improbably precise and salubrious figure mean? Is it, as it appears to be, evidence that if you send your boy to Yale you won't have to work in your old age and neither will he? Is this average a mean or is it a median? What kind of sample is it based on? You could lump one Texas oilman with two hundred hungry freelance writers and report *their* average income as $25,000-odd a year. The arithmetic is impeccable, the figure is convincingly precise, and the amount of meaning there is in it you could put in your eye.

In just such ways is the secret language of statistics, so appealing in a fact-minded culture, being used to sensationalize, inflate, confuse, and oversimplify. Statistical terms are necessary in reporting the mass data of social and economic trends, business conditions, "opinion" polls, this year's census. But without writers who use the words with honesty and understanding and readers who know what they mean, the result can only be semantic nonsense.

In popular writing on scientific research, the abused statistic is al- 5
most crowding out the picture of the white-jacketed hero laboring overtime without time-and-a-half in an ill-lit laboratory. Like the "little dash of powder, little pot of paint," statistics are making many an important fact "look like what she ain't." Here are some of the ways it is done.

The sample with the built-in bias. Our Yale men—or Yalemen, as they say in the Time-Life building—belong to this flourishing group. The exaggerated estimate of their income is not based on all members of the class nor on a random or representative sample of them. At least two interesting categories of 1924-model Yale men have been excluded.

First there are those whose present addresses are unknown to their classmates. Wouldn't you bet that these lost sheep are earning less than the boys from prominent families and the others who can be handily reached from a Wall Street office?

There are those who chucked the questionnaire into the nearest waste-basket. Maybe they didn't answer because they were not making enough money to brag about. Like the fellow who found a note clipped to his first pay check suggesting that he consider the amount of his salary confidential: "Don't worry," he told the boss. "I'm just as ashamed of it as you are."

Omitted from our sample then are just the two groups most likely to depress the average. The $25,111 figure is beginning to account for itself. It may indeed be a true figure for those of the Class of '24 whose addresses are known and who are willing to stand up and tell how much they earn. But even that requires a possibly dangerous assumption that the gentlemen are telling the truth.

To be dependable to any useful degree at all, a sampling study must use a representative sample (which can lead to trouble too) or a truly random one. If *all* the Class of '24 is included, that's all right. If every tenth name on a complete list is used, that is all right too, and so is drawing an adequate number of names out of a hat. The test is this: Does every name in the group have an equal chance to be in the sample?

You'll recall that ignoring this requirement was what produced the *Literary Digest's* famed fiasco. When names for polling were taken only from telephone books and subscription lists, people who did not have telephones or *Literary Digest* subscriptions had no chance to be in the sample. They possibly did not mind this underprivilege a bit, but their absence was in the end very hard on the magazine that relied on the figures.

This leads to a moral: You can prove about anything you want to by letting your sample bias itself. As a consumer of statistical data—a reader, for example, of a news magazine—remember that no statistical conclusion can rise above the quality of the sample it is based upon. In the absence of information about the procedures behind it, you are not warranted in giving any credence at all to the result.

The truncated, or gee-whiz, graph. If you want to show some statistical information quickly and clearly, draw a picture of it. Graphic presentation is the thing today. If you don't mind misleading the hasty looker, or if you quite clearly *want* to deceive him, you can save some space by chopping the bottom off many kinds of graphs.

Suppose you are showing the upward trend of national income month by month for a year. The total rise, as in one recent year, is 7 per cent. It looks like this:

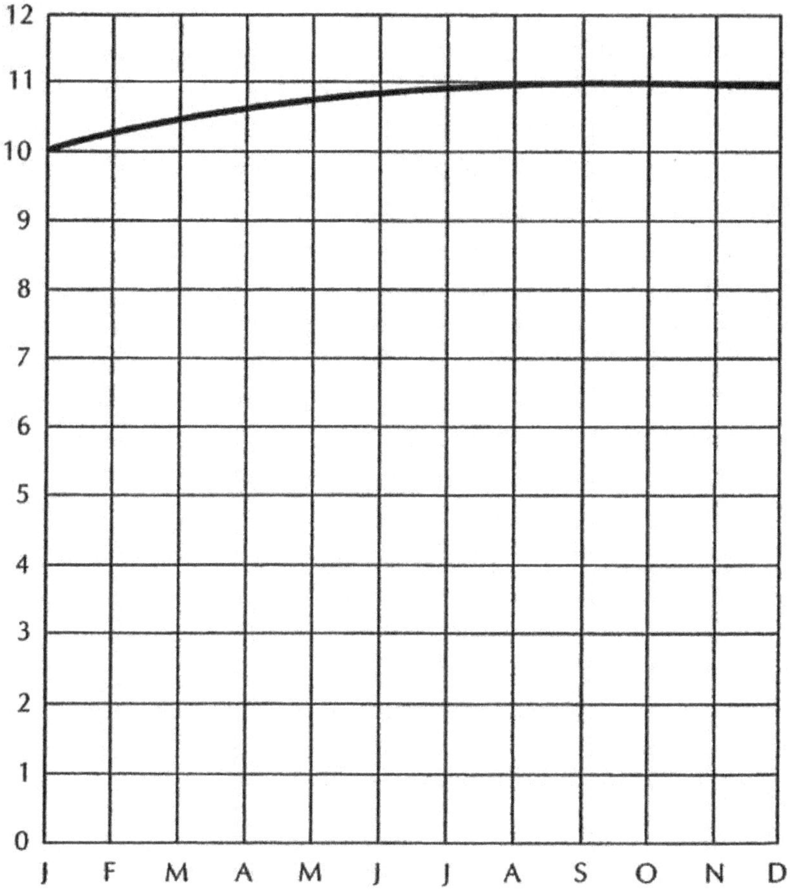

That is clear enough. Anybody can see that the trend is slightly upward. You are showing a 7 per cent increase and that is exactly what it looks like.

But it lacks schmaltz. So you chop off the bottom, this way:

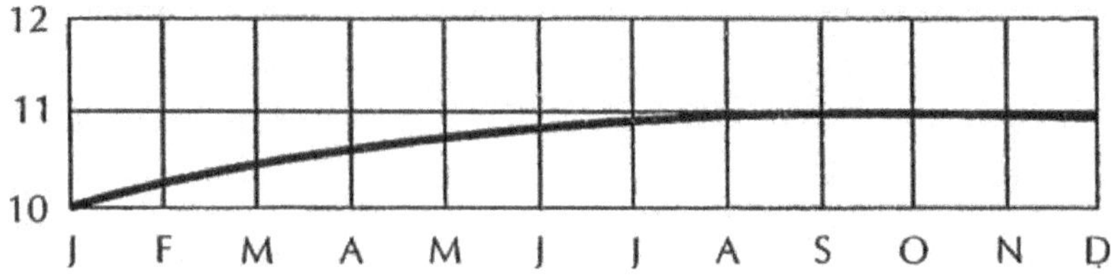

The figures are the same. It is the same graph and nothing has been falsified—except the impression that it gives. Anyone looking at it can just feel prosperity throbbing in the arteries of the country. It is a subtler equivalent of editing "National income rose 7 per cent" into ". . . climbed a whopping 7 per cent."

It is vastly more effective, however, because of that illusion of objectivity.

The souped-up graph. Sometimes truncating is not enough. The trifling rise in something or other still looks almost as insignificant as it is. You can make that 7 per cent look livelier than 100 per cent ordinarily does. Simply change the proportion between the ordinate and the abscissa. There's no rule against it, and it does give your graph a prettier shape.

But it exaggerates, to say the least, something awful (see page 2162).

The well-chosen average. I live near a country neighborhood for which I can report an average income of $15,000. I could also report it as $3,500.

If I should want to sell real estate hereabouts to people having a high snobbery content, the first figure would be handy. The second figure, however, is the one to use in an argument against raising taxes, or the local bus fare.

Both are legitimate averages, legally arrived at. Yet it is obvious that at least one of them must be as misleading as an out-and-out lie. The $15,000-figure is a mean, the arithmetic average of the incomes of all the families in the community. The smaller figure is a median; it might be called the income of the average family in the

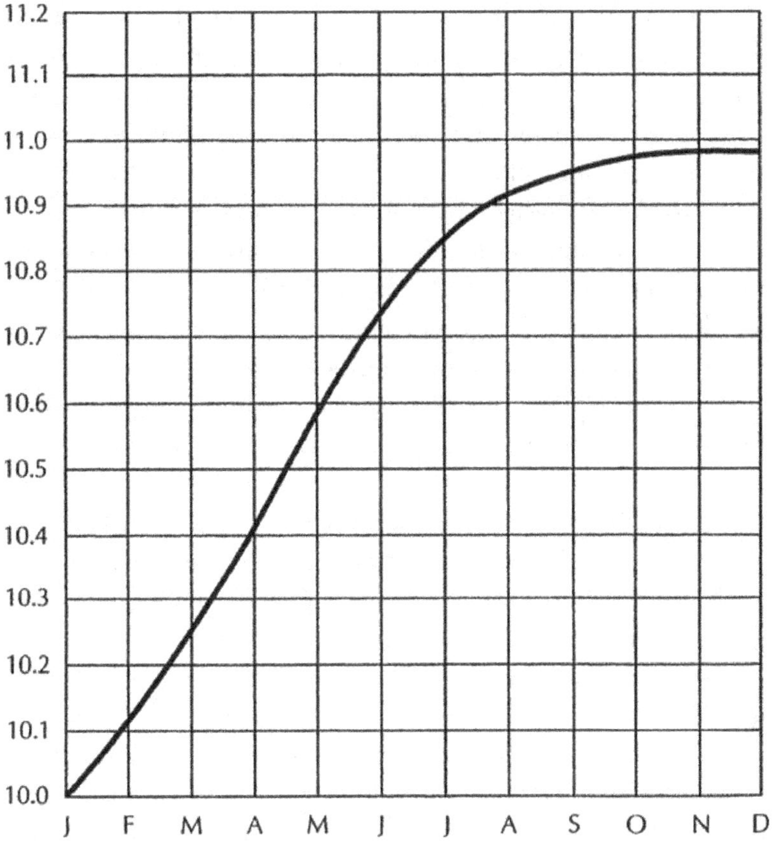

group. It indicates that half the families have less than $3,500 a year and half have more.

Here is where some of the confusion about averages comes from. Many human characteristics have the grace to fall into what is called the "normal" distribution. If you draw a picture of it, you get a curve that is shaped like a bell. Mean and median fall at about the same point, so it doesn't make very much difference which you use.

But some things refuse to follow this neat curve. Income is one of them. Incomes for most large areas will range from under $1,000 a year to upward of $50,000. Almost everybody will be under $10,000, way over on the left-hand side of that curve.

One of the things that made the income figure for the "average Yale-man" meaningless is that we are not told whether it is a mean or a median. It is not that one type of average is invariably better than the other; it depends upon what you are talking about. But neither gives you any real information—and either may be highly misleading—unless you know which of those two kinds of average it is.

In the country neighborhood I mentioned, almost everyone has less than the average—the mean, that is—of $10,500. These people are all small farmers, except for a trio of millionaire week-enders who bring up the mean enormously.

You can be pretty sure that when an income average is given in the form of a mean nearly everybody has less than that.

The insignificant difference or the elusive error. Your two children Peter and Linda (we might as well give them modish names while we're about it) take intelligence tests. Peter's IQ, you learn, is 98 and Linda's is 101. Aha! Linda is your brighter child.

Is she? An intelligence test is, or purports to be, a sampling of intellect. An IQ, like other products of sampling, is a figure with a statistical error, which expresses the precision or reliability of the figure. The size of this probable error can be calculated. For their test the makers of the much-used Revised Stanford-Binet have found it to be about 3 per cent. So Peter's indicated IQ of 98 really means only that there is an even chance that it falls between 95 and 101. There is an equal probability that it falls somewhere else—below 95 or above 101. Similarly, Linda's has no better than a fifty-fifty chance of being within the fairly sizeable range of 98 to 104.

You can work out some comparisons from that. One is that there is rather better than one chance in four that Peter, with his lower IQ rating, is really at least three points smarter than Linda. A statistician doesn't like to consider a difference significant unless you can hand him odds a lot longer than that.

Ignoring the error in a sampling study leads to all kinds of silly conclusions. There are magazine editors to whom readership surveys are gospel; with a 40 per cent readership reported for one article and a 35 per cent for another, they demand more like the first. I've seen even smaller differences given tremendous weight, because statistics are a mystery and numbers are impressive. The same thing goes for market surveys and so-called public-opinion polls. The rule is that you cannot make a valid comparison between two such figures unless you know the deviations. And unless the difference between the figures is many times greater than the probable error of each, you have only a guess that the one appearing greater really is.

Otherwise you are like the man choosing a camp site from a report of mean temperature alone. One place in California with a mean annual temperature of 61 is San Nicolas Island on the south coast, where it always stays in the comfortable range between 47 and 87. Another with a mean of 61 is in the inland desert, where the thermometer hops around from 15 to 104. The deviation from the mean marks the difference, and you can freeze or roast if you ignore it.

The one-dimensional picture. Suppose you have just two or three figures to compare—say the average weekly wage of carpenters in the United States and another country. The sums might be $60 and $30. An ordinary bar chart makes the difference graphic:

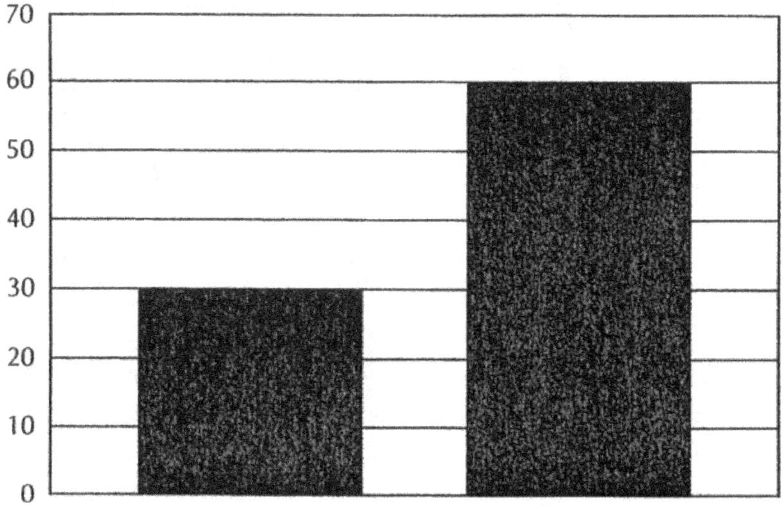

That is an honest picture. It looks good for American carpenters, but perhaps it does not have quite the oomph you are after. Can't you make that difference appear overwhelming and at the same time give it what I am afraid is known as eye-appeal? Of course you can. Following tradition, you represent these sums by pictures of money bags. If the $30 bag is one inch high, you draw the $60 bag two inches high. That's in proportion, isn't it? The catch is, of course, that the American's money bag, being twice as tall as that of the $30 man, covers an area on your page four times as great. And since your two-dimensional picture represents an object that would in fact have three dimensions, the money bags actually would differ much more than that. The volumes of any two similar solids vary as the cubes of their heights. If the unfortunate foreigner's bag holds $30 worth of dimes, the American's would hold not $60 but a neat $240:

You didn't say that, though, did you? And you can't be blamed, you're only doing it the way practically everybody else does.

The ever-impressive decimal. For a spurious air of precision that will lend all kinds of weight to the most disreputable statistics, consider the decimal.

Ask a hundred citizens how many hours they slept last night. Come out with a total of, say, 781.3. Your data are far from precise to begin with. Most people will miss their guess by fifteen minutes or more and some will recall five sleepless minutes as half a night of tossing insomnia.

But go ahead, do your arithmetic, announce that people sleep an average of 7.813 hours a night. You will sound as if you knew precise-
ly what you are talking about. If you were foolish enough to say 7.8 (or 35
"almost 8") hours it would sound like what it was—an approximation.

The semi-attached figure. If you can't prove what you want to prove, demonstrate something else and pretend that they are the same thing. In the daze that follows the collision of statistics with the human mind, hardly anybody will notice the difference. The semi-attached figure is a durable device guaranteed to stand you in good stead. It always has.

If you can't prove that your nostrum cures colds, publish a sworn laboratory report that the stuff killed 31,108 germs in a test tube in eleven seconds. There may be no connection at all between assorted germs in a test tube and the whatever-it-is that produces colds, but people aren't going to reason that sharply, especially while sniffling.

Maybe that one is too obvious and people are beginning to catch on. Here is a trickier version.

Let us say that in a period when race prejudice is growing it is to your advantage to "prove" otherwise. You will not find it a difficult assignment.

Ask that usual cross section of the population if they think
Negroes have as good a chance as white people to get jobs. Ask 40
again a few months later. As Princeton's Office of Public Opinion Research has found out, people who are most unsympathetic to Negroes are the ones most likely to answer yes to this question.

As prejudice increases in a country, the percentage of affirmative answers you will get to this question will become larger. What looks on the face of it like growing opportunity for Negroes actually is mounting prejudice and nothing else. You have achieved something rather remarkable: the worse things get, the better your survey makes them look.

The unwarranted assumption, or* post hoc *rides again. The interrelation of cause and effect, so often obscure anyway, can be most neatly hidden in statistical data.

Somebody once went to a good deal of trouble to find out if cigarette smokers make lower college grades than non-smokers. They did. This naturally pleased many people, and they made much of it.

The unwarranted assumption, of course, was that smoking had produced dull minds. It seemed vaguely reasonable on the face of it, so it was quite widely accepted. But it really proved nothing of the sort, any more than it proved that poor grades drive students to the solace of tobacco. Maybe the relationship worked in one direction, maybe in the other. And maybe all this is only an indication that the sociable sort of fellow who is likely to take his books less than seriously is also likely to sit around and smoke many cigarettes.

Permitting statistical treatment to befog causal relationships is little better than superstition. It is like the conviction among the people of the Hebrides that body lice produce good health. Observation over the centuries had taught them that people in good health had lice and sick people often did not. *Ergo*, lice made a man healthy. Everybody should have them.

Scantier evidence, treated statistically at the expense of common sense, has made many a medical fortune and many a medical article in magazines, including professional ones. More sophisticated observers finally got things straightened out in the Hebrides. As it turned out, almost everybody in those circles had lice most of the time. But when a man took a fever (quite possibly carried to him by those same lice) and his body became hot, the lice left.

Here you have cause and effect not only reversed, but intermingled.

There you have a primer in some ways to use statistics to deceive. A well-wrapped statistic is better than Hitler's "big lie": it misleads, yet it can't be pinned onto you.

Is this little list altogether too much like a manual for swindlers? Perhaps I can justify it in the manner of the retired burglar whose published reminiscences amounted to a graduate course in how to pick a lock and muffle a footfall: The crooks already know these tricks. Honest men must learn them in self-defense.

A Nation of Welfare Families

Stephanie Coontz [b. 1944]

The current political debate over family values, personal responsibility, and welfare takes for granted the entrenched American belief that dependence on government assistance is a recent and destructive phenomenon. Conservatives tend to blame this dependence on personal irresponsibility aggravated by a swollen welfare apparatus that saps individual initiative. Liberals are more likely to blame it on personal misfortune magnified by the harsh lot that falls to losers in our competitive market economy. But both sides believe that "winners" in America make it on their own, that dependence reflects some kind of individual or family failure, and that the ideal family is the self-reliant unit of traditional lore—a family that takes care of its own, carves out a future for its children, and never asks for handouts. Politicians at both ends of the ideological spectrum have wrapped themselves in the mantle of these "family values," arguing over *why* the poor have not been able to make do without assistance, or whether aid has exacerbated their situation, but never questioning the assumption that American families traditionally achieve success by establishing their independence from the government.

The myth of family self-reliance is so compelling that our actual national and personal histories often buckle under its emotional weight. "We always stood on our own two feet," my grandfather used to say about his pioneer heritage, whenever he walked me to the top of the hill to survey the property in Washington State that his family had bought for next to nothing after it had been logged off in the early 1900s. Perhaps he didn't know that the land came so cheap because much of it was part of a federal subsidy originally allotted to the railroad companies, which had received 183 million acres of the public domain in the nineteenth century. These federal giveaways were the original source of most major

Western logging companies' land, and when some of these logging companies moved on to virgin stands of timber, federal lands trickled down to a few early settlers who were able to purchase them inexpensively.

Like my grandparents, few families in American history—whatever their "values"—have been able to rely solely on their own resources. Instead, they have depended on the legislative, judicial, and social support structures set up by governing authorities, whether those authorities were the clan elders of Native American societies, the church courts and city officials of colonial America, or the judicial and legislative bodies established by the Constitution.

At America's inception, this was considered not a dirty little secret but the norm, one that confirmed our social and personal interdependence. The idea that the family should have the sole or even primary responsibility for educating and socializing its members, finding them suitable work, or keeping them from poverty and crime was not only ludicrous to colonial and revolutionary thinkers but dangerously parochial.

Historically, one way that government has played a role in the well-being of its citizens is by regulating the way that employers and civic bodies interact with families. In the early twentieth century, for example, as a response to rapid changes ushered in by a mass-production economy, the government promoted a "family wage system." This system was designed to strengthen the ability of the male breadwinner to support a family without having his wife or children work. This family wage system was not a natural outgrowth of the market. It was a *political* response to conditions that the market had produced: child labor, rampant employment insecurity, recurring economic downturns, an earnings structure in which 45 percent of industrial workers fell below the poverty level and another 40 percent hovered barely above it, and a system in which thousands of children had been placed in orphanages or other institutions simply because their parents could not afford their keep. The state policies involved in the establishment of the family wage system included abolition of child labor, government pressure on industrialists to negotiate with unions, federal arbitration, expansion of compulsory schooling—and legislation discriminating against women workers.

But even such extensive regulation of economic and social institutions has never been enough: government has always supported families with direct material aid as well. The two best examples of the government's history of material aid can be found in what many people consider the ideal models of self-reliant families: the Western pioneer family and the 1950s suburban family. In both cases, the ability of these families to establish and sustain themselves required massive underwriting by the government.

Pioneer families, such as my grandparents, could never have moved west without government-funded military mobilizations against the original Indian and Mexican inhabitants or state-sponsored economic investment in transportation systems. In addition, the Homestead Act of 1862 allowed settlers to buy 160 acres for $10—far below the government's cost of acquiring the land—if the homesteader lived on and improved the land for five years. In the twentieth century, a new form of public assistance became crucial to Western families: construction of dams and other federally subsidized irrigation projects. During the 1930s, for example, government electrification projects brought pumps, refrigeration, and household technology to millions of families.

The suburban family of the 1950s is another oft-cited example of familial self-reliance. According to legend, after World War II a new, family-oriented generation settled down, saved their pennies, worked hard, and found well-paying jobs that allowed them to purchase homes in the suburbs. In fact, however, the 1950s suburban family was far more dependent on government assistance than any so-called underclass family of today. Federal GI benefit payments, available to 40 percent of the male population between the ages of twenty and twenty-four, permitted a whole generation of men to expand their education and improve their job prospects without forgoing marriage and children. The National Defense Education Act retooled science education in America, subsidizing both American industry and the education of individual scientists. Government-funded research developed the aluminum clapboards, prefabricated walls and ceilings, and plywood paneling that comprised the technological basis of the postwar housing revolution. Government spending was also largely responsible for the new highways, sewer systems, utility services, and traffic-control programs that opened up suburbia.

In addition, suburban home ownership depended on an unprecedented expansion of federal regulation and financing. Before the war, banks often required a 50 percent down payment on homes and normally issued mortgages for five to ten years. In the postwar period, however, the Federal Housing Authority, supplemented by the GI bill, put the federal government in the business of insuring and regulating private loans for single-home construction. FHA policy required down payments of only 5 to 10 percent of the purchase price and guaranteed mortgages of up to thirty years at interest rates of just 2 to 3 percent. The Veterans Administration required a mere dollar down from veterans. Almost half the housing in suburbia in the 1950s depended on such federal programs.

The drawback of these aid programs was that although they worked well for recipients, nonrecipients—disproportionately poor and urban—were left far behind. While the general public financed the roads that suburbanites used to commute, the streetcars and trolleys that served urban and poor families received almost no tax revenues, and our previously thriving rail system was allowed to decay. In addition, federal loan policies, which were a boon to upwardly mobile white families, tended to systematize the pervasive but informal racism that had previously characterized the housing market. FHA redlining practices, for example, took entire urban areas and declared them ineligible for loans, while the government's two new mortgage institutions, the Federal National Mortgage Association and the Government National Mortgage Association (Fannie Mae and Ginny Mae) made it possible for urban banks to transfer savings out of the cities and into new suburban developments in the South and West.

Despite the devastating effects on families and regions that did not receive such assistance, government aid to suburban residents during the 1950s and 1960s produced in its beneficiaries none of the demoralization usually presumed to afflict recipients of government handouts. Instead, federal subsidies to suburbia encouraged family formation, residential stability, upward occupational mobility, and rising educational aspirations among youth who could look forward to receiving such aid. Seen in this light, the idea that government subsidies intrinsically induce dependence, undermine self-esteem, or break down family ties is exposed as no more than a myth.

I am not suggesting that the way to solve the problems of poverty and urban decay in America is to quadruple our spending on welfare. Certainly there are major reforms needed in our current aid policies to the poor. But the debate over such reform should put welfare in the context of *all* federal assistance programs. As long as we pretend that only poor or single-parent families need outside assistance, while normal families "stand on their own two feet," we will shortchange poor families, overcompensate rich ones, and fail to come up with effective policies for helping out families in the middle. Current government housing policies are a case in point. The richest 20 percent of American households receives three times as much federal housing aid—mostly in tax subsidies—as the poorest 20 percent receives in expenditures for low-income housing.

Historically, the debate over government policies toward families has never been over *whether* to intervene but *how:* to rescue or to warehouse, to prevent or to punish, to moralize about values or mobilize resources for education and job creation. Today's debate, lacking such historical perspective, caricatures the real issues. Our attempt to sustain the myth of family self-reliance in the face of all the historical evidence to the contrary has led policymakers into theoretical contortions and practical miscalculations that are reminiscent of efforts by medieval philosophers to maintain that the earth and not the sun was the center of the planetary system. In the sixteenth century, leading European thinkers insisted that the planets and the sun all revolved around the earth—much as American politicians today insist that our society revolves around family self-reliance. When evidence to the contrary mounted, defenders of the Ptolemaic universe postulated all sorts of elaborate planetary orbits in order to reconcile observed reality with their cherished theory. Similarly, rather than admit that all families need some kind of public support, we have constructed ideological orbits that explain away each instance of middle-class dependence as "exception," an "abnormality," or even an illusion. We have distributed public aid to families through convoluted bureaucracies that have become impossible to track; in some cases the system has become so cumbersome that it threatens to collapse around our ears. It is time to break through the old paradigm of self-reliance and substitute a new one that recognizes that assisting families is, simply, what government does.

Streets of Gold: The Myth of the Model Minority

Curtis Chang [b. 1968]

Over one hundred years ago, an American myth misled many of my ancestors. Seeking cheap labor, railroad companies convinced numerous Chinese that American streets were paved with gold. Today, the media portray Asian-Americans as finally mining those golden streets. Major publications like *Time, Newsweek, U.S. News & World Report, Fortune, The New Republic, the Wall Street Journal,* and the *New York Times Magazine* have all recently published congratulatory "Model Minority" headline stories with such titles as

America's Super Minority
An American Success Story
A "Model Minority"
Why They Succeed
The Ultimate Assimilation
The Triumph of Asian-Americans.

But the Model Minority is another "Streets of Gold" tale. It distorts Asian-Americans' true status and ignores our racial handicaps. And the Model Minority's ideology is even worse than its mythology. It attempts to justify the existing system of racial inequality by blaming the victims rather than the system itself.

The Model Minority myth introduces us as an ethnic minority that is finally "making it in America," as stated in *Time* (Doerner 42). The media consistently define "making it" as achieving material wealth, wealth that flows from our successes in the workplace and the schoolroom. This economic achievement allegedly proves a minority can, as *Fortune* says, "lay claim to the American dream" (Ramirez 149).

Trying to show how "Asian-Americans present a picture of affluence and economic success," as the New *York Times Magazine* puts it (Oxnam 72), nine out of ten of the major Model Minority stories of the last four years relied heavily on one statistic: the family median income. The median Asian-American family income, according to the U.S. Census Survey of Income and Education data, is $22,713 compared to $20,800 for white Americans. Armed with that figure, national magazines such as *Newsweek* have trumpeted our "remarkable, ever-mounting achievements" (Kasindorf et al. 51).

Such assertions demonstrate the truth of the aphorism "Statistics are like a bikini. What they reveal is suggestive, but what they conceal is vital." The family median income statistic conceals the fact that Asian-American families generally (1) have more children and live-in relatives and thus have more mouths to feed; (2) are often forced by necessity to have everyone in the family work, averaging *more* than two family income earners (whites only have 1.6) (Cabezas 402); and (3) live disproportionately in high cost of living areas (i.e., New York, Chicago, Los Angeles, and Honolulu) which artificially inflate income figures. Dr. Robert S. Mariano, professor of economics at the University of Pennsylvania, has calculated that

> when such appropriate adjustments and comparisons are made, a different and rather disturbing picture emerges, showing indeed a clearly disadvantaged group. . . . Filipino and Chinese men *are no better off than black men with regard to median incomes*. (55)[1]

Along with other racial minorities, Asian-Americans are still scrapping for the crumbs of the economic pie.

Throughout their distortion of our status, the media propagate two crucial assumptions. First, they lump all Asian-Americans into one monolithic, homogeneous, yellow-skinned mass. Such a view ignores the existence of an incredibly disadvantaged Asian-American underclass. Asians work in low-income and low-status jobs two to three times more than whites (Cabezas 438). Recent Vietnamese refugees in California are living like the Appalachian poor. While going to his Manhattan office, multimillionaire architect I. M. Pei's car passes Chinese restaurants and laundries where 72 percent of all New York Chinese men still work (U.S. Bureau of the Census qtd. in Cabezas 443).

But the media make an even more dangerous assumption. They suggest that (alleged) material success is the same thing as basic racial equality. Citing that venerable family median income figure, magazines claim Asian-Americans are "obviously nondisadvantaged folks," as stated in *Fortune* (Seligman 64). Yet a 1979 United States Equal Employment Opportunity Commission study on Asian-Americans discovered widespread anti-Asian hiring and promotion practices. Asian-Americans "in the professional, technical, and managerial occupations" often face "modern racism—the subtle, sophisticated, systemic patterns and practices ... which function to effect and to obscure the discriminatory outcomes" (Nishi 398). One myth simply does not prove another: Neither our "astonishing economic prosperity" (Ramirez 152) nor a racially equal America exist.

An emphasis on material success also pervades the media's stress on Asian-Americans' educational status at "the top of the class" ("Asian Americans" 4). Our "march into the ranks of the educational elite," as *U.S. News & World Report* puts it (McBee et al. 41), is significant, according to *Fortune*, because "all that education is paying off spectacularly" (Ramirez 149). Once again, the same fallacious assumptions plague this "whiz kids" image of Asian-Americans.

The media again ignore the fact that class division accounts for much of the publicized success. Until 1976, the U.S. Immigration Department only admitted Asian immigrants that were termed "skilled" workers. "Skilled" generally meant college educated, usually in the sciences since poor English would not be a handicap. The result was that the vast majority of pre-1976 Asian immigrants came from already well-educated, upper-class backgrounds—the classic "brain drain" syndrome (Hirschman and Wong 507–10).

The post-1976 immigrants, however, come generally from the 10
lower, less educated classes (Kim 24). A study by Professor Elizabeth Ahn Toupin of Tufts University matched similar Asian and non-Asian students *along class lines* and found that Asian-Americans "did not perform at a superior academic level to non-Asian students. Asian-Americans were more likely to be placed on academic probation than their white counterparts. . . . Twice as many Asian-American students withdrew from the university" (12).

Thus, it is doubtful whether the perceived widespread educational success will continue as the Asian-American population eventually balances out along class lines. When 16.2 percent of all Chinese have less than four years of schooling (*four times* the percentage of whites) (Azores 73), it seems many future Asian-Americans will worry more about being able to read a newspaper rather than a Harvard acceptance letter.

Most important, the media assume once again that achieving a certain level of material or educational success means achieving real equality. People easily forget that to begin with, Asians invest heavily in education since other means of upward mobility are barred to them by race. Until recently, for instance, Asian-Americans were barred from unions and traditional lines of credit (Yun 23–24).[2] Other "white" avenues to success, such as the "old-boy network," are still closed to Asian-Americans.

When *Time* claims "as a result of their academic achievement Asians are climbing the economic ladder with remarkable speed," it glosses over an inescapable fact: There is a white ladder and then there is a yellow one. Almost all of the academic studies on the *actual returns Asians receive* from their education point to prevalent discrimination. A striking example of this was found in a City University of New York research project which constructed résumés with equivalent educational backgrounds. Applications were then sent to employers, one group under an Asian name and a similar group under a Caucasian name. Whites received interviews five times more than Asians (Nishi 399). The media never headline even more shocking data that can be easily found in the U.S. Census. For instance, Chinese and Filipino males only earned respectively 74 percent and 52 percent as much as their *equally educated* white counterparts. Asian females fared even worse. Their salaries were only 44 percent to 54 percent as large as equivalent white males' paychecks (Cabezas 391). Blacks suffer from this same statistical disparity. We Asian-Americans are indeed a Model Minority—a perfect model of racial discrimination in America.

Yet this media myth encourages neglect of our pressing needs. "Clearly, many Asian-Americans and Pacific peoples are invisible to the governmental agencies," reported the California State Advisory Committee to the U.S. Commission on Civil Rights. "Discrimination against Asian-Americans and Pacific peoples is as much the result of omission as commission" (qtd. in Chun 7). In 1979, while the president praised Asian-Americans' "successful integration into American society," his administration revoked Asian-Americans' eligibility for minority small business loans, devastating thousands of struggling, newly arrived small businessmen. Hosts of other minority issues, ranging from reparations for the Japanese-American internment to the ominous rise of anti-Asian violence, are widely ignored by the general public.

The media, in fact, insist to the general populace that we are not a true racial minority. In an attack on affirmative action, the *Boston Globe* pointed out that universities, like many people, "obviously feel that Asian-Americans, especially those of Chinese and Japanese descent, are brilliant, privileged, and wrongly classified 15
as minorities" ("Affirmative Non-actions" 10). Harvard Dean Henry Rosovsky remarked in the same article that "It does not seem to me that as a group, they are disadvantaged. . . . Asian-Americans appear to be in an odd category among other protected minorities."

The image that we Asians aren't like "other minorities" is fundamental to the Model Minority ideology. Any elementary-school student knows that the teacher designates one student the model, the "teachers pet," in order to set an example for others to follow. One only sets up a "model minority" in order to communicate to the other "students," the blacks and Hispanics, "Why can't you be like that?" The media, in fact, almost admit to "grading" minorities as they headline Model Minority stories "Asian-Americans: Are They Making the Grade?" (McBee et al.). And Asians have earned the highest grade by fulfilling one important assignment: identifying with the white majority, with its values and wishes.

Unlike blacks, for instance, we Asian-Americans have not vigorously asserted our ethnic identity (a.k.a. Black Power). And the American public has historically demanded assimilation over racial pluralism.[3] Over the years, *Newsweek* has published titles from

"Success Story: Out-whiting the Whites" to "The Ultimate Assimilation," which lauded the increasing number of Asian-white marriages as evidence of Asian-Americans' "acceptance into American society" (Kantrowitz et al. 80).

Even more significant is the public's approval of how we have succeeded in the "American tradition" (Ramirez 164). Unlike the blacks and Hispanics, we "Puritan-like" Asians (Oxnam 72) disdain governmental assistance. A *New Republic* piece, "The Triumph of Asian-Americans," similarly applauded how "Asian-Americans pose no problems at all" (Bell 30). The media consistently compare the crime-ridden image of other minorities with the picture of law-abiding Asian parents whose "well-behaved kids" hit books and not the streets ("Asian Americans" 4).

Some insist there is nothing terrible about whites conjuring up our "tremendous" success, divining from it model American traits, then preaching, "Why can't you blacks and Hispanics be like that?" After all, one might argue, aren't those traits desirable?

Such a view, as mentioned, neglects Asian-Americans' true and pressing needs. Moreover, this view completely misses the Model Minority image's fundamental ideology, an ideology meant to falsely grant America absolution from its racial barriers.

David O. Sears and Donald R. Kinder, two social scientists, have recently published significant empirical studies on the underpinnings of American racial attitudes. They consistently discovered that Americans' stress on "values, such as 'individualism and self-reliance, the work ethic, obedience, and discipline'... can be invoked, however perversely, to feed racist appetites" (qtd. in Kennedy 88). In other words, the Model Minority image lets Americans' consciences rest easy. They can think: "It's not our fault those blacks and Hispanics can't make it. They're just too lazy. After all, look at the Asians."[4] Consequently, American society never confronts the systemic racial and economic factors underlying such inequality. The victims instead bear the blame.

This ideology behind the Model Minority image is best seen when we examine one of the first Model Minority stories, which suddenly appeared in the mid-1960s. It is important to note that the period was marked by newfound, strident black demands for equality and power.

> At a time when it is being proposed that hundreds of billions be spent to uplift Negroes and other minorities, the nation's 300,000 Chinese-Americans are moving ahead on their own—with no help from anyone else. . . . Few Chinese-Americans are getting welfare handouts—or even want them. . . . They don't sit around moaning. ("Success Story of One Minority Group" 73).

The same article then concludes that the Chinese-American history and accomplishment "would shock those now complaining about the hardships endured by today's Negroes."

Not surprisingly, the dunce-capped blacks and Hispanics resent us apple-polishing, "well-behaved" teacher's pets. Black comedian Richard Pryor performs a revealing routine in which new Asian immigrants learn from whites their first English word, "Nigger." And Asian-Americans themselves succumb to the Model Minority's deceptive mythology and racist ideology.[5] "I made it without help," one often hears among Asian circles; "why can't they?" In a 1986 nationwide poll, only 27% of Asian-American students rated "racial understanding" as "essential." The figure plunged 9 percent in the last year alone (a year marked by a torrent of Model Minority stories) (Hune). We "whitewashed" Asians have simply lost our identity as a fellow, disadvantaged minority.

But we don't even need to look beyond the Model Minority stories themselves to realize that whites see us as "whiter" than blacks—but not quite white enough. For instance, citing that familiar median family income figure, *Fortune* magazine of 17 May 1982 complained that the Asian-American community is in fact "getting *more* than its share of the pie" (Seligman 64). For decades, when white Americans were leading the nation in every single economic measure, editorials arguing that whites were getting more than *their* share of the pie were rather rare.

No matter how "well-behaved" we are, Asian-Americans are still excluded from the real pie, the "positions of institutional power and political power" (Kuo 289). Professor Harry Kitano of UCLA has written extensively on the plight of Asian-Americans as the "middleman minority," a minority supposedly satisfied materially but forever racially barred from a true, *significant* role in society. Empirical studies indicate that Asian-Americans "have been channeled into lower-echelon white-collar jobs having little or no decision making authority" (Suzuki 38). For example, in *Fortune's* 1,000 largest companies, Asian-American nameplates rest on a mere half of one percent of all officers' and directors' desks (a statistical disparity worsened by the fact that most of the Asians founded their companies) (Ramirez 152). While the education of the upper-class Asians may save them from the bread lines, their race still keeps them from the boardroom.

Our docile acceptance of such exclusion is actually one of our "model" traits. When Asian-Americans in San Francisco showed their first hint of political activism and protested Asian exclusion from city boards, the *Washington Monthly* warned in a long Asian-American article, "Watch out, here comes another group to pander to" ("The Wrong Way" 21). *The New Republic* praised Asian-American political movements because

> Unlike blacks or Hispanics, Asian-American politicians have the luxury of not having to devote the bulk of their time to an "Asian-American agenda," and thus escape becoming prisoners of such an agenda. . . . The most important thing for Asian-Americans... is simply "being part of the process." (Bell 31)

This is strikingly reminiscent of another of the first Model Minority stories:

> As the Black and Brown communities push for changes in the present system, the Oriental is set forth as an example to be followed—a minority group that has achieved success through adaptation rather than confrontation. *(Gidra* qtd. in Chun 7)

But it is precisely this "present system," this system of subtle, persistent racism that we all must confront, not adapt to. For example, we Asians gained our right to vote from the 1964 Civil Rights Act that blacks marched, bled, died, and, in the words of that original Model Minority story, "sat around moaning for." Unless we assert our true identity as a minority and challenge racial misconceptions and inequalities, we will be nothing more than techno-coolies—collecting our wages but silently enduring basic political and economic inequality.

This country perpetuated a myth once. Today, no one can afford to dreamily chase after that gold in the streets, oblivious to the genuine treasure of racial equality. When racism persists, can one really call any minority a "model"?

Notes

1. The picture becomes even more disturbing when one realizes the higher income figures do not necessarily equal higher quality of life. For instance, in New York Chinatown, more than one out of five work more than fifty-seven hours per week, almost one out of ten elderly must labor more than fifty-five hours per week (Nishi 503).
2. For further analysis on the role racism plays in Asian-Americans' stress on education and certain technical and scientific fields, see Suzuki (44).
3. A full discussion of racial pluralism versus assimilation is impossible here. But suffice it to say that pluralism accepts ethnic cultures as equally different; assimilation asks for a "melting" into the majority. An example of the assimilation philosophy is the massive "Americanization" programs of the late 1880s, which successfully erased Eastern European immigrants' customs in favor of Anglo-Saxon ones.
4. This phenomenon of blaming the victim for racial inequality is as old as America itself. For instance, southerners once eased their consciences over slavery by labeling blacks as animals lacking humanity. Today, America does it by labeling them as inferior people lacking "desirable" traits. For an excellent further analysis of this ideology, actually widespread among American intellectuals, see *Iron Cages: Race and Culture in 19th-century America* by Ronald T. Takaki.

5. America has a long history of playing off one minority against the other. During the early 1900s, for instance, mining companies in the west often hired Asians solely as scabs against striking black miners. Black versus Asian hostility and violence usually followed. This pattern was repeated in numerous industries. In a larger historical sense, almost every immigrant group has assimilated, to some degree, the culture of antiblack racism.

Works Cited

"Affirmative Non-actions." Op-ed. *Boston Globe* 14 Jan. 1985: 10.

"Asian Americans, The Drive to Excel." *Newsweek on Campus* April 1984: 4–13.

Asian American Studies: Contemporary Issues. Proc. from East Coast Asian American Scholars Conf. 1986.

Azores, Fortunata M. "Census Methodology and the Development of Social Indicators for Asian and Pacific Americans." United States Commission on Civil Rights 70–79.

Bell, David A. "The Triumph of Asian-Americans." *New Republic* 15 & 22 July 1985:24–31.

Cabezas, Armado. "Employment Issues of Asian Americans." United States Commission on Civil Rights.

Chun, Ki-Taek. "The Myth of Asian American Success and Its Educational Ramifications." *IRCD Bulletin* Winter/Spring 1980.

Doerner, William R. "To America with Skills." *Time* 8 July 1985: 42–44.

Dutta, Manoranjan. "Asian/Pacific American Employment Profile: Myth and Reality—Issues and Answers." United States Commission on Civil Rights 445–89.

Hirschman, Charles, and Morrison G. Wong. "Trends in Socioeconomic Achievement Among Immigrants and Native-Born Asian-Americans, 1960–1976." *Sociological Quarterly* 22.4 (1981): 495–513.

Hune, Shirley. Keynote address. East Coast Asian Student Union Conference. Boston University. 14 Feb. 1987.

Kahng, Anthony. "Employment Issues." United States Commission on Civil Rights 1980.

Kantrowitz, Barbara, et al. "The Ultimate Assimilation." *Newsweek* 24 Nov. 1986: 80.

Kasindorf, Martin, et al. "Asian-Americans: A 'Model Minority.'" *Newsweek* 6 Dec. 1982:39–51.

Kennedy, David M. "The Making of a Classic. Gunnar Myrdal and Black-White Relations: The Use and Abuse of *An American Dilemma.*" *Atlantic* May 1987: 86–89.

Kiang, Peter. Personal interview. 1 May 1987.

Kim, Illsoo. "Class Division Among Asian Immigrants: Its Implications for Social Welfare Policy." *Asian American Studies* 24–25.

Kuo, Wen H. "On the Study of Asian-Americans: Its Current State and Agenda." *Sociological Quarterly* 20.2 (1979): 279–90.

Mariano, Robert S. "Census Issues." United States Commission on Civil Rights 54–59.

McBee, Susanna, et al. "Asian-Americans: Are They Making the Grade?" *U.S. News & World Report* 2 Apr. 1984: 41–47.

Nishi, Setsuko Matsunaga. "Asian American Employment Issues: Myths and Realities." United States Commission on Civil Rights 397–99, 495–507.

Oxnam, Robert B. "Why Asians Succeed Here." *New York Times Magazine* 30 Nov. 1986:72+.

Ramirez, Anthony. "America's Super Minority." *Fortune* 24 Nov. 1986: 148–49.

Seligman, Daniel. "Keeping Up: Working Smarter." *Fortune* 17 May 1982: 64.

"Success Story of One Minority Group in the U.S." *U.S. News & World Report* 26 Dec. 1966: 73–76.

"Success Story: Outwhiting the Whites." *Newsweek* 21 June 1971: 24–25. Sung, Betty Lee. *A Survey of Chinese American Manpower and Employment*. New York: Praeger, 1976.

Suzuki, Bob H. "Education and the Socialization of Asian Americans: A Revisionist Analysis of the 'Model Minority' Thesis." *Amerasia Journal* 4.2 (1977): 23–51.

Toupin, Elizabeth Ahn. "A Model University for a Model Minority." *Asian American Studies* 10–12.

United States Commission on Civil Rights. *Civil Rights Issues of Asian and Pacific Americans: Myths and Realities*. 1980.

"The Wrong Way to Court Ethnics." *Washington Monthly* May 1986: 21–26.

Yun, Grace. "Notes from Discussions on Asian American Education." *Asian American Studies* 20–24.

The Human Cost of an Illiterate Society

Jonathan Kozol [b. 1960]

Jonathan Kozol (1936–) was born in Boston and graduated from Harvard University. He has taught at Yale University, Trinity College, and the University of Massachusetts at Amherst as well as several public schools. He is well known for his writing on social and educational issues, often calling for educational reform and more realistic examination of societal problems. His books include Death at an Early Age *(1967),* Free Schools *(1972),* On Being a Teacher *(1981),* Illiterate America *(1985),* Rachel and Her Children: Homeless Families in America *(1986), and* Savage Inequalities: Children in America's Schools *(1991). The following selection is an excerpt from* Illiterate America. *Kozol does not explore the causes of illiteracy in this selection, as he does elsewhere in this book, but instead looks at a wide range of effects, or costs, of illiteracy, both for society and the individual. Before beginning to read, think for a moment about what it might mean to be illiterate. Try to imagine how many ways your life would be different if you couldn't read. Regardless of how imaginative you are, you are likely to be shocked by all the ways illiteracy affects an illiterate person and society as a whole.*

> PRECAUTIONS. READ BEFORE USING.
> Poison: Contains sodium hydroxide (caustic soda-lye).
> Corrosive: Causes severe eye and skin damage, may cause blindness.
> Harmful or fatal if swallowed.
> If swallowed, give large quantities of milk or water.
> Do not induce vomiting.
> Important: Keep water out of can at all times to prevent contents from violently erupting . . .
>
> —WARNING ON A CAN OF DRĀNO

We are speaking here no longer of the dangers faced by passengers on Eastern Airlines or the dollar costs incurred by U.S. corporations and tax-payers. We are speaking now of human suffering and of the ethical dilemmas that are faced by a society that looks upon such suffering with qualified concern but does not take those actions which its wealth and ingenuity would seemingly demand.

Questions of literacy, in Socrates' belief, must at length be judged as matters of morality. Socrates could not have had in mind the moral compromise peculiar to a nation like our own. Some of our Founding Fathers did, however, have this question in their minds. One of the wisest of those Founding Fathers (one who may not have been most compassionate but surely was more prescient than some of his peers) recognized the special dangers that illiteracy would pose to basic equity in the political construction that he helped to shape.

"A people who mean to be their own governors," James Madison wrote, "must arm themselves with the power knowledge gives. A popular government without popular information or the means of acquiring it, is but a prologue to a farce or a tragedy, or perhaps both."

Tragedy looms larger than farce in the United States today. Illiterate citizens seldom vote. Those who do are forced to cast a vote of questionable worth. They cannot make informed decisions based on serious print information. Sometimes they can be alerted to their interests by aggressive voter education. More frequently, they vote for a face, a smile, or a style, not for a mind or character or body of beliefs.

The number of illiterate adults exceeds by 16 million the entire vote cast for the winner in the 1980 presidential contest. If even one third of all illiterates could vote, and read enough and do sufficient math to vote in their self-interest, Ronald Reagan would not likely have been chosen president. There is, of course, no way to know for sure. We do know this: Democracy is a mendacious term when used by those who are prepared to countenance the forced exclusion of one third of our electorate. So long as 60 million people are denied significant participation, the government is neither of, nor for, nor by, the people. It is a government, at best, of those two thirds whose wealth, skin color, or parental privilege allows them opportunity to profit from the provocation and instruction of the written word.

The undermining of democracy in the United States is one "expense" that sensitive Americans can easily deplore because it represents a contradiction that endangers citizens of all political positions. The human price is not so obvious at first.

Since I first immersed myself within this work I have often had the following dream: I find that I am in a railroad station or a large department store within a city that is utterly unknown to me and where I cannot understand the printed words. None of the signs or symbols is familiar. Everything looks strange: like mirror writing of some kind. Gradually I understand that I am in the Soviet Union. All the letters on the walls around me are Cyrillic. I look for my pocket dictionary but I find that it has been mislaid. Where have I left it? Then I recall that I forgot to bring it with me when I packed my bags in Boston. I struggle to remember the name of my hotel. I try to ask somebody for directions. One person stops and looks at me in a peculiar way. I lose the nerve to ask. At last I reach into my wallet for an ID card. The card is missing. Have I lost it? Then I remember that my card was confiscated for some reason, many years before. Around this point, I wake up in a panic.

This panic is not so different from the misery that millions of adult illiterates experience each day within the course of their routine existence in the U.S.A.

Illiterates cannot read the menu in a restaurant.

They cannot read the cost of items on the menu in the *window* of the restaurant before they enter.

Illiterates cannot read the letters that their children bring home 10
from their teachers. They cannot study school department circulars that tell them of the courses that their children must be taking if they hope to pass the SAT exams. They cannot help with homework. They cannot write a letter to the teacher. They are afraid to visit in the classroom. They do not want to humiliate their child or themselves.

Illiterates cannot read instructions on a bottle of prescription medicine. They cannot find out when a medicine is past the year of safe consumption; nor can they read of allergenic risks, warnings to diabetics, or the potential sedative effect of certain kinds of nonprescription pills. They cannot observe preventive health care admonitions. They cannot read about "the seven warning signs of cancer" or the indications of blood-sugar fluctuations or the risks of eating certain foods that aggravate the likelihood of cardiac arrest.

Illiterates live, in more than literal ways, an uninsured existence. They cannot understand the written details on a health insurance form. They cannot read the waivers that they sign preceding surgical procedures. Several women I have known in Boston have entered a slum hospital with the intention of obtaining a tubal ligation and have emerged a few days later after having been subjected to a hysterectomy. Unaware of their rights, incognizant of jargon, intimidated by the unfamiliar air of fear and atmosphere of ether that so many of us find oppressive in the confines even of the most attractive and expensive medical facilities, they have signed their names to documents they could not read and which nobody, in the hectic situation that prevails so often in those overcrowded hospitals that serve the urban poor, had even bothered to explain.

Childbirth might seem to be the last inalienable right of any female citizen within a civilized society. Illiterate mothers, as we shall see, already have been cheated of the power to protect their progeny against the likelihood of demolition in deficient public schools and, as a result, against the verbal servitude within which they themselves exist. Surgical denial of the right to bear that child in the first place represents an ultimate denial, an unspeakable metaphor, a final darkness that denies even the twilight gleamings of our own humanity. What greater violation of our biological, our biblical, our spiritual humanity could possibly exist than that which takes place nightly, perhaps hourly these days, within such overburdened and benighted institutions as the Boston City Hospital? Illiteracy has many costs; few are so irreversible as this.

Even the roof above one's head, the gas or other fuel for heating that protects the residents of northern city slums against the threat of illness in the winter months become uncertain guarantees. Illiterates cannot read the lease that they must sign to live in an apartment which, too often, they cannot afford. They cannot manage check accounts and therefore seldom pay for anything by mail.

Hours and entire days of difficult travel (and the cost of bus or other public transit) must be added to the real cost of whatever they consume. Loss of interest on the check accounts they do not have, and could not manage if they did, must be regarded as another of the excess costs paid by the citizen who is excluded from the common instruments of commerce in a numerate society.

"I couldn't understand the bills," a woman in Washington, D.C., reports, "and then I couldn't write the checks to pay them. We signed things we didn't know what they were."

Illiterates cannot read the notices that they receive from welfare offices or from the IRS. They must depend on word-of-mouth instruction from the welfare worker—or from other persons whom they have good reason to mistrust. They do not know what rights they have, what deadlines and requirements they face, what options they might choose to exercise. They are half-citizens. Their rights exist in print but not in fact.

Illiterates cannot look up numbers in a telephone directory. Even if they can find the names of friends, few possess the sorting skills to make use of the yellow pages; categories are bewildering and trade names are beyond decoding capabilities for millions of nonreaders. Even the emergency numbers listed on the first page of the phone book—"Ambulance," "Police," and "Fire"—are too frequently beyond the recognition of nonreaders.

Many illiterates cannot read the admonition on a pack of cigarettes. Neither the Surgeon General's warning nor its reproduction on the package can alert them to the risks. Although most people learn by word of mouth that smoking is related to a number of grave physical disorders, they do not get the chance to read the detailed stories which can document this danger with the vividness that turns concern into determination to resist. They can see the handsome cowboy or the slim Virginia lady lighting up a filter cigarette; they cannot heed the words that tell them that this product is (not "may be") dangerous to their health. Sixty million men and women are condemned to be the unalerted, high-risk candidates for cancer.

Illiterates do not buy "no-name" products in the supermarkets. They must depend on photographs or the familiar logos that are printed on the packages of brand-name groceries. The poorest people, therefore, are denied the benefits of the least costly products.

Illiterates depend almost entirely upon label recognition. Many labels, however, are not easy to distinguish. Dozens of different kinds of Campbell's soup appear identical to the nonreaders The purchaser who cannot read and does not dare to ask for help, out of the fear of being stigmatized (a fear which is unfortunately realistic), frequently comes home with something which she never wanted and her family never tasted.

Illiterates cannot read instructions on a pack of frozen food. Packages sometimes provide an illustration to explain the cooking preparations; but illustrations are of little help to someone who must "boil water, drop the food—*within* its plastic wrapper—in the boiling water, wait for it to simmer, instantly remove."

Even when labels are seemingly clear, they may be easily mistaken. A woman in Detroit brought home a gallon of Crisco for her children's dinner. She thought that she had bought the chicken that was pictured on the label. She had enough Crisco now to last a year—but no more money to go back and buy the food for dinner.

Recipes provided on the packages of certain staples sometimes tempt a semiliterate person to prepare a meal her children have not tasted. The longing to vary the uniform and often starchy content of low-budget meals provided to the family that relies on food stamps commonly leads to ruinous results. Scarce funds have been wasted and the food must be thrown out. The same applies to distribution of food-surplus produce in emergency conditions. Government inducements to poor people to "explore the ways" by which to make a tasty meal from tasteless noodles, surplus cheese, and powdered milk are useless to nonreaders. Intended as benevolent advice, such recommendations mock reality and foster deeper feelings of resentment and of inability to cope. (Those, on the other hand, who cautiously refrain from "innovative" recipes in preparation of their children's meals must suffer the opprobrium of "laziness," "lack of imagination. . . .")

Illiterates cannot travel freely. When they attempt to do so, 25
they encounter risks that few of us can dream of. They cannot read traffic signs and, while they often learn to recognize and to decipher symbols, they cannot manage street names which they haven't seen before. The same is true for bus and subway stops. While ingenuity can sometimes help a man or woman to discern directions from familiar landmarks, buildings, cemeteries, churches, and the like, most illiterates are virtually immobilized. They seldom wander past the streets and neighborhoods they know. Geographical paralysis becomes a bitter metaphor for their entire existence. They are immobilized in almost every sense we can imagine. They can't move up. They can't move out. They cannot see beyond. Illiterates may take an oral test for drivers' permits in most sections of America. It is a questionable concession. Where will they go? How will they get there? How will they get home? Could it be that some of us might like it better if they stayed where they belong?

Travel is only one of many instances of circumscribed existence. Choice, in almost all its facets, is diminished in the life of an illiterate adult. Even the printed TV schedule, which provides most people with the luxury of preselection, does not belong within the arsenal of options in illiterate existence. One consequence is that the viewer watches only what appears at moments when he happens to have time to turn the switch. Another consequence, a lot more common, is that the TV set remains in operation night and day. Whatever the program offered at the hour when he walks into the room will be the nutriment that he accepts and swallows. Thus, to passivity, is added frequency—indeed, almost uninterrupted continuity. Freedom to select is no more possible here than in the choice of home or surgery or food.

"You don't choose," said one illiterate woman. "You take your wishes from somebody else." Whether in perusal of a menu, selection of highways, purchase of groceries, or determination of affordable enjoyment, illiterate Americans must trust somebody else: a friend, a relative, a stranger on the street, a grocery clerk, a TV copywriter.

"All of our mail we get, it's hard for her to read. Settin' down and writing a letter, she can't do it. Like if we get a bill . . . we take it over to my sister-in-law . . . My sister-in-law reads it."

Billing agencies harass poor people for the payment of the bills for purchases that might have taken place six months before. Utility companies offer an agreement for a staggered payment schedule on a bill past due. "You have to trust them," one man said. Precisely for this reason, you end up by trusting no one and suspecting everyone of possible deceit. A submerged sense of distrust becomes the corollary to a constant need to trust. "They are cheating me . . . I have been tricked . . . I do not know . . ."

Not knowing: This is a familiar theme. Not knowing the right word for the right thing at the right time is one form of subjugation. Not knowing the world that lies concealed behind those words is a more terrifying feeling. The longitude and latitude of one's existence are beyond all easy apprehension. Even the hard, cold stars within the firmament above one's head begin to mock the possibilities for self-location. Where am I? Where did I come from? Where will I go?

"I've lost a lot of jobs," one man explains. "Today, even if you're a janitor, there's still reading and writing . . . They leave a note saying, 'Go to room so-and-so . . .' You can't do it. You can't read it. You don't know."

"The hardest thing about it is that I've been places where I didn't know where I was. You don't know where you are . . . You're lost."

"Like I said: I have two kids. What do I do if one of my kids starts choking? I go running to the phone . . . I can't look up the hospital phone number. That's if we're at home. Out on the street, I can't read the sign. I get to a pay phone. 'Okay, tell us where you are. We'll send an ambulance.' I look at the street sign. Right there, I can't tell you what it says. I'd have to spell it out, letter for letter. By that time, one of my kids would be dead . . . These are the kinds of fears you go with, every single day . . ."

"Reading directions, I suffer with. I work with chemicals . . . That's scary to begin with . . . "

"You sit down. They throw the menu in front of you. Where 35
do you go from there? Nine times out of ten you say, 'Go ahead. Pick out something for the both of us.' I've eaten some weird things, let me tell you!"

Menus. Chemicals. A child choking while his mother searches for a word she does not know to find assistance that will come too late. Another mother speaks about the inability to help her kids to read: "I can't read to them. Of course that's leaving them out of something they should have. Oh, it matters. You *believe* it matters! I ordered all these books. The kids belong to a book club. Donny wanted me to read a book to him. I told Donny: 'I can't read,' He said: 'Mommy, you sit down. I'll read it to you.' I tried it one day, reading from the pictures. Donny looked at me. He said, 'Mommy, that's not right.' He's only five. He knew I couldn't read . . .'"

A landlord tells a woman that her lease allows him to evict her if her baby cries and causes inconvenience to her neighbors. The consequence of challenging his words conveys a danger which appears, unlikely as it seems, even more alarming than the danger of eviction. Once she admits that she can't read, in the desire to maneuver for the time in which to call a friend, she will have defined herself in terms of an explicit impotence that she cannot endure. Capitulation in this case is preferable to self-humiliation. Resisting the definition of oneself in terms of what one cannot do, what others take for granted, represents a need so great that other imperatives (even one so urgent as the need to keep one's home in winter's cold) evaporate and fall away in face of fear. Even the loss of home and shelter, in this case, is not so terrifying as the loss of self.

"I come out of school. I was sixteen. They had their meetings. The directors meet. They said that I was wasting their school paper. I was wasting pencils . . ."

Another illiterate, looking back, believes she was not worthy of her teacher's time. She believes that it was wrong of her to take up space within her school. She believes that it was right to leave in order that somebody more deserving could receive her place.

Children choke. Their mother chokes another way: on more than chicken bones.

People eat what others order, know what others tell them, struggle not to see themselves as they believe the world perceives them. A man in California speaks about his own loss of identity, of self-location, definition:

"I stood at the bottom of the ramp. My car had broke down on the freeway. There was a phone. I asked for the police. They was nice. They said to tell them where I was. I looked up at the signs. There was one that I had seen before. I read it to them: ONE WAY STREET. They thought it was a joke. I told them I couldn't read. There was other signs above the ramp. They told me to try. I looked around for somebody to help. All the cars was going by real fast. I couldn't make them understand that I was lost. The cop was nice. He told me: 'Try once more,' I did my best. I couldn't read. I only knew the sign above my head. The cop was trying to be nice. He knew that I was trapped. 'I can't send out a car to you if you can't tell me where you are.' I felt afraid. I nearly cried. I'm forty-eight years old. I only said: 'I'm on a one-way street . . .'"

Perhaps we might slow down a moment here and look at the realities described above. This is the nation that we live in. This is a society that most of us did not create but which our President and other leaders have been willing to sustain by virtue of malign neglect. Do we possess the character and courage to address a problem which so many nations, poorer than our own, have found it natural to correct?

The answers to these questions represent a reasonable test of our belief in the democracy to which we have been asked in public school to swear allegiance.

The Limits to Growth

Donella Meadows
Dennis L. Meadows
Jorgen Randers

The following conclusions have emerged from our work so far. We are by no means the first group to have stated them. For the past several decades, people who have looked at the world with a global, long-term perspective have reached similar conclusions. Nevertheless, the vast majority of policy-makers seem to be actively pursuing goals that are inconsistent with these results.

Our conclusions are:

1. If the present growth trends in world population, industrialization, pollution, food production, and resource depletion continue especially unchanged, the limits to growth on this planet will be reached sometime within the next one hundred years. The most probable result will be a rather sudden and uncontrollable decline in both population and industrial capacity.
2. It is possible to alter these growth trends and to establish a condition of ecological and economic stability that is sustainable far into the future. The state of global equilibrium could be designed so that the basic material needs of each person on earth are satisfied and each person has an equal opportunity to realize his individual human potential.
3. If the world's people decide to strive for this second outcome rather than the first, the sooner they begin working to attain it, the greater will be their chances of success.

These conclusions are so far-reaching and raise so many questions for further study that we are quite frankly overwhelmed by the enormity of the job that must be done. We hope that this book will serve to interest other people, in many fields of study and in many countries of the world, to raise the space and time horizons of their concerns and join us in understanding and preparing for a period of great transition—the transition from growth to global equilibrium. . . .

All five elements basic to the study reported here—population, food production, industrialization, pollution, and consumption of nonrenewable natural resources are increasing. The amount of their increase each year follows a pattern that mathematicians call exponential growth. . . .

Most people are accustomed to thinking of growth as a *linear* process. A quantity is growing linearly when it increases by a constant amount in a constant time period. For example, a child who becomes one inch taller each year is growing linearly. If a miser hides $10 each year under his mattress, his horde of money is also increasing in a linear way. The amount of increase each year is obviously not affected by the size of the child nor the amount of money already under the mattress.

A quantity exhibits *exponential* growth when it increases by a constant percentage of the whole in a constant time period. A colony of yeast cells in which each cell divides into two cells every ten minutes is growing exponentially. For each single cell, after ten minutes there will be two cells, an increase of 100 per cent. After the next ten minutes there will be four cells, then eight, then sixteen. If a miser takes $100 from his mattress and invests it at 7 per cent (so that the total amount accumulated increases by 7 per cent each year), the invested money will grow much faster than the linearly increasing stock under the mattress. The amount added each year to a bank account or each ten minutes to a yeast colony is not constant. It continually increases, as the total accumulated amount increases. Such exponential growth is a common process in biological, financial, and many other systems of the world.

Common as it is, exponential growth can yield surprising results—results that have fascinated mankind for centuries. There is an old Persian legend about a clever courtier who presented a beautiful chessboard to his king and requested that the king give him in return one grain of rice for the first square on the board, two grains for the second square, four grains for the third, and so forth. The king readily agreed and ordered rice to be brought from his stores. The fourth square of the chessboard required eight grains, the tenth square took 512 grains, the fifteenth required 16,384, and the twenty-first square gave the courtier more than a million grains of rice. By the fortieth square a million million rice grains had to be brought from the storerooms. The king's entire rice supply was exhausted long before he reached the sixty-fourth square. Exponential increase is deceptive because it generates immense numbers very quickly.

A French riddle for children illustrates another aspect of exponential growth—the apparent suddenness with which it approaches a fixed limit. Suppose you own a pond on which a water lily is growing. The lily plant doubles in size each day. If the lily were allowed to grow unchecked, it would completely cover the pond in thirty days, choking off the other forms of life in the water. For a long time the lily plant seems small, and so you decide not to worry about cutting it back until it covers half the pond. On what day will that be? On the twenty-ninth day, of course. You have one day to save your pond. . . .

The earth's crust contains vast amounts of those raw materials which man has learned to mine and to transform into useful things. However vast those amounts may be, they are not infinite. Now that we have seen how suddenly an exponentially growing quantity approaches a fixed upper limit, the following statement should not come as a surprise. *Given present resource consumption rates and the projected increase in these rates, the great majority of the currently important non-renewable resources will be extremely costly a hundred years from now.* The above statement remains true regardless of the most optimistic assumptions about undiscovered reserves, technological advances, substitution, or recycling, as long as the demand for resources continues to grow exponentially. The prices of those resources with the shortest static reserve indices have already begun to increase. The price of mercury, for example, has gone up 500 per cent in the last twenty years; the price of lead has increased 300 per cent in the last thirty years. . . .

Are there enough resources to allow the economic development of the seven billion people expected by the year 2000 to a reasonably high standard of living? Once again the answer must be a conditional one. It depends on how the major resource-consuming societies handle some important decisions ahead. They might continue to increase resource consumption according to the present pattern. They might learn to reclaim and recycle discarded materials. They might develop new designs to increase the durability of products made from scarce resources. They might encourage social and economic patterns that would satisfy the need of a person while minimizing, rather than maximizing, the irreplaceable substances he possesses and disperses.

All of these possible courses involve trade-offs. The trade-offs are particularly difficult in this case because they involve choosing between present benefits and future benefits. In order to guarantee the availability of adequate resources in the future, policies must be adopted that will decrease resource use in the present. Most of these policies operate by raising resource costs. Recycling and better product design are expensive; in most parts of the world today they are considered 'uneconomic.' Even if they were effectively instituted, however, as long as the driving feedback loops of population and industrial growth continue to generate more people and a higher resource demand per capita, the system is being pushed toward its limit—the depletion of the earth's nonrenewable resources.

What happens to the metals and fuels extracted from the earth after they have been used and discarded? In one sense they are never lost. Their constituent atoms are rearranged and eventually dispersed in a diluted and unusable form into the air, the soil, and the waters of our planet. The natural ecological systems can absorb many of the effluents of human activity and reprocess them into substances that are usable by, or at least harmless to, other forms of life. When any effluent is released on a large enough scale, however, the natural absorptive mechanisms can become saturated.

The wastes of human civilization can build up in the environment until they become visible, annoying, and even harmful. Mercury in ocean fish, lead particles in city air, mountains of urban trash, oil slicks on beaches—these are the results of the increasing flow of resources into man's hands. It is little wonder, then, that another exponentially increasing quantity in the world system is pollution.

Pie in the Sky

Bill McKibben [b. 1960]

Question: should anyone who requires a "revolutionary new laser technology system" in order to figure out if they're parking in the right spot inside their own garage really be allowed behind the wheel in the first place? Compared with the other tasks of a driver—making right-hand turns, making left-hand turns, deciphering the red-amber-green vernacular of a stoplight—safely positioning your auto within the confines of your own garage seems like a fairly straightforward task, the kind of thing that might not require a laser.

But you'd be surprised how useful lasers can be. The Hairmax Laser Comb, for instance, used only fifteen minutes a day, three times a week, results in noticeably thicker locks and tresses. And not just lasers. Ions are also surprisingly useful—confusingly, negative ions. A lamp made of salt crystal mined from the Himalayas emits them, aiding you in the fight against "dust mites" and also "depression."

If there's any piece of writing that defines our culture, I submit it's the SkyMall catalogue, available in the seatback pocket of every airplane in North America. To browse its pages is to understand the essential secret of American consumer life: We've officially run out not only of things that we need, but even of things that we might plausibly desire.

But we in the airline traveling class still have a few problems to solve in our lives. Judging from the joys on offer, our particular worries at the moment might be categorized as follows:

I'm overworked and overtired. In which case, I need a $4,000 massaging recliner with voice control, synthetic leather ("softer, more plush than leather"), and thirty-three airbags—a machine that "pampers your body and soothes your soul." And if perchance I drift off to sleep, "the peaceful progression wake-up clock" will rouse me with infinite care. "Thirty minutes before wake-up time, the light glows softly, brightening over the next half hour, while faint aromatherapy scents release into the air. Fifteen minutes before wake up, the clock generates one of six soft nature sounds." In case that isn't quite enough, I might want to back it up with the "sensory assault alarm clock," whose large, wired vibrating pad placed under the mattress shakes you awake in time to turn off the clock before it emits a ninety-five-decibel alarm and starts flashing a strobe light.

I have an immense supply of trousers, and hence require the closet organizer trouser rack to keep twenty pairs of slacks neatly hung and readily accessible. The five-eighths-inch-diameter birch dowels "reduce creasing of even fine fabrics," and "nylon washers between the dowels ensure smooth swing motion."

I distrust my neighbors and government, and so would benefit from a giant-capacity mailbox that holds up to two weeks of mail (catalogues, presumably). "Don't bother a neighbor to get your mail, and don't tell the post office you'll be away."

I am extremely, extremely clean. I'm therefore thankful that my toothbrush has been ultravioletly cleansed overnight to remove the "millions of germs" that would otherwise accumulate, and my room is protected against "airborne bacteria, viruses, and germs" by a Germ Guardian machine, "proven by a Harvard researcher," which "takes ultraviolet C energy and multiplies its germ-killing power in our exclusive Intensifier Chamber." Also, I have another very similar-looking machine "now with exclusive Ozoneguard" in case any ozone is nearby. And a soap dispenser with infrared sensor technology for my shower, a "no-touch approach that dramatically reduces the chance of spreading germs."

I have way too many watches, and therefore might benefit from a $300 case that will shake them all with "intermittent timers and directional controls" to mimic the action of a human wrist and hence keep them fully wound at all times.

10 *I have plugged in so many things that the planet has warmed considerably, reducing the chances that my children will experience a natural winter*. So I have purchased a "weatherproof light projection box that rests on your front lawn and transforms the entire facade of your house into an illuminated snowscape. The box creates the illusion of gently falling snow flurries by directing a bright white beam onto a rotating mirror-ball." Flake size and fall rate are,

pleasingly, adjustable. I have opted also to purchase an "exclusive heavy duty vinyl snow castle" that will "set up almost anywhere in just minutes with the included electric pump." A real snow castle would, SkyMall notes, "take hours to build and require lots of snow," but this version "encourages children to use their imaginations while having fun."

I have an enormous number of remote controls, and hence need caddies to store them, small "buddy lights" to illuminate them, and locator devices to find them when I have mislaid them.

I may be devolving. Though for eons my ancestors have grilled meat over flames, I am no longer very clear on the concept and so would like a digital barbecue fork that I can stick into my burger or steak and receive a readout indicating whether it is currently rare, medium, or well done. Also, it would help a lot to have all the lights already strung on my artificial Christmas tree, and the difficult task of marinating would be much easier if I had a $199.95 marinating machine. Frankly, I've lately found grilled cheese sandwiches more trouble than I want, but with my dishwasher-safe Toastabag I can simply place a slice of cheese between two slices of bread and pop it in my toaster. (Depressing the toaster lever still requires my thoughtful attention, as does chewing the resulting treat.)

There are a few problems SkyMall can't solve (the lack of community that comes when you live in a giant stuff-filled house marooned on its half-acre lot, the lack of security that comes when your country is spending its money on remote-control golf balls instead of, say, healthcare and retirement savings). And there's always the vexing question of what the people who are making these items think about the people who will buy them.

(I was in a shower curtain factory in rural China last year where the very nice people sewing the curtains told another visitor that they'd never actually encountered a shower curtain outside the factory. If that's true for a shower curtain, one wonders what their fellow workers make of the traveling wine trolley, the pop-up hot dog cooker, the hand-held paper shredder with wood-grain plastic handle.)

But this kind of talk sounds tired, clichéd, left over from the '60s. Everyone knows that the most important thing we can do is grow the economy. When you buy the Designated Driver, a faux golf club that you store in your bag to dispense forty-eight ounces of cold beverages, then you grow the economy. No doubt about it. Also, the Vintage Express Aging Accelerator that ages your bottle of wine ten years in ten seconds by surrounding it with "extremely powerful Neodymium magnets to replicate the Earth's magnetic field." Only a real jerk or a Christian or something would point out that there might possibly be items in this world that it would make more sense to spend our money on. (Insecticide-impregnated bed-nets to stop the spread of malaria run about five dollars. If only they came in self-erecting pastel versions that would also rouse you out of bed with gentle nature sounds.)

No Logo

Naomi Klein [b. 1970]

As a private person, I have a passion for landscape, and I have never seen one improved by a billboard. Where every prospect pleases, man is at his vilest when he erects a billboard. When I retire from Madison Avenue, I am going to start a secret society of masked vigilantes who will travel around the world on silent motor bicycles, chopping down posters at the dark of the moon. How many juries will convict us when we are caught in these acts of beneficent citizenship?

—David Ogilvy, founder of the Ogilvy&Mather advertising agency, in *Confessions of an Advertising Man*, 1963

The astronomical growth in the wealth and cultural influence of multinational corporations over the last fifteen years can arguably be traced back to a single, seemingly innocuous idea developed by management theorists in the mid-1980s: that successful corporations must primarily produce brands, as opposed to products.

Until that time, although it was understood in the corporate world that bolstering one's brand name was important, the primary concern of every solid manufacturer was the production of goods. This idea was the very gospel of the machine age. An editorial that appeared in *Fortune* magazine in 1938, for instance, argued that the reason the American economy had yet to recover from the Depression was that America had lost sight of the importance of making *things*.

> This is the proposition that the basic and irreversible function of an industrial economy is *the making of things:* that the more things it makes the bigger will be the income, whether dollar or real; and hence that the key to those lost recuperative powers lies . . . in the factory where the lathes and the drills and the fires and the hammers are. It is in the factory and on the land and under the land that purchasing power *originates*. [italics theirs].

And for the longest time, the making of things remained, at least in principle, the heart of all industrialized economies. But by the eighties, pushed along by that decade's recession, some of the most powerful manufacturers in the world had begun to falter. A consensus emerged that corporations were bloated, oversized; they owned too much, employed too many people, and were weighed down with *too many things*. The very process of producing—running one's own factories, being responsible for tens of thousands of fulltime permanent employees—began to look less like the route to success and more a clunky liability.

At around this same time a new kind of corporation began to rival the traditional all-American manufacturers for market share; these were Nikes and Microsofts, and later, the Tommy Hilfigers and Intels. These pioneers made the claim that producing goods was only an incidental part of their operations, and that thanks to recent victories in trade liberalization and labor-law reform, they were able to have their products made for them by contractors, many of them overseas. What these companies produced primarily were not things they said, but *images* of their brands. Their real work lay not in manufacturing but in marketing. This formula, needless to say, has proved enormously profitable, and its success has companies competing in a race toward weightlessness: whoever owns the least, has the fewest employees on the payroll and produces the most powerful images, as opposed to products, wins the race.

And so the wave of mergers in the corporate world over the 5
last few years is a deceptive phenomenon: it only *looks* as if the giants, by joining forces, are getting bigger and bigger. The true key to understanding these shifts is to realize that in several crucial ways—not their profits, of course—these merged companies are actually shrinking. Their apparent bigness is simply the most effective route toward their real goal: divestment of the world of things.

Since many of today's best-known manufacturers no longer produce products and advertise them, but rather buy products and "brand" them, these companies are forever on the prowl for creative new ways to build and strengthen their brand images. Manufacturing products may require drills, furnaces, hammers and the like, but creating a brand calls for a completely different set of tools and materials. It requires an endless parade of brand extensions, continuously renewed imagery for marketing and, most of all, fresh new spaces to disseminate the brand's idea of itself. In this section of the book, I'll look at how, in ways both insidious and overt, this corporate obsession with brand identity is waging a war on public and individual space: on public institutions such as schools, on youthful identities, on the concept of nationality and on the possibilities for unmarketed space.

THE BEGINNING OF THE BRAND

It's helpful to go back briefly and look at where the idea of branding first began. Though the words are often used interchangeably, branding and advertising are not the same process. Advertising any given product is only one part of branding's grand plan, as are sponsorship and logo licensing. Think of the brand as the core meaning of the modern corporation, and of the advertisement as one vehicle used to convey that meaning to the world.

The first mass-marketing campaigns, starting in the second half of the nineteenth century, had more to do with advertising than with branding as we understand it today. Faced with a range of recently invented products—the radio, phonograph, car, light bulb and so on—advertisers had more pressing tasks than creating a brand identity for any given corporation; first, they had to change the way people lived their lives. Ads had to inform consumers about the existence of some new invention, then convince them that their lives would be better if they used, for example, cars instead of wagons, telephones instead of mail and electric light instead of oil lamps. Many of these new products bore brand names—some of which are still around today—but these were almost incidental. These products were themselves news; that was almost advertisement enough.

The first brand-based products appeared at around the same time as the invention-based ads, largely because of another relatively recent innovation: the factory. When goods began to be produced in factories, not only were entirely new products being introduced but old products—even basic staples—were appearing in strikingly new forms. What made early branding efforts different from more straightforward salesmanship was that the market was now being flooded with uniform mass-produced products that were virtually indistinguishable from one another. Competitive branding became a necessity of the machine age—within a context of manufactured sameness, image based difference had to be manufactured along with the product.

So the role of advertising changed from delivering product news bulletins to building an image around a particular brand-name version of a product. The first task of branding was to bestow proper names on generic goods such as sugar, flour, soap and cereal, which had previously been scooped out of barrels by local shopkeepers. In the 1880s, corporate logos were introduced to mass-produced products like Campbell's Soup, H.J. Heinz pickles and Quaker Oats cereal. As design historians and theorists Ellen Lupton and J. Abbott Miller note, logos were tailored to evoke familiarity and folksiness, in an effort to counteract the new and unsettling anonymity of packaged goods. "Familiar personalities such as Dr. Brown, Uncle Ben, Aunt Jemima, and Old Grand-Dad came to replace the shopkeeper, who was traditionally responsible for measuring bulk foods for customers and acting as an advocate for products . . . a nationwide vocabulary of brand names replaced the small local shopkeeper as the interface between consumer and product." After the product names and characters had been established, advertising gave them a venue to speak directly to would-be consumers. The corporate "personality," uniquely named, packaged and advertised, had arrived.

For the most part, the ad campaigns at the end of the nineteenth century and the start of the twentieth used a set of rigid, pseudoscientific formulas: rivals were never mentioned, ad copy used declarative statements only and headlines had to be large, with lots of white space—according to one turn-of-the-century adman, "an advertisement should be big enough to make an impression but not any bigger than the thing advertised."

But there were those in the industry who understood that advertising wasn't just scientific; it was also spiritual: Brands could conjure a feeling—think of Aunt Jemima's comforting presence—but not only that, entire corporations could themselves embody a meaning of their own. In the early twenties, legendary adman Bruce Barton turned General Motors into a metaphor for the American family, "something personal, warm and human," while GE was not so much the name of the faceless General Electric Company as, in Barton's words, "the initials of a friend." In 1923 Barton said that the role of advertising was to help corporations find their soul. The son of a preacher, he drew on his religious upbringing for uplifting messages: "I like to think of advertising as something big, something splendid, something which goes deep down into an institution and gets hold of the soul of it. . . . Institutions have souls just as men and nations have souls," he told GM president Pierre du Pont. General Motors ads began to tell about the people who drove its cars—the preacher, the pharmacist or the country doctor who, thanks to his trusty GM, arrived "at the bedside of a dying child" just in time "to bring it back to life."

By the end of the 1940s, there was a burgeoning awareness that a brand wasn't just a mascot or a catchphrase or a picture printed on the label of a company's product; the company as a whole could have a brand identity or a "corporate consciousness," as this ephemeral quality was termed at the time. As this idea evolved, the adman ceased to see himself as a pitchman and instead saw himself as "the philosopher-king of commercial culture," in the words of ad critic Randall Rothberg. The search for the true meaning of brands—or the "brand essence," as it is often called—gradually took the agencies away from individual products and their attributes and toward a psychological/anthropological examination of what brands mean to the culture and to people's lives. This was seen to be of crucial importance, since corporations may manufacture products, but what consumers buy are brands.

It took several decades for the manufacturing world to adjust to this shift. It clung to the idea that its core business was still production and that branding was an important add-on. Then came the brand equity mania of the eighties, the defining moment of which arrived in 1988 when Philip Morris purchased Kraft for

$12.6 billion—six times what the company was worth on paper. The price difference, apparently, was the cost of the word "Kraft." Of course Wall Street was aware that decades of marketing and brand bolstering added value to a company over and above its assets and total annual sales. But with the Kraft purchase, a huge dollar value had been assigned to something that had previously been abstract and unquantifiable—a brand name. This was spectacular news for the ad world, which was now able to make the claim that advertising spending was more than just a sales strategy: it was an investment in cold hard equity. The more you spend, the more your company is worth. Not surprisingly, this led to a considerable increase in spending on advertising. More important, it sparked a renewed interest in puffing up brand identities, a project that involved far more than a few billboards and TV spots. It was about pushing the envelope in sponsorship deals, dreaming up new areas in which to "extend" the brand, as well as perpetually probing the zeitgeist to ensure that the "essence" selected for one's brand would resonate karmically with its target market. For reasons that will be explored in the rest of this chapter, this radical shift in corporate philosophy has sent manufacturers on a cultural feeding frenzy as they seize upon every corner of unmarketed landscape in search of the oxygen needed to inflate their brands. In the process, virtually nothing has been left unbranded. That's quite an impressive feat, considering that as recently as 1993 Wall Street had pronounced the brand dead, or as good as dead.

THE BRAND'S DEATH (RUMORS OF WHICH HAD BEEN GREATLY EXAGGERATED)

On April 2, 1993, advertising itself was called into question by the very brands the industry had been building, in some cases, for over two centuries. That day is known in marketing circles as 15
"Marlboro Friday," and it refers to a sudden announcement from Philip Morris that it would slash the price of Marlboro cigarettes

by 20 percent in an attempt to compete with bargain brands that were eating into its market. The pundits went nuts, announcing in frenzied unison that not only was Marlboro dead, all brand names were dead. The reasoning was that if a "prestige" brand like Marlboro, whose image had been carefully groomed, preened and enhanced with more than a billion advertising dollars, was desperate enough to compete with no-names, then clearly the whole concept of branding had lost its currency. The public had seen the advertising, and the public didn't care. The Marlboro Man, after all, was not any old campaign; launched in 1954, it was the longest-running ad campaign in history. It was a legend. If the Marlboro Man had crashed, well, then, brand equity had crashed as well. The implication that Americans were suddenly thinking for themselves en masse reverberated through Wall Street. The same day Philip Morris announced its price cut, stock prices nose-dived for all the household brands: Heinz, Quaker Oats, Coca-Cola, PepsiCo, Procter and Gamble and RJR Nabisco. Philip Morris's own stock took the worst beating.

Bob Stanojev, national director of consumer products marketing for Ernst and Young, explained the logic behind Wall Street's panic: "If one or two powerhouse consumer products companies start to cut prices for good, there's going to be an avalanche. Welcome to the value generation."

Yes, it was one of those moments of overstated instant consensus, but it was not entirely without cause. Marlboro had always sold itself on the strength of its iconic image marketing, not on anything so prosaic as its price. As we now know, the Marlboro Man survived the price wars without sustaining too much damage. At the time, however, Wall Street saw Philip Morris's decision as symbolic of a sea change. The price cut was an admission that Marlboro's name was no longer sufficient to sustain the flagship position, which in a context where image is equity meant that Marlboro had blinked. And when Marlboro—one of the quintessential global brands—blinks, it raises questions about branding that reach beyond Wall Street, and way beyond Philip Morris.

The panic of Marlboro Friday was not a reaction to a single incident. Rather, it was the culmination of years of escalating anxiety in the face of some rather dramatic shifts in consumer habits that were seen to be eroding the market share of household-name brands, from Tide to Kraft. Bargain-conscious shoppers, hit hard by the recession, were starting to pay more attention to price than to the prestige bestowed on their products by the yuppie ad campaigns of the 1980s. The public was suffering from a bad case of what is known in the industry as "brand blindness."

Study after study showed that baby boomers, blind to the alluring images of advertising and deaf to the empty promises of celebrity spokespersons, were breaking their lifelong brand loyalties and choosing to feed their families with private-label brands from the supermarket—claiming, heretically, that they couldn't tell the difference. From the beginning of the recession to 1993, Loblaw's President's Choice line, Wal-Mart's Great Value and Marks and Spencer's St. Michael prepared foods had nearly doubled their market share in North America and Europe. The computer market, meanwhile, was flooded by inexpensive clones, causing IBM to slash its prices and otherwise impale itself. It appeared to be a return to the proverbial shopkeeper dishing out generic goods from the barrel in a prebranded era.

THE BRANDS BOUNCE BACK

There were some brands that were watching from the sidelines as Wall Street declared the death of the brand. Funny, they must have thought, we don't feel dead. 20

Just as the admen had predicted at the beginning of the recession, the companies that exited the downturn running were the ones who opted for marketing over value every time: Nike, Apple, the Body Shop, Calvin Klein, Disney, Levi's and Starbucks. Not only were these brands doing just fine, thank you very much, but the act of branding was becoming a larger and larger focus of their businesses. For these companies, the ostensible product was mere filler for the real production: the brand. They integrated the idea of branding into the very fabric of their companies. Their corporate cultures were so tight and cloistered that to outsiders they appeared to be a cross between fraternity house, religious cult and sanitarium. Everything was an ad for the brand: bizarre lexicons for describing employees (partners, baristas, team players, crew members), company chants, superstar CEOs, fanatical attention to design consistency, a propensity for monument-building, and New Age mission statements. Unlike classic household brand names, such as Tide and Marlboro, these logos weren't losing their currency, they were in the midst of breaking every barrier in the marketing world—becoming cultural accessories and lifestyle philosophers. These companies didn't wear this image like a cheap shirt—their image was so integrated with their business that other people wore it as *their* shirt. And when the brands crashed, these companies didn't even notice—they were branded to the bone.

So the real legacy of Marlboro Friday is that it simultaneously brought the two most significant developments in nineties marketing and consumerism into sharp focus: the deeply unhip big-box bargain stores that provide the essentials of life and monopolize a disproportionate share of the market (Wal-Mart *et al.*) and the extra-premium "attitude" brands that provide the essentials of lifestyle and monopolize ever-expanding stretches of cultural space (Nike *et al.*). The way these two tiers of consumerism developed would have a profound impact on the economy in the years to come. When overall ad expenditures took a nosedive in 1991, Nike and Reebok were busy playing advertising chicken, with each company increasing its budget to outspend the other. In 1991 alone, Reebok upped its ad spending by 71.9 percent, while Nike pumped an extra 24.6 percent into its already soaring ad budget, bringing the company's total spending on marketing to a staggering $250 million annually. Far from worrying about competing on price, the sneaker pimps were designing ever more intricate and pseudoscientific air pockets, and driving up prices by signing star athletes to colossal sponsorship deals. The fetish strategy seemed to be working fine: in the six years prior to 1993, Nike had gone from a $750 million company to a $4 billion one and Phil Knight's Beaverton, Oregon, company emerged from the recession with profits 900 percent higher than when it began.

Benetton and Calvin Klein, meanwhile, were also upping their spending on lifestyle marketing, using ads to associate their lines with risque art and progressive politics. Clothes barely appeared in these high-concept advertisements, let alone prices. Even more abstract was Absolut Vodka, which for some years now had been developing a marketing strategy in which its product disappeared and its brand was nothing but a blank bottle-shaped space that could be filled with whatever content a particular audience most wanted from its brands: intellectual in *Harper's*, futuristic in *Wired*, alternative in *Spin*, loud and proud in *Out* and "Absolut Centerfold" in *Playboy*. The brand reinvented itself as a cultural sponge, soaking up and morphing to its surroundings.

Saturn, too, came out of nowhere in October 1990 when GM launched a car built not out of steel and rubber but out of New Age spirituality and seventies feminism. After the car had been on the market a few years, the company held a "homecoming" weekend for Saturn owners, during which they could visit the auto plant and have a cookout with the people who made their cars. As the Saturn ads boasted at the time, "44,000 people spent their vacations with us, at a car plant." It was as if Aunt Jemima had come to life and invited you over to her house for dinner.

In 1993, the year the Marlboro Man was temporarily hobbled by "brand-blind" consumers, Microsoft made its striking debut on *Advertising Age's* list of the top 200 ad spenders—the very same year that Apple computer increased its marketing budget by 30 percent after already making branding history with its Orwellian takeoff ad launch during the 1984 Super Bowl. Like Saturn, both companies were selling a hip new relationship to the machine that left Big Blue IBM looking as clunky and menacing as the now-dead Cold War.

And then there were the companies that had always understood that they were selling brands before product. Coke, Pepsi, McDonald's, Burger King and Disney weren't fazed by the brand crisis, opting instead to escalate the brand war, especially since they had their eyes firmly fixed on global expansion. They were joined in this project by a wave of sophisticated producer/retailers who hit full stride in the late eighties and early nineties. The Gap, Ikea and the Body Shop were spreading like wildfire during this period, masterfully transforming the generic into the brand-specific, largely through bold, carefully branded packaging and the promotion of an "experiential" shopping environment. The Body Shop had been a presence in Britain since the seventies, but it wasn't until 1988 that it began sprouting like a green weed on every street corner in the U.S. Even during the darkest years of the recession, the company opened between forty and fifty American stores a year. Most baffling of all to Wall Street, it pulled off the expansion without spending a dime on advertising. Who needed billboards and magazine ads when retail outlets were three-dimensional advertisements for an ethical and ecological approach to cosmetics? The Body Shop was all brand.

The Starbucks coffee chain, meanwhile, was also expanding during this period without laying out much in advertising; instead, it was spinning off its name into a wide range of branded projects: Starbucks airline coffee, office coffee, coffee ice cream, coffee beer. Starbucks seemed to understand brand names at a level even deeper than Madison Avenue, incorporating marketing into every fiber of its corporate concept—from the chain's strategic association with books, blues and jazz to its Euro-latte lingo. What the success of both the Body Shop and Starbucks showed was how far the branding project had come in moving beyond splashing one's logo on a billboard. Here were two companies that had fostered powerful identities by making their brand concept into a virus and sending it out into the culture via a variety of channels: cultural sponsorship, political controversy, the consumer experience and brand extensions. Direct advertising, in this context, was viewed as a rather clumsy intrusion into a much more organic approach to image building.

Scott Bedbury, Starbucks' vice president of marketing, openly recognized that "consumers don't truly believe there's a huge difference between products," which is why brands must "establish emotional ties" with their customers through "the

Starbucks Experience." The people who line up for Starbucks, writes CEO Howard Shultz, aren't just there for the coffee. "It's the romance of the coffee experience, the feeling of warmth and community people get in Starbucks stores."

Interestingly, before moving to Starbucks, Bedbury was head of marketing at Nike, where he oversaw the launch of the "Just Do It!" slogan, among other watershed branding moments. In the following passage, he explains the common techniques used to infuse the two very different brands with meaning:

> Nike, for example, is leveraging the deep emotional connection that people have with sports and fitness. With Starbucks, we see how coffee has woven itself into the fabric of people's lives, and that's our opportunity for emotional leverage. . . . A great brand raises the bar—it adds a greater sense of purpose to the experience, whether it's the challenge to do your best in sports and fitness or the affirmation that the cup of coffee you're drinking really matters.

This was the secret, it seemed, of all the success stories of the late eighties and early nineties. The lesson of Marlboro Friday was that there never really was a brand crisis—only brands that had crises of confidence. The brands would be okay, Wall Street concluded, so long as they believed fervently in the principles of branding and never, ever blinked. Overnight, "Brands, not products!" became the rallying cry for a marketing renaissance led by a new breed of companies that saw themselves as "meaning brokers" instead of product producers. What was changing was the idea of what—in both advertising and branding—was being sold. The old paradigm had it that all marketing was selling a product. In the new model, however, the product always takes a back seat to the real product, the brand, and the selling of the brand acquired an extra component that can only be described as spiritual. Advertising is about hawking product. Branding, in its truest and most advanced incarnations, is about corporate transcendence.

It may sound flaky, but that's precisely the point. On Marlboro Friday, a line was drawn in the sand between the lowly price slashers and the high-concept brand builders. The brand builders conquered, and a new consensus was born: the products that will flourish in the future will be the ones presented not as "commodities" but as concepts: the brand as experience, as lifestyle.

Ever since, a select group of corporations has been attempting to free itself from the corporeal world of commodities, manufacturing and products to exist on another plane. Anyone can manufacture a product, they reason (and as the success of private-label brands during the recession proved, anyone did). Such menial tasks, therefore, can and should be farmed out to contractors and subcontractors whose only concern is filling the order on time and under budget (ideally in the Third World, where labor is dirt cheap, laws are lax and tax breaks come by the bushel). Headquarters, meanwhile, is free to focus on the real business at hand—creating a corporate mythology powerful enough to infuse meaning into these raw objects just by signing its name.

The corporate world has always had a deep New Age streak, fed—it has become clear—by a profound need that could not be met simply by trading widgets for cash. But when branding captured the corporate imagination, New Age vision quests took center stage. As Nike CEO Phil Knight explains, "For years we thought of ourselves as a production-oriented company, meaning we put all our emphasis on designing and manufacturing the product. But now we understand that the most important thing we do is market the product. We've come around to saying that Nike is a marketing-oriented company, and the product is our most important marketing tool." This project has since been taken to an even more advanced level with the emergence of on-line corporate giants such as Amazon.com. It is on-line that the purest brands are being built: liberated from the real-world burdens of stores and product manufacturing, these brands are free to soar, less as the disseminators of goods or services than as collective hallucinations.

Tom Peters, who has long coddled the inner flake in many a hard-nosed CEO, latched on to the branding craze as the secret to financial success, separating the transcendental logos and the earthbound products into two distinct categories of companies. "The top half—Coca-Cola, Microsoft, Disney, and so on—are pure 'players' in brainware. The bottom half [Ford and GM] are still lumpy-object purveyors, though automobiles are much 'smarter' than they used to be," Peters writes in *The Circle of Innovation* (1997), an ode to the power of marketing over production.

When Levi's began to lose market share in the late nineties, the trend was widely attributed to the company's failure—despite lavish ad spending—to transcend its products and become a free- 35
standing meaning. "Maybe one of Levi's problems is that it has no Cola," speculated Jennifer Steinhauer in *The New York Times*. "It has no denim-toned house paint. Levi makes what is essentially a commodity: blue jeans. Its ads may evoke rugged outdoorsmanship, but Levi hasn't promoted any particular life style to sell other products."

In this high-stakes new context, the cutting-edge ad agencies no longer sold companies on individual campaigns but on their ability to act as "brand stewards": identifying, articulating and protecting the corporate soul. Not surprisingly, this spelled good news for the U.S. advertising industry, which in 1994 saw a spending increase of 8.6 percent over the previous year. In one year, the ad industry went from a near crisis to another "best year yet." And that was only the beginning of triumphs to come. By 1997, corporate advertising, defined as "ads that position a corporation, its values, its personality and character" were up 18 percent from the year before.

With this wave of brand mania has come a new breed of businessman, one who will proudly inform you that Brand X is not a product but a way of life, an attitude, a set of values, a look, an idea. And it sounds really great—way better than that Brand X is a screwdriver, or a hamburger chain, or a pair of jeans, or even a very successful line of running shoes. Nike, Phil Knight announced in the late eighties, is "a sports company"; its mission is not to sell shoes but to "enhance people's lives through sports and fitness" and to keep "the magic of sports alive." Company president-cum-sneaker-shaman Tom Clark explains that "the inspiration of sports allows us to rebirth ourselves constantly."

Reports of such "brand vision" epiphanies began surfacing from all corners. "Polaroid's problem," diagnosed the chairman of its advertising agency, John Hegarty, "was that they kept thinking of themselves as a camera. But the '[brand] vision' process taught us something: Polaroid is not a camera—it's a social lubricant." IBM isn't selling computers, it's selling business "solutions." Swatch is not about watches, it is about the idea of time. At Diesel Jeans, owner Renzo Rosso told *Paper* magazine, "We don't sell a product, we sell a style of life. I think we have created a movement. . . . The Diesel concept is everything. It's the way to live, it's the way to wear, it's the way to do something." And as Body Shop founder Anita Roddick explained to me, her stores aren't about what they sell, they are the conveyers of a grand idea—a political philosophy about women, the environment and ethical business. "I just use the company that I surprisingly created as a success—it shouldn't have been like this, it wasn't meant to be like this—to stand on the products to shout out on these issues," Roddick says.

The famous late graphic designer Tibor Kalman summed up the shifting role of the brand this way: "The original notion of the brand was quality, but now brand is a stylistic badge of courage."

The idea of selling the courageous message of a brand, as opposed to a product, intoxicated these CEOs, providing as it did an opportunity for seemingly limitless expansion. After all, if a brand was not a product, it could be anything! And nobody embraced branding theory with more evangelical zeal than Richard Branson, whose Virgin Group has branded joint ventures in everything from music to bridal gowns to airlines to cola to financial services. Branson refers derisively to the "stilted Anglo-Saxon view of consumers," which holds that a name should be associated with a product like sneakers or soft drinks; and opts instead for "the Asian 'trick'" of the *keiretsus* (a Japanese term meaning a network of linked corporations). The idea, he explains, is to "build brands not around products but around reputation. The great Asian names imply quality, price and innovation rather than a specific item. I call these 'attribute' brands: They do not relate directly to one product—such as a Mars bar or a Coca-Cola—but instead to a set of values."

Tommy Hilfiger, meanwhile, is less in the business of manufacturing clothes than he is in the business of signing his name. The company is run entirely through licensing agreements, with Hilfiger commissioning all its products from a group of other companies: Jockey International makes Hilfiger underwear, Pepe Jeans London makes Hilfiger jeans, Oxford Industries make Tommy shirts, the Stride Rite Corporation makes its footwear. What does Tommy Hilfiger manufacture? Nothing at all.

So passé had products become in the age of lifestyle branding that by the late nineties newer companies like Lush cosmetics and Old Navy clothing began playing with the idea of old-style commodities as a source of retro marketing imagery. The Lush chain serves up its face masks and moisturizers out of refrigerated stainless-steel bowls, spooned into plastic containers with grocery-store labels. Old Navy showcases its shrink-wrapped T-shirts and sweatshirts in deli-style chrome refrigerators, as if they were meat or cheese. When you are a pure, concept-driven brand, the aesthetics of raw product can prove as "authentic" as loft living.

And lest the branding business be dismissed as the playground of trendy consumer items such as sneakers, jeans and New Age beverages, think again. Caterpillar, best known for building tractors and busting unions, has barreled into the branding business, launching the Cat accessories line: boots, back-packs, hats and anything else calling out for a postindustrial *je ne sais quoi*. Intel Corp., which makes computer parts no one sees and few understand, transformed its processors into a fetish brand with TV ads featuring line workers in funky metallic space suits dancing to "Shake Your Groove Thing." The Intel mascots proved so popular that the company has sold hundreds of thousands of bean-filled dolls modeled on the shimmery dancing technicians. Little wonder, then, that when asked about the company's decision to diversify its products, the senior vice president for sales and marketing, Paul S. Otellini, replied that Intel is "like Coke. One brand, many different products."

And if Caterpillar and Intel can brand, surely anyone can.

There is, in fact, a new strain in marketing theory that holds that even the lowliest natural resources, barely processed, can develop brand identities, thus giving way to hefty premium-price markups. In an essay appropriately titled "How to Brand Sand," advertising executives Sam Hill, Jack McGrath and Sandeep Dayal team up to tell the corporate world that with the right marketing plan, nobody has to stay stuck in the stuff business. "Based on extensive research, we would argue that you can indeed brand not only sand, but also wheat, beef, brick, metals, concrete, chemicals, corn grits and an endless variety of commodities traditionally considered immune to the process."

Over the past six years, spooked by the near-death experience of Marlboro Friday, global corporations have leaped on the brand-wagon with what can only be described as a religious fervor. Never again would the corporate world stoop to praying at the altar of the commodity market. From now on they would worship only graven media images. Or to quote Tom Peters, the brand man himself: "Brand! Brand!! Brand!!! That's the message . . . for the late '90s and beyond."

Why I Want a Wife

Judy Brady [b. 1937]

Judy Brady (1937–), born in San Francisco, studied painting and received a B.F.A. in 1962 in art from the University of Iowa. Then she married and raised a family in a traditional housewife role. She later commented that her male professors had talked her out of pursuing a career in education. In the late 1960s, she became active in the women's movement and began writing articles on feminism and other social issues. In 1990, she was the editor of Women and Cancer, an anthology by women. The essay "Why I Want a Wife" appeared in the first issue of Ms. magazine in 1972.

I belong to that classification of people known as wives. I am a Wife. And, not altogether incidentally, I am a mother.

Not too long ago a male friend of mine appeared on the scene fresh from a recent divorce. He had one child, who is, of course, with his ex-wife. He is looking for another wife. As I thought about him while I was ironing one evening, it suddenly occurred to me that I, too, would like to have a wife. Why do I want a wife?

I would like to go back to school so that I can become economically independent, support myself, and, if need be, support those dependent upon me. I want a wife who will work and send me to school. And while I am going to school I want a wife to take care of my children. I want a wife to keep track of the children's doctor and dentist appointments. And to keep track of mine, too. I want a wife to make sure my children eat properly and are kept clean. I want a wife who will wash the children's clothes and keep them mended. I want a wife who is a good nurturant attendant to my children, who arranges for their schooling, makes sure that they have an adequate social life with their peers, takes them to the park, the zoo, etc. I want a wife who takes care of the children when they are sick, a wife who arranges to be around when the children need special care, because, of course, I cannot miss classes at school. My wife must arrange to lose time at work and not lose the job. It may mean a small cut in my wife's income from time to time, but I guess

I can tolerate that. Needless to say, my wife will arrange and pay for the care of the children while my wife is working.

I want a wife who will take care of *my* physical needs. I want a wife who will keep my house clean, a wife who will pick up after me. I want a wife who will keep my clothes clean, ironed, mended, replaced when need be, and who will see to it that my personal things are kept in their proper place so that I can find what I need the minute I need it. I want a wife who cooks the meals, a wife who is a *good* cook. I want a wife who will plan the menus, do the necessary grocery shopping, prepare the meals, serve them pleasantly, and then do the cleaning up while I do my studying. I want a wife who will care for me when I am sick and sympathize with my pain and loss of time from school. I want a wife to go along when our family takes a vacation so that someone can continue to care for me and my children when I need a rest and change of scene.

I want a wife who will not bother me with rambling complaints about a wife's duties. But I want a wife who will listen to me when I feel the need to explain a rather difficult point I have come across in my course of studies. And I want a wife who will type my papers for me when I have written them.

I want a wife who will take care of the details of my social life. When my wife and I are invited out by friends, I want a wife who will take care of the babysitting arrangements. When I meet people at school that I like and want to entertain, I want a wife who will have the house clean, will prepare a special meal, serve it to me and my friends, and not interrupt when I talk about the things that interest me and my friends. I want a wife who will have arranged that the children are fed and ready for bed before my guests arrive so that the children do not bother us. I want a wife who takes care of the needs of my guests so that they feel comfortable, who makes sure that they have an ashtray, that they are passed the hors d'oeuvres, that they are offered a second helping of the food, that their wine glasses are replenished when necessary, that their coffee is served to them as they like it. And I want a wife who knows that sometimes I need a night out by myself.

I want a wife who is sensitive to my sexual needs, a wife who makes love passionately and eagerly when I feel like it, a wife who makes sure that I am satisfied. And, of course, I want a wife who will not demand sexual attention when I am not in the mood for it. I want a wife who assumes the complete responsibility for birth control, because I do not want more children. I want a wife who will remain sexually faithful to me so that I do not have to clutter up my intellectual life with jealousies. And I want a wife who understands that *my* sexual needs may entail more than strict adherence to monogamy. I must, after all, be able to relate to people as fully as possible.

If, by chance, I find another person more suitable as a wife than the wife I already have, I want the liberty to replace my present wife with another one. Naturally, I will expect a fresh, new life; my wife will take the children and be solely responsible for them so that I am left free.

When I am through with school and have a job, I want my wife to quit working and remain at home so that my wife can more fully and completely take care of a wife's duties.

My God, who *wouldn't* want a wife? 10

On Colored Women and Work

Sojourner Truth (1797–1893)

Born into slavery as Isabella Baumfree, Sojourner Truth began life in Ulster County, New York. At nine years of age, she was sold to a vicious slaveholder who beat and raped her repeatedly. She would be sold three more times before New York State abolished slavery in 1827. The mother of five children, Baumfree became a devout Christian after gaining her freedom. A fiery orator with a strong voice and a sharp sense of humor, she became a traveling evangelist, and, in 1843, took the name Sojourner Truth.

Never able to read or write, she dictated her autobiography, The Narrative of Sojourner Truth, *which was published in 1850. She toured the country, advocating an end to slavery and promoting equal rights for women. During the Civil War, she encouraged blacks to fight for the North. In 1864, she moved to Washington, DC, and organized a campaign to allow blacks to sit with whites on trains. Abraham Lincoln was so impressed with Sojourner Truth that he welcomed her to the White House. In addition to advocating against slavery and for women's rights, Truth spoke in favor of prison reform and against capital punishment.*

Address to the First Annual Meeting of the American Equal Rights Association, delivered by Sojourner Truth on May 9, 1867

New York City, May 9, 1867

My friends, I am rejoiced that you are glad, but I don't know how you will feel when I get through. I come from another field—the country of the slave. They have got their liberty—so much good luck to have slavery partly destroyed; not entirely. I want it root and branch destroyed. Then we will all be free indeed. I feel that if I have to answer for the deeds done in my body just as much as a man, I have a right to have just as much as a man.

There is a great stir about colored men getting their rights, but not a word about the colored women; and if colored men get their rights, and not colored women theirs, you see the colored men will be masters over the women, and it will be just as bad as it was before.

So I am for keeping the thing going while things are stirring; because if we wait till it is still, it will take a great while to get it going again. White women are a great deal smarter, and know more than colored women, while colored women do not know scarcely anything.

They go out washing, which is about as high as a colored woman gets, and their men go about idle, strutting up and down; and when the women come home, they ask for their money and take it all, and then scold because there is no food.

I want you to consider on that, chil'n. I call you chil'n; you are somebody's chil'n, and I am old enough to be mother of all that is here. I want women to have their rights. In the courts women have no right, no voice; nobody speaks for them. I wish woman to have her voice there among the pettifoggers. If it is not a fit place for women, it is unfit for men to be there.

I am above eighty years old; it is about time for me to be going. I have been forty years a slave and forty years free, and would be here forty years more to have equal rights for all. I suppose I am kept here because something remains for me to do; I suppose I am yet to help to break the chain.

I have done a great deal of work; as much as a man, but did not get so much pay. I used to work in the field and bind grain, keeping up with the cradler; but men doing no more, got twice as much pay; so with the German women. They work in the field and do as much work, but do not get the pay.

We do as much, we eat as much, we want as much. I suppose I am about the only colored woman that goes about to speak for the rights of the colored women. I want to keep the thing stirring, now that the ice is cracked.

What we want is a little money. You men know that you get as much again as women when you write, or for what you do. When we get our rights we shall not have to come to you for money, for then we shall have money enough in our own pockets; and may be you will ask us for money. But help us now until we get it. It is a good consolation to know that when we have got this battle once fought we shall not be coming to you any more.

You have been having our rights so long, that you think, like a slaveholder, that you own us. I know that it is hard for one who has held the reins for so long to give up; it cuts like a knife. It will feel all the better when it closes up again. I have been in Washington about three years, seeing about these colored people. Now colored men have the right to vote. There ought to be equal rights now more than ever, since colored people have got their freedom. I am going to talk several times while I am here; so now I will do a little singing. I have not heard any singing since I came here.

Accordingly, suiting the action to the word, Sojourner sang, "We are going home." "There, children," said she, "in heaven we shall rest from all our labors; first do all we have to do here. There I am determined to go, not to stop short of that beautiful place, and I do not mean to stop till I get there, and meet you there, too."

Plane Wreck At Los Gatos (Deportee)

Woody Guthrie (1912–1967)

Having lived through some of the most significant historic movements and events of the Twentieth-Century–the Great Depression, the Great Dust Storm, World War II, the social and political upheavals resulting from Unionism, the Communist Party and the Cold War–Woody absorbed it all to become a prolific writer whose songs, ballads, prose and poetry captured the plight of "everyman." While traveling throughout the American landscape during the 1930s, 40s, and 50s, Woody's observations of what he saw and experienced has left for us a lasting and sometimes haunting legacy of images, sounds, and voices of the marginalized, disenfranchised, and oppressed people with whom he struggled to survive despite all odds. Although the corpus of original Woody Guthrie songs, or as Woody preferred "people's songs," are, perhaps, his most recognized contribution to American culture, the stinging honesty, humor, and wit found even in his most vernacular prose writings exhibit Woody's fervent belief in social, political, and spiritual justice.

Recognition of Woody Guthrie's work lives on. He has been inducted into The Songwriters' Hall of Fame (1971), the Nashville Songwriters Hall of Fame (1977), and The Rock and Roll Hall of Fame and Museum (1988). He has received numerous awards, including the U.S. Department of the Interior's Conservation Award (1966), The Folk Alliance Lifetime Achievement Award (1996), and from the National Academy of Recording Arts and Sciences (1999). Colleges and universities such as Case Western Reserve University have sponsored symposia and lectures. Popular and folk musicians such as Bruce Springsteen, Billy Bragg, Wilco, Ani DiFranco, and countless others continue to draw inspiration from Woody Guthrie, re-interpreting and re-invigorating his songs for new audiences. Pete Seeger, Bob Dylan, Arlo Guthrie, and Ramblin' Jack Elliot, are among the legions of folk musicians, of every age-group, who are carrying the tradition of the harmonica and guitar-playing singer/songwriter into the future.

The crops are all in and the peaches are rott'ning,
The oranges piled in their creosote dumps;
They're flying 'em back to the Mexican border
To pay all their money to wade back again

Goodbye to my Juan, goodbye, Rosalita,
Adios mis amigos, Jesus y Maria;
You won't have your names when you ride the big airplane,
All they will call you will be "deportees"

My father's own father, he waded that river,
They took all the money he made in his life;
My brothers and sisters come working the fruit trees,
And they rode the truck till they took down and died.

Some of us are illegal, and some are not wanted,
Our work contract's out and we have to move on;
Six hundred miles to that Mexican border,
They chase us like outlaws, like rustlers, like thieves.

We died in your hills, we died in your deserts,
We died in your valleys and died on your plains.
We died 'neath your trees and we died in your bushes,
Both sides of the river, we died just the same.

The sky plane caught fire over Los Gatos Canyon,
A fireball of lightning, and shook all our hills,
Who are all these friends, all scattered like dry leaves?
The radio says, "They are just deportees"

Is this the best way we can grow our big orchards?
Is this the best way we can grow our good fruit?
To fall like dry leaves to rot on my topsoil
And be called by no name except "deportees"?

1948